CHRISTIAN VALUES

Theory and Practice in Christian Ethics Today

CHRISTIAN VALUES

Theory and Practice in Christian Ethics Today

by

J. Ian H. McDonald

with contributions from:

Ruth Harvey, Marion Keston, Sharon Kyle,
David Molyneaux, Elisabeth Spence,
Pauline Steenbergen, Una Stewart,
Heather Wraight and John Young

T&T CLARK
EDINBURGH

T&T CLARK LTD
59 GEORGE STREET
EDINBURGH EH2 2LQ
SCOTLAND

First published 1995

ISBN 0 567 29282 7

British Library Cataloguing-in-Publication Data
A catalogue record for this book is available from the British Library

Page make-up by Trinity Typesetting, Edinburgh
Printed and bound in Great Britain by Page Bros, Norwich

11-6-97

CONTENTS

v

PREFACE

It is a pleasure to acknowledge interest and practical help from many sources in the making of this book. First, there are my fellow contributors – all of them present or former students of Christian Ethics at Edinburgh University. Their interest and enthusiasm has meant much to me. They are also the channels by which the experiences of other individuals and groups flow into the book: to them also a debt of gratitude is owed. A wider group of students – at second year, honours and post-graduate level – unknowingly contributed through their responses in class.

I warmly thank my colleagues who showed a keen interest in the book's preparation. In particular, Professor Duncan Forrester gave selflessly of his time to read the manuscript and comment helpfully on it. Dr David Lyall gave valuable advice on the earlier chapters, as did my friend and former co-author, Ian C. M. Fairweather. My wife Jenny has been, as ever, a valued collaborator in the preparation of the manuscript. Other colleagues also gave material assistance. It is the hope of all the contributors that the book will commend the study and discussion of Christian ethics to a growing constituency of students and readers.

Ian McDonald

INTRODUCTION

THINKING ABOUT CHRISTIAN VALUES

A university chaplain commented on a very constructive question session on 'Faith in Sexuality' as follows:

> The spontaneous round of applause of the evening went to the young woman who articulated the feelings of the whole room.... The churches, she declared, were failing her generation on the issues of sexuality. Conservative Christians presented a moral absolute which could be summed up as 'no sex outside marriage', but in today's world few if any young people could or would adhere to that. Most people were like her, in the middle somewhere, not helped by the rigidities of the Christian right but not helped either by the liberal churches, who tended to say nothing on the subject at all. Her generation felt itself to be facing complex moral issues without the help of a church. The applause was eloquent.... Predictably, the issue of homosexuality came up repeatedly. For many students the homophobia and sexism of the church are a considerable stumbling block. They know injustice when they see it, and the church's discrimination against women and gays flies in the face of the gospel it proclaims.[1]

The dilemma expressed here is as urgent for Christian ethics as it is perplexing for the churches. Indeed, it could hardly be more accurately portrayed, at least in so far as a wide range of interested students is concerned: other constituencies might

---

[1] John Turner, 'Faith in the university: Two weeks of exploration', *Avenue* 16, University of Glasgow, 1994, p. 5.

see matters somewhat differently. One would not wish simply to discount the loyalty to 'traditional values' which some conscientiously profess: a case can be made for such a stance. If, however, this involves closing the mind to important factors in the modern situation (including a modern understanding of sexuality and society), and if it becomes unsympathetically judgemental (in total contrast to Jesus' attitude),[2] it must be challenged in the name of ethics and the gospel. The failure of the 'liberals' to communicate is equally significant. They too have traded on an ideological consensus which is crumbling: hence their apparent impotence. There is more here than a simple failure to communicate. However, surely the most damning indictment is that the students felt they could make a moral critique of the churches – ostensibly the guardians of the high moral ground – and find them wanting. The charges, based on a keen sense of justice, relate to the failure of the churches to rethink the moral priorities and to express them meaningfully in the context of the realities of life today.[3]

All this would seem to argue the crying need for a basic book on Christian values! Not only does it specify areas of concern and make a plea for realism in Christian moral teaching, but it also implies the need for a fresh understanding of Christian moral discourse. How are we to discuss such highly charged issues? What are the ground rules? If our discussion must be 'true to life' today, how is it to handle moral tradition and authority? And what of ourselves, as potential ethicists and moral agents? Must not our horizons be enlarged and our prejudices recognised and controlled before we are fit for the contest? These, at any rate, are the kinds of issues which will be before us constantly.

Christian ethics stands for disciplined reflection on the issues raised by Christian faith and life. It is not concerned

---

[2] Cf. the story of the 'woman taken in adultery': John 8:2–11 (in some mss), especially 8:11.
[3] This is not to deny that some churches have tried nobly to come to terms with modern issues in morality, through reports and publications, but have often run into difficulties either from ultra-traditionalists or from media misrepresentations of their intentions.

merely with the life-style of Christian communities: if it were so, it would simply be an exercise in the social sciences. It *is* concerned with the moral issues people meet in real life and with faith perspectives upon them – and the social sciences, as well as theological and ethical reflection, are certainly relevant to this task. Christian ethics is thus concerned with the interaction of faith and practice (or *theoria* and *praxis*, to use the technical terms): the normal movement being from the present situation, observed and analysed, through theological and ethical reflection, to renewed practice – *praxis> theoria> praxis.*

The model adopted, however, is not that of the ethicist or moral teacher who knows all the answers in advance, so that it is simply a matter, as the politicians would say, of 'putting the message across'. Rather, what is envisaged is a learning community exploring how one is led to truth, articulates truth and 'does the truth': a community grappling with the problem of expressing Christian values in the world, as authentically as possible. The book contains contributions from a number of people who have belonged to a community of this kind.

Introducing the team

All the contributors to the book have been ethics students at Edinburgh. In the course of their studies, they submitted projects or essays which have been adapted for publication here. As the reader will readily detect, their work was oriented towards the empirical, or 'real life'. Hence they conducted interviews, investigated problems, researched cases and wrote studies, conducted experiments and stimulated dialogue…. As is evident from reading their work, all of them brought to their studies not only a deep concern for ethics but also personal involvement in the selected topic and, in some cases, professional practice in the field. Their readiness to allow their work to be included here and the enthusiasm they showed for this joint venture is much appreciated. It is notable that so many female students have contributed so effectively. Since the author of the rest of the book is male, it can be fairly claimed that an acceptable gender ratio has been achieved.

There is also — without giving away too many secrets — a pleasing blend of youthfulness and maturity!

The contributors were:

Ruth Harvey: a dedicated member of the Iona Community, she has served as Deputy Warden at the Abbey and is currently an assistant minister in the Church of Scotland; a graduate of Aberdeen, she took her BD at Edinburgh. She contributed material on liturgy as pastoral response, together with a case study, for Chapter 4.

Marion Keston: a very experienced medical practitioner and specialist, she has recently been ordained priest in the Scottish Episcopal Church and is currently an M.Th. student in Ethics at Edinburgh. She contributed the case study at the beginning of Chapter 1.

Sharon Kyle: recently ordained deacon in the Scottish Episcopal Church and now working in an Edinburgh parish, she trained originally as a journalist and then spent seventeen years in the Scottish Office, during which time she took a BA with the Open University: she then took a BD at Edinburgh. She contributed material on human sexuality and the church, with particular reference to homosexuality, together with a case study, for Chapter 4.

David Molyneaux: studied classics and early church history before qualifying as a chartered accountant in London. After working in East Africa, he came to Edinburgh where for six years he was a partner in a major international accountancy practice. Following acceptance as a candidate for the ordained ministry of the Church of Scotland, he became a BD student at New College, Edinburgh (1992–95). He contributed the special study on 'Disclosure of Life Assurance Commission' for Chapter 5.

Elisabeth Spence: spent eight years as a professional worker with emotionally disturbed children and young people in the

Highlands of Scotland; after graduating BD, she completed her probationer assistantship in an Edinburgh parish. She contributed the material on 'Fractured Families – Broken Children?' for Chapter 3.

Pauline Steenbergen: currently probationer assistant minister at South Queensferry: a graduate in English and Philosophy at Aberdeen, she lived and worked in the Grassmarket Mission in Edinburgh while studying for her BD. She contributed the special study on 'Caring – The Ethics of Community Care and Development' for Chapter 5.

Una Stewart: has a background in teaching; served five years as a parish deaconess in the Borders; she has also worked for the World Trade Centre in Rotterdam; completed her BD at New College; currently a probationer minister in the Church of Scotland. She contributed four brief case studies on the theme of reconciliation in Chapter 2.

Heather Wraight: spent twenty years making radio programmes for the Third World with Radio Worldwide; was director for nine years before taking her MTh in the Theology and Ethics of Communication at Edinburgh; is now Assistant Director of Christian Research in London. She contributed the special study on 'Some Dilemmas in Professional Ethics in the Media' for Chapter 5.

John Young: after completing research for his doctoral thesis in Social Anthropology, he spent several years in education in Scotland before working in research and lay-training with the Church in Southern Pakistan; now completing his BD at New College in preparation for ministry. He contributed the special study on Northern Ireland for Chapter 5.

Ian McDonald: as tutor in Christian ethics, he has had the privilege of working with the above students, as well as with others of their contemporaries whose labours could not be included here. It has been exciting to see how their very different contributions have come together to form a coherent expression of Christian ethics in practice. As author of the rest of the book and co-ordinator of the contributed work, it has been his task to supply the theoretical material which the special studies have presupposed.

Aims and objectives

It may be helpful to clarify the aims and objectives of the book at this point. The *general aims* may be stated as follows:

1. to provide an introduction to Christian ethics which will be a useful learning tool for new students in the field as well as for other readers with an interest in Christian ethics;
2. to promote an understanding of what is involved in 'thinking about ethics' and 'doing the truth in love' in such a way that moral dialogue may be resumed for reflective people who have not found conventional teaching either interesting or convincing;
3. to present the subject as part of the interpretive cycle described above: *praxis>theoria>praxis* – and so promote methods and skills appropriate to moral discourse;
4. to encourage independent thinking and reflection, in the belief that in a rapidly changing world the priority is not so much to preserve traditional values at all costs as to rediscover Christian values in today's world in all its complexity.

The *particular objectives* are as follows:

1. to present a structured study encompassing basic orientations and the Bible as ground of value (Chapter 1), a review of major elements in personal and social values (Chapter 2), family values as a special area of concern (Chapter 3), the question of sexual orientation and preference, with particular reference to homosexuality (Chapter 4), and social values and public policy (Chapter 5);
2. to follow a strategy – through the use of case studies or similar material – which combines empirical studies

     with theoretical reflection, both in the more general
     chapters and in the special studies of selected issues;

3. to relate the material to real life situations or dilemmas
     in the contemporary world;

4. to present the material in such a way as to encourage a
     high degree of participation on the part of readers in
     the issues in question.

A living tradition – like living scholarship – is characterised by openness, by a willingness to listen to others' encounters with life and its riddles, and by a commitment to 'doing the truth in love'. It will respect traditional authority but expect it to be alive to the possibility that new situations ask new questions for which old answers to old questions may not suffice. The scrutiny of presuppositions and assumptions – one's own and others' – is a major part of 'thinking about values'.

Even determining the approach and scope of a book on Christian values involves presuppositions. Let us declare some of them at the outset. This book assumes that Christian values are important at a personal level, for churches or faith communities, and for society. It presupposes that balanced judgement is important: between theory and practice, the academic and the practical, and the traditional and the contemporary. It rejects superficial judgements on ethics or moral values – for example, that they are 'subjective', or depend on 'how one feels', or are mere social conditioning. It similarly rejects the marginalising of theology or Christian perspectives on ethics, as if they were unworthy contributors to serious debate today. It also rejects the suggestion that in studying religion in the modern world one can only be descriptive and not deal with matters such as value or the validity of belief; or that a departure from such descriptiveness involves one in prescriptive authoritarianism! It assumes, and hopes to demonstrate, that it is possible to have an open 'discovery approach' to Christian values, and that Christian moral discourse is in fact a civilised and enlightened area of enquiry.

Of course, this book represents only *one* possible approach to the subject. It doubtless reveals preferences not declared above: for biblical interpretation; for a personal and social stance; and for contemporary relevance to society. None of these, however, should detract from the open, exploratory view which it is our aim to commend. It is in this context and in this spirit that we can approach questions of gender and sexuality which rightly command the attention of ethicists and which the churches are often felt to address inadequately.

But first, since clarification of basic terms is important, some primary definitions of terms are called for.

Definitions

Morality This term, as used in current debate, relates to the *mores* or actual behaviour patterns of persons, groups or communities, complete with a marking of the boundaries of action (laws, rules, taboos), penalties, goals and aspirations actually sponsored within society. Its rootedness in empirical contexts opens it to investigation by the social sciences. The term is also used in connection with specific issues within society – for example, the morality of deterrence or the free market – where the emphasis is on the practices and policies in operation or advocated in society. 'Immorality' is often used in relation to the infringement of such *mores*. It is not restricted to personal or sexual misdemeanour.

Ethics is reflection on morality. It requires that one can achieve sufficient detachment from the situation to allow rational argumentation, critical analysis and general reflection. It tends to move through a spectrum, one end of which is close to or overlaps morality while the other end is academic in nature. This latter end of the spectrum is represented by the tradition of moral philosophy which originated with the ancient Greeks, as well as by the discipline of Christian ethics. Its task is to clarify moral criteria, to test philosophical or theological theories of moral value, and to reveal the nature of assumptions made both in the sphere of morality itself and in academic interpretation and reflection. At the other end of the spectrum, moral philosophers now engage more freely than they once did in specific moral issues such as abortion and animal rights.

Christian ethics has always been concerned to relate theory and practice.

Christian ethics is a branch of ethics which relates to the same kind of spectrum as ethics itself but which is grounded in the Christian tradition of moral understanding. This means that the tradition of Christian faith and the Bible is brought to bear on moral reality and provides the groundwork of a Christian life-style. This activity presupposes a moral and interpretive community to which Christian ethics relates, for the Bible, like the Christian faith itself, found articulation in faith communities; and it is not self-explanatory but requires interpretation and application, which again presupposes community. Different kinds of communities contribute to Christian ethics. Some are indeed involved in practical ministry, where the insights of ordinary people sharpened by experience are seen to be valid even when not well articulated, and where the resources of the Christian community help to develop ethical perspectives. Some may be professional groups, concerned to relate the ethics of business or profession to open scrutiny. Others may be learning communities: this book emerges from just such a context, where the teacher is also a learner even when teaching Christian ethics as an academic subject, while the students actively explore moral reality in Christian perspectives. It is interesting that some moral philosophers are also rediscovering the importance of community for ethics.[4]

Values is a term which denotes elements of moral worth in the character of a person or group: elements which show what a person prizes most in living – rather like the 'pearl of great price' in Jesus' parable. They are variously described as general guides to behaviour, as giving direction to life, as maturing and evolving with experience, as patterns of evaluating and behaving, or simply as goals. To adopt the term *Christian values*, as we have done, is to suggest a focus on the moral

[4] Cf. A. MacIntyre, *After Virtue* (1981).

priorities of Christian experience, on Christian ways of evaluating moral experience, on Christian life-style and Christian action. This kind of reflection, however, is never done in a holy huddle where the group reduces reality to fit the limitations of its own world view but opens out on the world of human experience, with all its imponderables and apparent contradictions. 'Values' is thus a more sharply focussed term than morality, ethics or Christian ethics. Occasionally, the term *disvalue* is used in this book. This denotes lack of moral worth in an action, which may have to be accepted on occasion for the sake of positive values achieved by the course of action in question.

Agape   There was a time when three Greek words were taken to distinguish three different types of love. *Eros* was the desire for the other, as in sexual longing and the yearning of the soul for eternal bliss. *Philia* was affection: the love of brothers and sisters. *Agape* was disinterested love: a love not evoked by any quality of the beloved and offered without thought of return. Anders Nygren wrote a classic on the essential distinction between *agape* and *eros*.[5] It is important to have a clear picture of the priority and quality of *agape*, such as that offered in 1 Corinthians 13; and also to find its motivation not only in our awareness of the quality of experienced love but also, beyond our immediate experience, in the story of God's love for us in Christ. It is also important, however, *not* to distinguish too sharply between these terms nor to ignore areas of overlap. *Eros* needs to be enriched, if not transformed, by *agape* to create mutuality and impart the self-giving which is involved in an enduring relationship. And *philia* can be a channel for *agape*: as John Ferguson has put it, 'it is surprising that the Christian tradition has not made more of the value of friendship.... We are the poorer because we have not developed it.'[6]

There are many different foci in Christian ethics, and a distinctive view can be based on almost any one of them. It may

[5] A. Nygren, *Agape and Eros* (1954).
[6] J. Ferguson, *Moral Values in the Ancient World* (1958), p. 75.

be useful to clarify the following terms and perspectives. (Some readers may prefer simply to use this material for reference purposes and proceed directly to the first chapter.)

Biblical ethics Reformed ethics in particular has given prominence to the moral teaching of the Old and New Testaments. At a popular level, it is often supposed that the ten commandments or the teaching of Jesus offer direct commands and counsels for today. But, in view of the diversity of the material and its historical and social distance, major questions of interpretation and understanding have to be faced. Yet biblical perspectives remain important for determining the ground of value. (See Chapter 1 below.)

Natural law The Catholic tradition has long prized the notion that, in some sense, there is a moral law written in our hearts and informing our moral world, in which every form of life can be seen to move towards its proper goal. Yet such is the variety in life that a concept of this kind may be viable only if used in general terms. Nevertheless, moral theology has been plagued by attempts to argue that certain acts are *intrinsically* right or wrong – irrespective of situation. In the modern age, ecological problems raise the question of natural law in a different form, arguing for the right relationship of *homo sapiens* to the global and cosmic totality: a difficult, controversial but important and potentially creative perspective. (See Chapter 1 below.)

Rules and principles Some forms of Christian ethics which stress action have advocated a normative basis of rules, principles, commands and maxims. Since the supreme value is usually recognised as *agape* or Christian love, this approach has tended to speak paradoxically of 'the law of love', 'loving in principle', or 'in-principled love'. Justice is an important principle, though its nature requires definition. Casuistry (case law) or the principle of accommodation relates the binding norm to the particularity of situations. While this general approach can impart rigidity to Christian ethics, it is of great importance for social ethics and public questions. (See Chapter 1 below.)

Moral philosophy   This has influenced Christian ethics in a variety of ways. Immanuel Kant presented a normative theory of ethics, involving 'categorical imperatives' (i.e., universally binding norms) in conjunction with the *motive* of good will. The 'Golden Rule' – 'Do unto others as you would that they should do to you' – is a biblical example of a categorical imperative. On the other hand, the Utilitarians rejected norms in favour of an ethics which had utility as its primary goal. Hence, *goal* and *consequence* became important criteria, especially in (Christian) social ethics. One of the services moral philosophy performed for Christian ethics was its insistence that criteria should be properly clarified. (See Chapters 1 and 2 below.)

Context or situation   Others countered the emphasis on norm with an emphasis on the context of action. The 'situationist', rejecting permanent norms apart from the principle of *agape*, finds out as much as possible about the situation and then acts in love to bring about the most loving outcome. 'Situation ethics' provides guidelines for personal and even professional action, but is of doubtful relevance to social ethics, where norms appear essential. Others emphasise not only the situation in which a specific action is performed but also the context which informs the agent's decision. Such contextualism recognises that the agent seldom acts purely as an individual but is influenced, if not determined, by the community and culture to which he or she belongs: a perception of importance to the Christian community. (Discussed briefly in Chapter 1.)

Personalism   From the sixties onwards, there was an increasing impatience with formalistic ethics. Should Christian ethics not be insisting that 'people matter'? What was needed was an ethics of the person. This focused in the first instance on motive, on the person as moral agent, on personal formation and interaction, and on moral learning. It may well represent the recovery of the fundamental nature of Christian ethics, but it requires careful handling since it can be misrepresented as relating characteristically to personal 'feelings'. Its relation to social ethics is also problematic. (See Chapter 2.)

Virtue The traditional way, since Aristotle, of expressing personalist perspectives has been through the concept of virtue. Priority is given not to a person's acts as such but to the kind of person one is. It thus relates to character and the virtues or moral qualities of the good person. It gives rise to the popular notion of 'the mean between two extremes', sometimes applied to the public realm at least at a pragmatic level. (See Chapter 2.)

Community The moral community is increasingly recognised, in moral philosophy as in Christian ethics, as the matrix of ethics. An emphasis on community has obvious relevance to churches and faith communities. It also underlines the social interaction which shapes and conditions personal formation, moral discernment and even views of society or 'moral worlds'. It provides commentary on the pluralism which obtains in the area of values, and raises the question whether there are broad 'fiduciary foundations' in the moral realm. (See Chapters 2–5.)

Narrative Every moral agent, like every moral community, has a story. It is 'my story', 'our story'. Stories affirm the historical, social and personal nature of human experience and identity. Stories interact: 'my story' may then be enriched, even transformed. At the centre of Christian ethics is the interaction of 'my story' and 'the Christian story', conveyed through the Christian community. Here is yet another perspective on personal and social value. (See Chapters 2–5.)

Structures Human behaviour is constrained by the structures of human society. These may be social, educational, cultural, religious, business or political. They may be liberating or oppressive. In its social dimension, ethics is directly involved with them: whether in a reinforcing or oppositional role, or through interaction with their implicit values. (See Chapters 3–5.)

Secularity Society is not neutral! It generates its own sets of values, dictated not only by broad consensus but by the structures of authority. Religion is often seen to represent not only residual values of a traditional kind but also marginal views. It may also be seen as divisive. Christian ethics has a complicated role here: to temper worldly wisdom with a higher wisdom (as in the biblical 'wisdom' tradition) and thus influence it for good; to have a critical role in relation to the values explicitly advocated or implicitly acted upon (or rejected) in society; to promote dialogue in matters of ethics; and to point to 'fiduciary foundations' or the bases of moral values. (See Chapter 5 in particular.)

CHAPTER 1

BASIC PERSPECTIVES

I *Right Action and Relevant Circumstances*

CASE STUDY

A doctor writes:

A fourteen year old girl was brought by an anxious mother to my
surgery. The mother, an extremely sensible and caring person, was
a nursing sister in our local hospital. She had known for the past
week that her daughter was pregnant and though saddened by the
news felt it important that she did not add blame and guilt to the
difficulties her daughter was facing. Both the girl and her parents
were active church members and this had made it more difficult for
the mother and daughter to tell her father. Because they knew of my
deep Christian faith and also because the child was afraid to talk to
a male doctor they had waited until my return from holiday. By then
the pregnancy was nearing the twelve week gestation after which
time termination by evacuation of the uterus would be difficult.

During the course of the consultation, it became obvious that
the child regretted her sexual behaviour and she felt that to have
the baby was her punishment. Both her parents felt acutely the
moral dilemma of their Christian belief, seeing abortion as sinful,
yet also aware that the girl had suffered considerably and that their
most loving action might be to suggest that the pregnancy be
ended. The social consequences were also considered. The girl's
partner seemed to have disappeared since hearing of the pregnancy
and he certainly did not wish to be associated with any decision.
The girl was still at school, in an academic stream, and would have
been expected eventually to go to college or university. Both
mother and daughter realised that to continue with these plans
would be unrealistic unless the mother gave up her nursing career

or the baby was placed for adoption. Neither of these options seemed right to the family.

The situation was further complicated by the girl's medical history. She had been an insulin-dependent diabetic since birth and I sensed that one of the factors in her having had sexual intercourse at this age was a desperate need to prove herself 'normal' in the eyes of her peers. In spite of twice daily injections, her blood sugar level was still difficult to control, and to continue the pregnancy would increase the risk to this young girl's life. At the very least, her health and that of the baby were threatened by the serious consequences of unstable diabetes.

Together we discussed all aspects as openly and fully as possible. I suggested that they talk together as a family and that they also speak to their parish minister. They returned the following day, and asked me directly for my advice. Until this time I had always believed that abortion was wrong, though when there was a grave risk to the health of either the woman or child it may be the more caring decision. On this occasion I felt that my medical duty was to recommend referral for termination and I told them that I believed it would be wrong to delay any further. The mother was obviously relieved when I voiced this opinion but the girl still remained convinced that she had to live with the consequences of her actions.

Counselling of patients is normally non-directive. However I found myself actively trying to persuade her that it would be the responsible decision to end the pregnancy. Though unhappy about using my influence in this way, I was aware that I was entrusted by the family to help them work through the moral as well as the medical aspects of the dilemma. My own acceptance of the role of actively advocating the taking of life was difficult. I believed that the God I knew in Christ cared about the girl more than moral law. I could not accept that God wished her life to be endangered in order to punish. Above all there was a sense of God's generosity, which would forgive if we were misguided.

Although she listened, the young girl wished to continue the pregnancy and refused the opportunity of receiving further counselling.

Sadly, in spite of the girl spending the following weeks in hospital receiving specialist care, the baby died *in utero*. Subsequently, the girl was gravely ill for many months and has since been advised to have no further pregnancies. Her health has been permanently damaged. If faced with the same situation today she says that she would have chosen differently. (Marion Keston)

This case touches on many perspectives on ethics. One is professional ethics and the close relationship it bears to pastoral care and counselling: e.g., advice giving or 'taking over' from the client. Another is personal ethics, involving feelings of shame and guilt, and also the need for acceptance on the human plane and forgiveness at an even deeper level. Yet another is family ethics, where feelings of alarm and disappointment coexist with loving support, a willingness to understand and the desire to do what is best for all concerned. A further dimension is the conflict of roles; between nurse and mother; father and churchman; the girl in relation to her family and in relation to her peers; even the doctor as professional and believer. The question of autonomy is also apparent: mother, father and doctor advise, but the decision is finally the girl's – even if it is the wrong decision. Religion also emerges as a complicating factor, supplying firm notions of right and wrong action, which to some extent make the resolution of the problem more intense; while there are distorted notions of punishment on the girl's part. There is also, certainly on the doctor's side, a mature theological perspective, including a strong awareness of divine generosity and infinite understanding.

Why should religion be a complicating factor? Let us emphasise at the outset that it is also a fundamental element, reaching to the depths of human existence. Let us also discount the notion that religion simply reinforces conventional elements, such as 'What will the neighbours think?' or 'How will this affect my social standing – or my esteem in the church?' Such social dimensions are, of course, a part of the scene, but we must try to set them in perspective. Nor do we set religion aside in favour of some shallow secular notion that 'these things happen' and it is better not to make a fuss about them.

Religion is a complicating factor because its moral emphasis is often not understood in its wholeness. Frequently, the focus is placed on the moral demand. In a case like the above, people remember a familiar commandment such as 'Thou shalt not kill' or a principle such as 'respect for life' and *assume* that this rules out abortion, no matter what the circumstances are. Or they remember church teaching which lists abortion as an intrinsically evil act. Again, they might link religion with chaste behaviour in sexual matters and hold that there should be 'no sex outside marriage'. If the moral demand is isolated in this way, the result may be a heightened crisis of guilt when failure occurs and even a sense that punishment is deserved. Law breakers should pay the penalty for their crimes! The girl in the case study clearly had a guilt complex and was determined to punish herself.

But religion – and a discussion of Christian ethics presupposes the Christian religion here – has another side, which springs from the heart of things even more directly than moral demand. The doctor spoke of 'God's generosity': 'I believed that the God I knew in Christ cared about the girl more than moral law.' The centre of the Christian faith is God's grace: his infinite understanding and forgiveness. His judgement falls on those who cannot or will not accept that he accepts them! This is not theological day-dreaming. Deep down within ourselves we *need* the assurance that we are accepted, understood and forgiven – not simply by those we have offended but at a fundamental level, so that we do not become moral and spiritual cripples for life. Nor should religion be a vehicle for aggressive condemnation or self-hate.

It is essential to hold together God's grace and the moral life to which he calls us. They are not held together satisfactorily if we presuppose the primacy of moral demand and regard God's forgiveness as a kind of emergency service, mopping up when things have gone wrong. Nor is it satisfactory to weaken the moral demand and assume that 'anything goes'. God's grace calls us to respond in kind to his nature, which is love and truth. We understand only some aspects of truth, even through the witness of Bible and church. Truth is transcendent – in its totality, always beyond our grasp. We follow the signals of it, which are sufficient to enable us, in St Paul's words, to 'speak the truth in love' – relying on the infinite understanding of God, who alone understands all things.

It behoves us, then, to be careful when we pronounce any action to be intrinsically wrong, irrespective of the circumstances in which it is performed. Circumstances include not only special factors in the situation of the agent – such as provocation or peer pressure, inner disturbance or external constraint – but also questions of motive and intention. Even if we take the ten commandments as statements of unchanging moral norms, their interpretation necessarily includes consideration of circumstances and intention. For example, 'thou shalt not kill' literally denotes, 'thou shalt do no murder'; but murder is specifically deliberate and unjustified killing. Many types of killing are not *explicitly* denoted here: including self-defence (*justifiable* homicide), killing in war, capital punishment and a whole list of specific issues, such as killing animals for food, and abortion. All of these require careful interpretation and application of the commandment, taking into account all relevant circumstances and intentions, and recognising the limitations and fallibility of our own judgements.

To make this point as strongly as we have is not to undermine 'the moral law' but rather to set it firmly within human experience and to interpret it theologically. The divine law, as Thomas Aquinas recognised, is known fully only to God. The Bible speaks of the righteousness of God. As human beings, we are not left with our feeble perceptions alone, but are guided through the witness of the Bible and the experience of the faithful through the ages. All such witness is relative to context: we must make our moral judgements in today's world. We do so within the parameters of the 'Great Commandments': love to God, and love to neighbour; and of the maxim of the 'Golden Rule' (or the principle of reciprocity): 'Do (not) to others as you would that they should do (not) to you'.[1] We

[1] Matt. 22:37–39; Mark 12:29–31; Luke 10:27; cf. Matt. 7:12; Luke 26:27–28; V. P. Furnish, *The Love Command in the New Testament* (1973), esp. pp. 24–45; J. I. H. McDonald, 'The Great Commandment and the Golden Rule', in A. G. Auld (ed), *Understanding Poets and Prophets* (1993), pp. 213–276. The matter is discussed further below, in Chapter 2. One form of Immanuel Kant's categorical imperative, which combined duty and goodwill, was very

have, above all, the teaching of Jesus, with its emphasis on living in response to God's graciousness: hence, the beatitudes, love to enemy, overcoming prejudice, attending to the deeper purpose of scriptural teaching, rejecting the distorting features of bad religion, and so on. The 'moral law' is really a moral direction, which requires us to know who we are and where we are heading in life.

To return for a moment to our opening case study: it shows clearly the *dilemma* presented by the unwanted pregnancy. None of the people involved found abortion an attractive solution (it is a 'disvalue', something not desirable in itself), but the parents and the doctor eventually concluded that, *given all the circumstances of the case*, it was the right course to take. It is all too easy for those not involved in the case to pontificate about the rights and wrongs of abortion, but viewed from the standpoint of involvement the case is seen differently – and much more painfully. For this reason, we do not present here the traditional arguments for and against abortion – these are readily obtainable elsewhere.[2] One of the aims of Christian ethics is to develop not only a rational analysis of the general arguments in a case but also an understanding of the particular circumstances and personal dilemmas involved.

*****

The type of ethics which appeals to principles, commands, maxims and exhortations is known in ethics as 'deontology' (from the Greek, *dei, deontos*, it is necessary or required). One form (*narrow rule deontology*) specifies actions or classes of actions which are intrinsically wrong. Thus the encyclical letter *Veritatis Splendor* (1993), which was designed to reaffirm the fundamental principles of Roman Catholic moral teaching, includes 'artificial' contraception, abortion, homosexual

similar to the 'Golden Rule'. For him, the principle of reciprocity was clearly important.
  [2] Cf. article by R. Gardner, 'Abortion and abortion Counselling', in A. V. Campbell (ed.), *A Dictionary of Pastoral Care* (1987) – including bibliography.

behaviour and pre-marital sex as intrinsically wrong acts.[3] In rule deontology, the action is wrong in itself, although it may inhere in a wider authority, such as that of a church (cf. the *magisterium* of the Roman Catholic Church), or the scriptures, or in a view of the moral order of the universe. Acts are intrinsically wrong simply because that's the way things are in the God-given moral order.

It is fair to say that many Roman Catholic moral theologians find this approach unsatisfactory, for reasons similar to those which emerged in our case study. While traditional Protestant examples have included, at certain periods, gambling, card playing, drinking, even theatre-going, more typically appeal is made to a biblical basis such as the ten commandments and the teaching of Jesus. However, because of the importance of circumstances and context, many Protestant and Roman Catholic ethicists prefer to think in terms of 'biblical principles'. This is to invoke *wide rule deontology*. Unlike rules, which are specific, principles are generalised and therefore better suited to indicate or relate to the grounds of ethics. Justice, equality and fraternity, for example, are fundamental principles. Other examples include veracity or truthfulness, fidelity or trustworthiness, integrity, loyalty, prudence, benevolence, beneficence, humility, reciprocity, and – very important in Christian ethics – neighbour love (*agape*). Hence, in the Hebrew prophetic tradition it is possible to sum up moral obligation in the language of principles:

> The Lord has told you mortals what is good,
> and what it is that the Lord requires of you:
> only to act justly, to love loyalty,
> to walk humbly with your God. (Micah 6.8, *REB*)

St Paul speaks of three abiding virtues: faith, hope and love:

---

[3] 'Encyclical Letter *Veritatis Splendor* Addressed by the Supreme Pontiff Pope John II to all the Bishops of the Catholic Church Regarding Certain Fundamental Questions of the Church's Moral Teaching', dated 6 August 1993, released to press 5 October 1993. For responses to *Veritatis Splendor*, cf. J. Wilkins (ed), *Understanding Veritatis Splendor*, (1994), and particularly J. Selling and J. Jans (eds.), *The Splendor of Accuracy* (1994). There was also a useful series of articles in *The Tablet*, Oct.–Dec., 1993. See also the subsequent encyclical, *Evangelium Vitae*, March 1995.

'and the greatest of the three is love' (1Cor. 13:13) In Romans 13:10, he observes that love is the fulfilment of the law. But neither the prophets nor Paul reduce ethics to principles alone, as is apparent from the wider context of the passages cited. They always presuppose an active relationship with God.

Rules and principles – narrow and wide deontology – have thus greater moral significance when linked to motive and inner disposition, to the awakening of moral and spiritual understanding (as they are in the biblical tradition), and to the particularities of cases. This is not to restrict their value unduly. They are of particular service in social ethics, as we shall see in later chapters, and in moral education, where clear guidance is required.[4]

---

[4] For a detailed discussion of deontology, cf. I. C. M. Fairweather and J. I. H. McDonald, *The Quest for Christian Ethics* (1984), pp. 3–37; P. Ramsey, *Deeds and Rules in Christian Ethics* (1967). The importance of circumstances led to an emphasis on situation as in J. Fletcher, *Situation Ethics* (1966); *Moral Responsibility* (1967); and on the perspective of the faith community which provides the context for moral decision-making, as in P. L. Lehmann, *Ethics in a Christian Context* (1963). On deontology, the following qualifications and observations may be made in brief:

(i) *Prescriptive rules and principles are too specific* to constitute a moral theory in themselves. What happens if two rules clash, and how does one allow for exceptions?

(ii) Rule deontology should be distinguished carefully from *legalism*. Legalism holds that all that matters is obeying the law (or rule or regulation); i.e., to carry out the rule is the 'necessary and sufficient condition' of morality. It often occurs in petty officialdom ('it's more than my job's worth'). Rule deontology is not in itself legalistic, but the danger must be recognised.

(iii) *The danger of rationalisation* must be recognised. One may profess the highest moral principles but have ulterior motives of a different sort. Human beings are complex, and have the capacity to reorganise their world from an egocentric standpoint. There is need for self-knowledge and awareness of the complexity of motivation.

(iv) Attention needs to be paid to the *rhetoric* of moral discourse, which can also be deceptive. Moral discourse can become entangled with other forms of discourse – polemics, propaganda, homiletics, catechetics, to name but a few. These can have a distorting effect on the moral content, which requires critical analysis.

(v) *Sanctions* frequently accompany deontological ethics. An ethics of rules presupposes obedience to the rules. Disobedience incurs penalty. In law, these penalties are imposed by courts. Much thought is given to the function of such sanctions. Deontology is often considered 'realistic' in its assessment

Because rules cannot apply neatly to every situation and are not well adapted to deal with exceptions, *casuistry* or *case law* is an essential procedure. Sometimes this term has a bad connotation ('twisting' the rule), but its task, as in case law, is to relate rules to situations. Many examples occur in the Bible: for example, the case of the dangerous ox in Ex. 21:28–30. Here one notes how crucial the assessment of the empirical factors is, including the nature of the animal, the official cautioning of the owner, and the foreseeable consequences of not restraining its movements. There is also a fundamental concern for justice, including appropriate penalties for harm caused to others.

N. Wolterstorff has presented a view of moral education in which the emphasis is on right action and relevant circumstances: in short, on casuistry. He distinguished six phases of casuistic discussion, which are meant to be understood and applied with some flexibility (the comments in brackets refer to the case study cited above and do not originate with Wolterstorff):

1. Describe the facts of the situation as accurately as possible and as elaborately as necessary... (the assessment of empirical factors and relevant circumstances is always essential).
2. Try to discover the various options actually available to the agent.... Specify the possible choices... (cf. the agonising choices facing the girl and those concerned for her).
3. Decide whether some of these options are clearly ruled out by moral law... (abortion is often held to be morally wrong on the grounds that it breaks the sixth

of human nature and in its insistence on the need to curb human lawlessness and to require the punishment of offenders. In religious discourse, the whole notion of divine judgement reflects this kind of thinking. Disobedience to the law of God incurs divine judgement, and images of hell emphasise the point. Both the moral and the religious outworking of this view have severe limitations. If one acts mainly or solely out of fear of punishment, this may be effective in curbing social misbehaviour but it does not engender moral or spiritual maturity. At worst, it completely distorts moral reality and the Christian gospel.

commandment or the principle of 'the right to life'; but this is to overstate the moral rule or principle and to prejudge the case; abortion is a disvalue, but the moral judgement depends on the circumstances).

4. Try to predict the consequences of each of the remaining options... (that is what the doctor and parents were doing – and possibly the girl herself: 'consequences' are important and are discussed in the next section).

5. Decide which of one's moral standards seem to apply to the case as thus outlined... (one line is 'good is to be done and promoted, evil avoided'; the 'law of love' applies, as always: what is the most loving action in the situation?).

6. If necessary, decide which of the standards that apply ought to receive priority... (loving care transcends any formal commandment: cf. the doctor's comment, 'I believed that the God I knew in Christ cared about the girl more than moral law').[5]

Such an outline hardly does justice to Wolterstorff's proposals but it provides an illustration of an approach to the case in question in terms of one particular strategy of moral education. Other interpretations of this model are possible, and it is not suggested that the view taken here necessarily coincides with that of Wolterstorff.

In the above discussion, appeal was made to the foreseeable consequences of possible lines of action or inaction. This raises the question of a further type of moral criterion, namely, consequences of action, which we are now about to discuss. Moral education always presupposes a growing moral awareness, which guides one in the choices that have to be made. Such concerns will receive further attention in the next chapter.

---

[5] N. Wolterstorff, *Educating for Responsible Action* (1980), p. 105.

II *Consequences and Goal of Action*

A DEBATE: MORAL ISSUES IN BOXING

The debating chamber is well filled. The chairperson has taken her seat, with the leaders of the opposing views on either side. She calls the meeting to order and announces the motion: 'This house believes that boxing is a violent activity and should be banned as a sport.' She calls for the motion to be presented.

The speaker begins by referring to well known pictures of boxers who have suffered brain damage or grave impairment of faculties. He cites several well known cases. He goes on to speak of several notorious instances where boxers have died soon after being beaten in the ring. He thunders: 'The consequences of engaging in this so-called sport undoubtedly include life-threatening injury and death. This fact is incontrovertible.' But, he says, he is not going to rest his case on such evocative cases alone. There are sober rational arguments against this so-called sport to which such a discriminating audience will attach weight. He summarised the case in four propositions:

(i)   The sport involves a higher level of pain and injury than other sports. The evidence, he claims, speaks for itself.

(ii) The inflicting of pain and injury is inseparable from the actual objective of boxing. Accidental injury may occur in other sports, but in boxing it is the aim of the game!

(iii) Violence is inherent in the activity of boxing: boxing therefore promotes an indefensible end. No matter what euphemisms are used, the fact remains!

(iv) As a spectator sport, boxing encourages violent and aggressive feelings in the audience. The speaker cites a recent incident where a fight broke out between rival factions in the audience and almost wrecked the auditorium. Violence begets violence!

In his peroration, he urges the house to face facts. Boxing is out of keeping with a civilised society – let alone a society which has some claim to Christian values. Other violent sports have been outlawed ages ago: bear baiting, badger baiting, dog fighting, cock fighting.... It is high time boxing suffered the same fate. The house should endorse the motion.

Called to reply, the opposer begins by attempting to calm the audience's evident excitement. Boxing is a controversial sport.

Every time an accident occurs and receives widespread publicity, exaggerated claims and the propaganda of the opposing camp whip up emotions that blind people to the real state of affairs. Boxing is not to everyone's taste. Fine! 'I dislike football. I hate its violence. I think kicking games are particularly dangerous. But I don't stop others who like to watch them.' Tolerance and diversity of taste must be accommodated in a modern society. And in a debate such as this, the power of reasoned argument and the cogency of balanced judgement must win the day. He advances the following case:

(i)   Viewed dispassionately, boxing is so carefully supervised and controlled that it is certainly no more dangerous than other sporting activities. Other competitive sports entail a high level of pain and injury: what about rugby football, or long distance running, or squash?

(ii)   Boxing is totally misrepresented if construed as a violent attack. The rules strictly forbid violence. Points are scored by landing blows, many without injury. Besides, the referee's word is law in boxing ('unlike some other games I could mention'), and he intervenes to protect against injury or undue physical punishment.

(iii) Boxing aims to perfect the skills of pugilism, not to promote or reward violence. Controlled aggression may serve to reduce violence. A degree of self-knowledge accrues from pitting oneself in controlled conditions against a worthy opponent: this has been described as 'a conscious celebrating of one's strength in vulnerability' ('oohs' and 'ahs' from the audience!).

(iv)   The spectators enjoy the skills, not the violence (a hint of scepticism from the opposition here!); the excitement is a useful social safety valve; in any case, many sports evoke expressions of aggression from the spectators; boxing should not be singled out for attack in this respect.

In his final appeal, the speaker underlined the personal and social benefits of boxing. If adequate provision was made, there would be fewer louts in our housing schemes and inner cities, for youngsters would gain enormously from being taught the skills and self-control that boxing encourages. They would find a legitimate and healthy outlet for their frustrated energy. Some sports *are* objectionable: the house might consider fox hunting in that category. There is no parallel with boxing. This is a sport in which people engage and which they watch voluntarily. Opposition to it is ill informed and often arises out of a misdirected puritanism which has no place in a broadminded, pluralist society. Let the house decide on the merits of the case.

The Chair called for questions and discussion. There was a lively session. Some wanted to emphasise the nature and seriousness of the injuries which do occur in boxing. Others argued that, especially in professional boxing, the knock-out cannot be separated from pain and injury, and this is true of some other blows as well. Pain and injury are not simply contingent factors, as in other sports. Several speakers refuted misrepresentations of the sport and indicated possible benefits from it.

The house then divided. How would you have voted? And why?[1]

For our purpose here, it is important to note that a large part of the debate was conducted in terms of consequences and goals. It would be useful for the reader to go back over the debate and identify the appeals made to the consequences of the activity of boxing.

Perhaps the most important contribution from the side of Christian ethics is the insistence that the issue be debated in moral terms. To do so, the ethicist requires to use arguments from goal and consequence, which are the coinage of social ethics. As we have noted, this type of argument enshrines hidden values: for example, that violence is not a good end in itself, it is a disvalue. To this, Christian ethics gives an unequivocal endorsement: the ethos of Jesus' ministry was one of non-violence; and there is a basic principle that it is wrong to inflict harm or injury on others. It is important not to 'jump the gun' here and conclude that boxing is thus ruled out on *a priori* grounds. The whole process of argumentation must be gone through, for the issue is whether boxing is unqualifiedly violent or harmful. As the debate suggests, the arguments are finely balanced. If the balance of the case is judged to be against boxing, then the moral arguments should be put forward clearly in the forum which a pluralist society offers.

[1] Some material in this discussion is derived from Paul Davis and Cheryl Foster, 'Aestheticising violence: ethical issues in Boxing', *P. E. News* (University of Edinburgh), 4.1.1991, p. 1.

Another possibility is to argue that the controls on the sport should be further developed to obviate harmful or violent features.

*****

Consequences represent an accepted criterion of moral value, which is subsumed under the term *teleology* (Greek *telos*, end or goal) as opposed to deontology (norm or rule). But does it provide a viable alternative to rule deontology? Value is located in the good end or outcome of action: for example, happiness, alleviation of suffering, excellence. No action is intrinsically right or wrong: it all depends on its consequences; in particular, the *foreseeable consequences* of the action. If the consequences were intended or reasonably foreseeable, the agent is morally responsible for them. Actual or accidental consequences are not morally culpable if they could not reasonably have been foreseen. Thus intentions enter the equation, although one still has a responsibility to assess the likely consequences of one's actions. Pleading 'I never meant to...' may not be adequate.

The criterion of consequences and goal occurs frequently in social ethics, where *utilitarianism*, which is found in the works of philosophers such as Locke, Bentham, Mill and Moore, is its most celebrated expression. The good end is that which is useful to (has utility for) society. An outline discussion of it is found in the footnote below.[2]

---

[2] Following Frankena (*Ethics*, 1973), we distinguish three different types:

(i) *Act Utilitarianism* The basic question in this case is: which action of mine will provide the greatest balance of good over evil? However, in achieving this end, I may be forced to face up to questions about the means used to attain it, and to answer such challenges, one may have to resort to some *deontological* principle such as justice.

(ii) *General Utilitarianism* places action in a general context: 'Suppose everyone did the same?' One can see the popular force of such arguments (e.g., in moral education), but too often they ignore the extent to which situations alter cases. We would certainly have to insert a qualifying clause, 'everyone, *placed in similar circumstances*, would act with this end in view...'. The trouble lies precisely in the generality.

Perhaps the best way forward is to take a public issue – say, euthanasia – to illustrate the importance of this criterion in public debate. Yet we find at the outset that, since the problem centres on the prohibition of killing, deontology is also involved. As we have already seen, the commandment was understood in Israel to relate to murder.[3] Other forms of killing have to be assessed on the merits of the case, which frequently turn on teleological concerns such as aim or goal in acting, intention and foreseeable consequences. Intention is clearly important: accidental killing is a completely different matter. It is sometimes suggested in relation to euthanasia that to introduce exceptions to the prohibition of killing would have the *consequence* of devaluing life; but exceptions occur in most cultures – war, self-defence, capital punishment, for example – without at least a general devaluation of life. Sometimes it is argued that an act of compassion, such as terminating acute suffering, is justified *teleologically*: it has a good end in view. Is not 'a good death' a desirable goal? Popular debate about the possibility of legalising euthanasia frequently appeals to consequences. Would it not have the effect of putting the patient (whose assent is required) under too great pressure – for example, not to be a burden on others? Would it be similarly devastating for relatives – not to appear to want to be rid of the patient, or to be thought mercenary, or to have to take such a momentous decision? Would it not put the doctors under a corresponding strain? And so on.

Discussions of euthanasia usually centre around questions such as the 'active' or 'passive' (direct or indirect) nature of the steps taken. Direct euthanasia, even with the assent of the patient (in itself problematic), is illegal in many countries. Indirect euthanasia relates to termination of life as the outcome of treatment which was directly aimed at another end, namely

---

(iii) *Rule Utilitarianism* tries to combine 'useful end' with 'moral rule'. Not only would everyone, similarly situated, observe a particular moral rule, but the moral rule is validated by reference to the good end or consequence. Here we have, ostensibly, a way of distinguishing between good rules (laws) and bad.

[3] See above on abortion, and cf. the discussion of the Bible in IV below.

relief from pain.[4] As long as euthanasia remains illegal in a given country, the intention of treatment must be to relieve pain.

The difficulty about this position is that it may involve an element of 'double think'. Even if the intention is to relieve pain, the *foreseeable consequence* is that the patient dies. The method used to obviate this exposed ethical position is to lean heavily on the importance of intention. The intended outcome is the relief of pain. One cannot even say that death is the secondary intention, for that would still be intention! One has to distinguish between intention and knowledge. The doctor *knows* the likely outcome – but he or she does not *intend* it. Of course, the doctor cannot be said to have complete pre-knowlege of the outcome. Resort is often made to 'possibility' or 'probability': one suspects, for euphemistic purposes.

One way of handling what we have called, rather crudely, the element of double think is to invoke the 'principle of double effect', which has been succinctly outlined by Richard McCormick as follows:

1.   The action from which evil results is good or indifferent in itself; it is not morally evil.
2.   The intention of the agent is upright - i.e., the evil effect is sincerely not intended.
3.   The evil effect must be equally immediate causally with the good effect, for otherwise it would be a means to the good effect and would be intended.
4.   There must be a proportionately good reason for allowing the evil to occur.[5]

The first point establishes the principle that we may not do evil that good may come of it ('principle' denotes a deontological point, but consequence is also involved in the notion of evil *results*). The second invokes intention (teleology) and has the effect of insisting that the action is not done from malice,

---

[4] Cf. R. Gill, *A Textbook of Christian Ethics* (1985), pp. 420–21.
[5] R. A. McCormick in J. Macquarrie and J. Childress, *A New Dictionary of Christian Ethics* (1986), p. 162. On intention, cf. Fairweather and McDonald, *The Quest*, pp. 70–71.

caculated self-interest or other unworthy motive (motive as a criterion of action will be discussed later). The third deals with consequences and enforces the absence of a separate act designed to inflict death. The fourth invokes the notion of 'proportion': the balance of good must outweigh the evil (consequences again). This whole line of argument takes place largely within the tradition of moral theology and is fiercely debated.

Intention and consequences of action are clearly important criteria, yet as so often, they are not the whole story. Apart from the obvious deontological concern about not killing, there remains the theological and existential question of how death is to be regarded. What picture do we have of moral reality, indeed, of life itself? Humanistic Western society sees death as the enemy, a threat to one's being, and the terminus of meaningful life. It is possible to see it also as a release from suffering. In religious terms, it is the gateway to eternity. Here we reach the theological frontier of ethics and perhaps feel the need for a more holistic view of living and dying than most of us have.

> And thou, most kind and gentle death,
> Waiting to hush our latest breath,
>   O praise him, Alleluia!
> Thou leadest home the child of God,
> And Christ our Lord the way has trod.[6]

---

[6] St Francis of Assisi, tr. W. H. Draper, as in *The Church Hymnary*, Third Edition, no. 30.

III   *Natural Law*

CASE STUDY

An ethics class is discussing the case of 'the test-tube twins'. Specifically, a woman, aged 59, who was refused infertility treatment at a London clinic on the advice of its ethics committee on the grounds that she was too old to face the emotional stress of pregnancy, subsequently went to Italy and received treatment by an eminent specialist. She gave birth to twins in a London hospital, becoming apparently the world's oldest woman to have twins.

Since the case involved the decision of an ethics committee, it is not surprising that it produced lively, even heated, discussion in class. Initial reaction was as sharply divided as were reported comments in the press. Some agreed with one medical opinion that the case 'bordered on the Frankenstein syndrome'. It was *unnatural,* one student declared; and an older student directed something of an emotional outburst against the woman (which he subsequently withdrew). Clearly, it was an emotive issue – and also a complicated one. Objections were advanced on the issue of private health care (the woman was well off). Many people could not have such treatment: was this ethical? While some questioned IVF (*in vitro* fertilisation), also as 'an interference with nature' or 'playing God' or on grounds of medical priority, many readily agreed that the anguish of infertile couples could be very great and that to relieve such distress was a proper medical end. It was pointed out that such treatment was life enhancing and did not raise problems of life termination, as in abortion and euthanasia. But still there was unease: which is not surprising since an ethics committee in London advised against treatment in the first place!.

Two related issues seemed to worry many. One concerned the age of the woman. When the children are eighteen, she will be 77. Does this suggest a suitable home life? Yet her husband is considerably younger, thus at least moderating the force of the contention. Official opinion tended to be a little unsympathetic: no British centre, it was suggested, would be happy about allowing the test-tube baby procedure for people 'in significant middle age'. A BMA spokesman said the woman and her doctor should 'search their consciences as to where their responsibilities lie'. Others were more sympathetic to the woman's plight, 'even if she has left it rather late'. It could well be that many critics are betraying an 'ageist' prejudice. Had the woman been fifteen years younger, the controversy would have been much less. Perhaps this is no more than prejudice masquerading under the guise of affirming what is 'natural'! But, as the class began to see, medical care not only works with nature, it also intervenes in nature. A cancerous growth is 'natural', but medical science intervenes. Barrenness is a natural condition; why should medical science not intervene when new life is strongly desired? Several students declared that they had changed their views in the course of the discussion. Many were not convinced. Notions of 'the law of nature' die hard.

We all tend to use the term 'natural' in a loose way. It implies that what we affirm as 'natural' is somehow rooted in the nature of things. Often it is simply a view which has been shaped by social convention or custom. Assumptions about age, gender, and social or economic status can operate both surreptitiously and powerfully, as the above discussion suggests. In ethics, however, it is important to be clear about what we mean by 'natural law'. If we claim that there is an ultimate basis to moral obligation, and that humankind has a 'moral sense' which in some ways transcends the limitations of culture, then we must make doubly sure that we know what we are talking about!

*****

The recognition that there is a 'law of nature' goes back a long way. Stoicism used the concept of *logos* to denote the rational principle of the universe. As Cleanthes' *Hymn to Zeus* illustrates, the recipe for a happy life is to obey the universal law of God.[1]

---

[1] Human beings must seek to be true to the *logos* within them. Stoics therefore sought *apatheia*, detachment from corroding emotions or 'passions' which bound one to external goods. Yet many Stoics did not withdraw from society, but devoted themselves to public duty, distinguishing between classes of externals: those categorised as 'preferred' (such as health), 'undesirable' (such as sickness) and 'completely indifferent' (life and death). One can reasonably pursue 'preferred' ends and avoid their opposite: here is virtually a second form of 'natural law'. In public life, one does 'what is fitting' and thus performs one's reasonable duty.

It is possible to argue that some kind of notion of natural law informs moral understanding in the Old Testament, although it is seldom given precise articulation.[2] St Paul appealed to a model of natural law in his ministry to Jew and Gentile in Romans 1 and 2.

> When Gentiles who do not possess the law carry out its precepts by the light of nature, then, although they have no law, they are their own law; they show that what the law requires is written on their hearts, and to this their conscience gives supporting witness, since their own thoughts argue the case, sometimes against them, sometimes even for them. (Rom. 2:14–15)

It is only fair to say that this is not a recurring theme in Paul, although there is a suggestion of similar thinking in his Areopagus speech in Acts (cf. Acts 17:22–31). But it is so integral to his argument in Romans that its significance can hardly be denied. The 'light of nature' and the role of 'conscience' are morally significant in Paul: the latter term certainly embracing moral discernment.

St Thomas Aquinas (thirteenth century) is the fountainhead of natual law thinking in the Christian tradition. The influence of Aristotle provided a strongly teleological perspective. Aristotle deduced from his biological studies that everything tends towards a goal or end, and that each living thing progresses through its life cycle towards maturity or completion. In ethics, the good is that at which all things aim. Aristotle defined it as *eudaimonia*, which may be briefly characterised not simply as 'wellbeing' but as 'action in line with moral virtue'. Thus, the first precept of natural law is that *good is to be done and promoted, evil avoided*. Such a position presupposes that human beings have a degree of freedom: they ought to

---

[2] For example, tribal society had strong moral conventions which included the sanctity of hospitality and the right of asylum. Divine wisdom is immanent in creation and can be known through study and training. The prophet Amos' condemnation of the war atrocities of non-Israelite peoples presupposes that the latter were aware that their actions were morally inexcusable (Amos 1:3–2:3). All this is caught up and clarified in the laws of the covenant at Sinai/Horeb: cf. J. Barr, *Biblical Faith and Natural Theology* (1993).

make rational choices – but they may not. Aware of cultural relativity, Aquinas distinguished between the general principles of the moral law, which are valid for all, unchanging and ineradicable from the human heart, and secondary principles (such as mores or customs more susceptible to social conditioning), which may evince a degree of relativity and error, and may change from time to time. They may also be overridden by divine command. Also important for Aquinas was *synderesis,* or 'conscience', by which he denoted the inborn grasp of moral principles, essential to practical reason. He used *conscientia* in connection with the applying of moral principles to particular actions (we speak today of 'acting conscientiously').[3]

There have, of course, been great challenges to the world view Aquinas took for granted: the Renaissance, the Reformation and the Age of Enlightenment all played their part, not to speak of modern science and cosmology, and the rise of the social sciences. Yet in its interpretation of the moral quest of humankind, Aquinas' approach – if not his entire position – retains significance even for those whose world is very different from his. Moral values are not simply the by-products of particular ages and cultures, although many particular examples may be little more than that. They arise also through the human sense of involvement, within the time-flow of experience, in a moral reality which transcends individuals, community and cultural apprehension: a moral sense which looks towards a goal not yet achieved, towards which one may grow and to which one may aspire, yet with an awareness that the quest is not pursued on one's own but in interaction with others and with a sense that much is given one on the way. And the condition governing this quest for moral truth is human freedom. James Mackey speaks of the essential bond between human freedom and truth:

> That bond is sensed by every human being involved in the moral quest who feels that the good that is sought is beyond

---

[3] *Summa Theologica* 1a2ae, 96, 4–6: cf. R. Gill, *Textbook,* pp. 76–88; Fairweather and McDonald, *The Quest,* pp. 144–151.

human whim, and a matter of truth rather than one of arbitrary human decision, yet each one is free in pursuit of it. Indeed the often dim perception that the human moral quest is anchored in some truly transcendent prospect and promise for this world, of a sacred nature, is one which is shared, not just by non-Christians but by many a secular humanist who is otherwise agnostic.[4]

One further modern example may be offered here. Reinhold Niebuhr offered a thoughtful analysis of 'natural law' in relation to Christian ethics. Following up the duality evident in it from the time of the Stoics, he distinguished between 'relative natural law', applicable to this conditioned world, and 'absolute natural law', which enjoined freedom and equality. The latter, the *ius naturale*, embodies the ultimate requirement of reason, while the former, the *ius gentium*, represented the compromise reason must effect with the contingent and arbitrary forces of 'the real world'. Niebuhr believed that the pessimism of the Christian tradition regarding the sinful world had inclined it to put too much emphasis on the *ius gentium*. The ultimate requirement, expressed for example as 'equality before God', was dispatched to a kind of transcendental isolation, while institutions such as slavery were complacently accepted as a necessary part of the divine ordering of a sinful world. On the other hand, there is little mileage in a moral sentimentalism which fails to recognise the extent to which all human activity is contextually conditioned and regulated. A rational analysis finds the right balance between the two types of 'natural law'. Granted the need to come to terms with the actual situation with which one is confronted, the ideal possibility – freedom and equality – has a just claim on moral persons, even in a disfigured world: the freedom to develop their personal being, and the insistence on equal personal worth in a world of conflict and competition.

It offers immediate possibilities of a higher good in every given situation. We may never realise equality, but we

---

[4] James P. Mackey, 'Dogged by the dogma': a response to *Veritatis Splendor*, in *The Scotsman*.

cannot accept the inequalities of capitalism or any other unjust social system complacently.[5]

Disadvantages arising from the gender and class inequalities which are part of the 'real world' of nature and history can thus be rationally addressed. It is interesting that in the case study discussion above objections were made to private medicine precisely on the grounds of unequal provision based on economic class.

*****

Natural law is organically related to the understanding of the natural order as a whole. In the modern world, this may be the most important aspect of the subject. In physics, quantum mechanics and the theory of relativity not only prepared the way for the identifying of 'black holes', 'Hawking's radiation' and exciting cosmological theories about the beginnings of the universe; they also overturned the old mechanistic ways of thinking and, even more important, the old subject–object divide which sponsored the notion of the rational mind dominating recalcitrant matter. Developmental studies show constant interaction with our environment, by which we are shaped and advanced. Biology has also indicated, most notably with the discovery of the DNA molecule, that we are all integral parts of the whole creation.

No man is an island, entire of itself;
every man is a piece of the Continent, a part of the main.[6]

Several features of this picture may be underlined for the purposes of moral discussion:

(i) *Kinship with the animal world* Humankind is part of creation and specifically part of the animal world. To speak of distinguishing 'man' from the animals is less appropriate than

---

[5] R. Niebuhr, *An Interpretation of Christian Ethics* (1937), pp. 154–60.
[6] John Donne, *Devotions* XVII.

to ask what distinguishes humankind *within* the animal kingdom. Too often the 'pat' answer is given, by theists and humanists alike: reason, intellect, rationality, morality. Yet valuing – to focus on the aspect that interests us most here – takes place in relation to the meeting of needs, a factor common to 'man' and animals. Needs suggest objectives. Experiments with squirrels, for example, have shown the extraordinarily complex obstacle course they can master in order to achieve the goal of a valued nut. Animals can use complex means to achieve their end, and they can apparently have conflicting motives.[7] True, non-human animals do not write books on ethics! Before we congratulate the other animals on their lucky escape, we do well to reflect that one of the distinguishing features is the ability of *homo sapiens* to reflect critically on values, obligations, goals, consequences, intentions... and, as a moral being, to apply reason, feeling and will to the pursuit of the good rather than the evil. *Corruptio optimi pessima*: when we fail, we say we are 'behaving like animals' – a remarkably unjust, anthropocentric description! The conclusion to be drawn at this point is that we are true to our nature as members of the creation when we express our kinship with animals in appropriate ways: for example, by acknowledging our interdependence as living beings, by respecting our several needs, and by enhancing life for all creatures so far as it lies within our power.

(ii) *Kinship with all creation* 'Any man's death diminishes me, because I am involved in Mankind.' Again, Donne's insight can be given wider application today. Any damage to the world diminishes me, because I am involved in the world. I am dust of its dust; I breathe its air and its pollution; if I poison it, I poison myself. But it is not just a matter of damage limitation, largely on a self-interested basis. One can speak of having a proper feeling for the world of nature. This should not be interpreted simply in a romantic sense but rather as an acknowledgement of *affinity*, such as is evident in Celtic or Franciscan spirituality.

[7] J. M. Gustafson, *Theology and Ethics* (1981), p. 286.

I bind unto myself today
   the virtues of the star-lit heaven,
the glorious sun's life-giving ray,
   the whiteness of the moon at even,
the flashing of the lightning free,
   the whirling wind's tempestuous shocks,
the stable earth, the deep salt sea
   around the old eternal rocks.[8]

A number of ideas come together in ecological responsibility
in Christian perspective: Nature as *gift*, realised in living and
cherished with thanksgiving; Nature as the totality of our inter-
relationships and interdependence; Nature as *the world with
which we interact*. Stewardship is a valid concept as long as we
remember that we are part of that which is entrusted to us. We
are enhanced or diminished by the stance we take, just as the
world is enhanced or diminished by our actions. It is important,
therefore, to give careful consideration to *in vitro* fertilisation
and its applications in the context of our awareness of nature
and our responsibility for it.

(iii) *Domination or co-operation*   Ecological ethics can be taken
to revolve around this moral dilemma. Domination has been
the role of exploitive man. The earth is there to be worked for
human benefit and profit. The earth is almost an enemy, as in
the curse in Gen. 3:17–19, a passage doubtless reflecting the
age old struggle of the peasant with what Alexander Gray
called the 'ungrateful' soil.[9] This puts a rather different
complexion on the problem. The peasant farmer has to
'subdue' the earth, but he does so by co-operating with it to
grow his crops and control its floods and thus foster
'socionatural renewal'. Rather different is the rape of the earth
for mineral wealth or quick gain, the exhaustion of soil, the
intensive breeding of animals, and the poisoning of rivers and

[8] St Patrick (337–466), version by C. F. Alexander: *The Church Hymnary*,
Third Edition (1973), no. 402.
[9] Alexander Gray, 'Scotland', cited as the prologue to R. L. Mackie, *A Short
History of Scotland* (1930).

atmosphere with industrial and other waste products. Here is mindless and soulless exploitation, a denial of affinity between 'man' and nature, or harmony between the human community and natural systems. How far do our scientific and technological advances – *in vitro* fertilisation, for example – express domination or co-operation?

(iv) *Natural order and 'natural law'*   In the light of this discussion, we need to revise our notion of *ius naturale*. It is no longer adequate to speak of it as the ultimate requirement of reason but rather as the holistic requirement of being-in-the-world. 'Reason' is not a separate entity, like a character in a drama interacting with other personae such as 'emotion' and 'will'.[10] Reasoning is the process of choosing, which is integrated into a person's entire being. The challenge of the *ius naturale* is that the choice shall be *for* the whole created order, *for* the preservation of the earth, *for* global liberation and wellbeing. At the same time, we live with the *ius gentium*: compromised by it at every turn (unless we live on a desert island, and even there we will not escape completely). The tension can be creative: it is so whenever we bear witness, in word and action, to the *ius naturale* and let its gravitational pull be felt in the world as it is. Here is an important groundwork of Christian ethics today. On this basis it is possible to enter moral dialogue with people of many faiths and persuasions, and to express our common participation in the created order rather than simply the particularities which divide.

---

[10] Mary Midgley, *Beast and Man* (1978), p. 258; cf. also Rosemary Reuther, *New Woman, New Earth* (1975).

IV *The Biblical Ground of Value*

1 *Reading the Bible*

Throughout the ages, people have found the ground of moral value in the Bible; and, as a classic of Christendom (to put it no higher), the impact of the Bible on the moral awareness of humankind cannot be denied. The Bible is one of the primary pillars of Christian ethics. Yet the matter is not without difficulty. More exactly, there are problems about *the reading of the Bible* in this connection. Everyone reads the Bible selectively: it is such a diverse collection of books that we can do no other, even if we accept its cumulative witness to God and his ways. What is important is that our reading of it in relation to Christian ethics should be true to its moral witness and to the Spirit of Christ.

Certain readings of the Bible have been patently immoral: the warmonger who has called on 'the Lord of Hosts' to bless his nefarious endeavours; the tyrant who has appealed to Romans 13 to legitimise his oppression; the church authority that has invoked biblical revelation to sanction inquisition or witch-hunt; or the dogmatist who knows on 'biblical' grounds that everyone else is wrong. Non-contextual exegesis – the urge to pluck texts from the Bible without reference to the fact that its writings span many centuries and reflect the time-flow of history and cultural situation – is an elementary error in interpretation which can distort moral perspective. The pervasive human tendency towards rationalisation is another factor which requires to be recognised. Non-contextual exegesis (or 'biblicism') can combine with entrenched presuppositions to produce an intractable legalism. Thus it is not uncommon to find an obscure reference in a list of vices or ancient purity regulations cited as irrefutable biblical condemnation of homosexuality (whatever that term may be taken to mean), raising at least the suspicion of heterosexual self-endorsement on the interpreter's part; or selective appeal may be made to alleged Pauline policy in first-century churches, in order to refute the case for fuller participation of women in ministry, when patriarchal prerogatives, even if hallowed by tradition, may well be a factor in the interpretation. At the same time, liberal cultural assumptions may distort biblical perspectives on ethics and effectively reduce them to some kind of ideology. Such reflections point to the need for a 'hermeneutics of suspicion' – an approach to interpretation which subjects interpreters and texts to searching examination to assess the nature of their presuppositions and to identify prejudice.

An understanding of what is involved in reading the Bible – including the reading process itself – is critically important. This task, however, requires that we go beyond conventional claims to 'objectivity' or 'orthodoxy' or 'liberalism', each of which has its own axe to grind. The trouble is that, as readers, we ourselves participate in the reading of texts. The texts are independent of us, but we have to engage with them in order that meaning may be generated. If we allow ourselves and our presuppositions to dominate the text, we will take from it precisely what is agreeable to us. If we push the text too far away from us, it becomes no more than an ancient text in an ancient setting. If we place the text in a dogmatic straitjacket, the dogmatic presuppositions we have imposed on it will also confine and perhaps confuse our notion of the biblical ground of morality. The challenge is therefore to engage with the Bible in such a way that we can discern the grounds on which moral teaching is given in the context which has shaped the text, and by careful correlation of contexts determine how far particular texts can become a meaningful and authentic witness to the ground of value today.[1]

What do we mean by 'meaningful and authentic witness'? If it is claimed for a text that it represents the ground of morality or is based on such, then that text must be true to the moral concern of the Bible as a whole: for example, it must adequately reflect the story of God's dealings with his people and the dynamics of biblical morality. Furthermore, the text must deepen our knowledge of the ground of all moral value. Not all biblical texts nor all readings of them will meet these criteria. The Bible presents a diverse commentary on the human condition in the sight of God, and thus contains

[1] Cf. J . I. H. McDonald, *Biblical Interpretation and Christian Ethics* (1993).

expressions of obtuseness as well as insight, of closed-mindedness as well as openness to the Spirit – even when the text in question is not designed to express any one of these features! Readers may find qualities and perspectives which the writer never envisaged. Such diversity has always characterised the people of God, so that it has always been necessary to 'test the spirits' to see whether they be of God (cf. 1 John 4:1). Every text – every reading of a text – must be similarly tested, just as every interpreter is placed under God's judgement in every interpretation he or she makes. Some texts therefore do not illuminate the ground of moral value. If one read them as if they did, text and interpreter alike might well be vulnerable to the charge of operating at a lower level of morality than is found outside the Christian tradition.

In order to attempt to limit misunderstandings of what is being said here (and it is an area where misunderstandings abound), let us try to unpack this position more systematically. Key issues are:

(i) *Self-knowledge*

Socrates took the maxim 'know thyself' as the prerequisite of wisdom. It is no less required of the biblical interpreter. A Catholic commentator on the nineteenth century 'lives of Jesus' (most of which were written by Protestants keen to dispel centuries of Catholic darkness) suggested that their pictures of Jesus were like the reflections of liberal Protestant faces seen at the foot of a deep well.[2] Our biblically based ethics must not be of similar kind. If we are to reach out to the voice of the Other in the text and hear that voice as the call of God, then we must be prepared to be confronted by a ground of value that does not proceed from ourselves. If it simply confirms our previous stance, then it may be no more than the reflection of our own faces or the rationalisation of our desires. As in religious studies, where we study other people's religions, we need *'epoche'*, at least as one movement in interpretation: a bracketing or suspension of our presuppositions in order to

---

[2] G. Tyrrell, *Christianity at the Crossroads* (1909), p. 44.

enter this new world and to discover its structure and inner meaning. Biblical interpretation therefore requires a willingness to grow in self-awareness, in sensitivity to others, in historical and literary imagination and, above all, in openness to the many dimensions of the text. In other words, it demands – or creates – its own spirituality.

(ii) *Community*

Neither self-knowledge nor spirituality can be attained in isolation. Human beings grow as people through interaction with others. Community has been described as 'a group of people who are socially interdependent, who participate together in discussion and decision-making, and who share certain practices that both define the community and are nurtured by it'.[3] Community is therefore essential to growth in 'wisdom and understanding', whether we think of a study group or seminar which discusses and shares insight or of a worshipping community that incorporates within itself the love of God and intercession for his creation, and celebrates and is sustained by the story that is fundamental to Christian faith and life. Without idealising them, both types of community involvement provide a locus for the reading and re-reading of the Bible, and for helping members to discover and rediscover the ground of Christian value. Not that this is a simple process: it is not merely a matter of knowledge to be acquired. Christian values are prompted by the Spirit. To discover them and be true to them is a life-long process, a growing up in faith, hope and love. The dynamics of the group are therefore important. Academic groups still need to be supportive. Christian communities are best able to assist the process when they give mutual help in overcoming the undoubted disequilibrium (or 'unlearning') which such a moral spirituality entails and in thus bearing one another's burdens. Indeed, they need the love that is patient and kind...

---

[3] R. Gill, *Christian Ethics in Secular Worlds* (1991), p. 16.

(iii) *Approach to the text*

Without suggesting that every reader of the Bible must become an academic, to study the text today means that we are at least prepared to be open to guidance about appropriate methods of scientific criticism, such as would be applied to any text. As a preliminary, this involves, as we have seen, suspending dogmatic approaches which would pre-empt the search for meaning. In particular, it means recognising the kind of text we are dealing with and the considerations which apply to our reading of it. We note below questions of *genre*, context, rhetoric and diversity.

Genre There are, of course, many different types of text in the Bible – narratives of various kinds, letters, sayings, parables, poetry and song, apocalypses – not always in neat compartments. The *genre* of a text affects the way we interpret it. Narratives of events always raise the question of bias or point of view (on the part of the narrator, not simply the interpreter). The inherent purpose of the narrative must be carefully assessed, along with the methods used in the text to achieve it. Narratives tend to deal with events, real or imagined, in which some religious or moral point is made. Poetry or poetic narratives, with their richness of metaphor and imagery, attempt to express deeper truth – or sometimes simply to express the believer's feelings, which may include anger or outrage as well as penitence and faith. We will not be detained by the old chestnut about the primacy of the literal or the symbolic. Metaphor and parable are as relevant to ethics as they are to theology: Nathan the prophet brought David to moral awareness by means of a parabolic story (the poor man's pet lamb), which used situation and imagination to open up moral reality in a way which eventually shattered David's defensive rationalisations (cf. 2 Samuel 12).

Context Apart from *genre*, perhaps the most important step in biblical interpretation is to view the text *in its own world*. The ethics of historical interpretation insist that we appreciate the strangeness and integrity of this world which is opened out for us in the text. Also, as the sociology of knowledge insists, the text can only be understood in terms of the world from which it arises. None of the people involved, whether as characters in the story or as authors, can be modernised. What we can do is apply our knowledge of human needs and relationships, and of social, economic and political forces, to interpret the events described. Through such analogical procedures, situations in the text can be seen to highlight moral issues and dilemmas – such as paying taxes to Caesar, which occurs both in the Gospels and in Paul. Granted that obeying the will of God constitutes the supreme ground of value: is it to be expressed in 'messianic' resistance to Roman economic and political imperialism, or in some kind of eschatological transcending of such a policy, or in a positive attitude towards those who, under God, maintain order in society? Or take the issue of divorce: is it an expression of the will of God? Sometimes, or never? It is permitted in the *torah* (Deut. 24:1–4). Does it then reflect God's will? The *torah* permits it in the face of human intransigence, says Jesus (cf. Mark 10:5). We might observe that law is normally formulated precisely in view of human intransigence! But Jesus goes on to point to a higher level of awareness of God's will: his primordial purpose in creation. He therefore exhorts his hearers to accept the indissolubility of marriage as the fullest expression of the divine will. Such a concept is a calling or vocation: it cannot properly be legislation, nor does it invalidate Deut. 24:1–4. Such legislation represents the actuality of the human situation, characterised as it is by alienation. It must not be turned into the divine norm: it is a concession to human weakness. Hence, in Christian ethics the ground of value transcends law. A similar issue, in a different context, is worked through by Paul in 1 Corinthians 7. He relays to the Christians at Corinth the Lord's message not to break up their marriages, even when the other partner is an unbeliever (7:10–11); but in certain circumstances – for example, the insistence of the unbelieving partner on separation – it is unavoidable.

Rhetoric   One must not overlook the linguistic and rhetorical features of the text. Texts are designed to communicate with

and to persuade intended readers who are often broadly
contemporary with the writer. They are written for a purpose,
which is discernible in the text itself. Latter-day readers must
exercise care and discrimination, so that the rhetorical purpose
of each text is recognised. It is immoral, for example, to use a
polemical passage dealing with disputes with ancient Pharisees
in order to give a general characterisation either of ancient
Judaism or of Jewish practice today (some New Testament
exposition about 'the Jews', hopefully less common today, is
unintentionally racist!). At most, such passages provide
evidence of Jewish–Christian conflicts in the ancient world.
We must recognise also that when Paul, for example, was
presenting a case to persuade his intended hearers, he could
well resort to arguments – like his appeal to the Adam and Eve
story to suggest the subordination of women[4] – which carry no
weight with the modern reader and are untrue to his better
insights. Again, stories of the divine deliverance of God's
people – such as the Exodus story – may contain accounts of
the destruction of enemies which provide no moral warrant
for today. A story written with a specific purpose in mind – for
example, to proclaim the saving work of God – may be grossly
misleading when viewed in a different perspective.

Take, as a case in point, Jesus' reply to the contention that
the cost of the unguent lavished upon him by a woman
follower should have been given to the poor. 'The poor are
always with you,' he said, justifying the woman's devotion
(Matt. 26:11; Mark 14:7). As interpreters, we set the passage in
its context and note how it is narrated. It is the prelude to Jesus'
death, a proleptic anointing for burial. Do we say that the act

---

[4] Cf. 1 Tim. 2:13–14. The situation appears somewhat different from that
which obtains in the major Pauline epistles. Here, the submissiveness of
women (all creatures must be submissive before God) is interpreted as a ban
on having any authority over men, including any role in teaching. This
androcentric stance is justified by appeal to the Adam and Eve story in which
Adam is declared not to have been deceived(!) and the sin is laid at the
woman's door. This interpretation is considerably worse than the original
story, in which Adam was indeed created first but the subordination of
woman is part of the curse (Gen. 3:16) and of the enmity between the sexes
(3:15): hardly the basis on which to build church community.

of anointing is singularly appropriate here, overriding normal concerns? For everything there is a season, and this is when the act of devotion counts for more than the charitable use of the assets. The poor are part of the continuing distress of the world; the concern of the moment is Jesus' departure from it. Continuing duties are temporarily suspended in the presence of such a crisis. Is it at the same time a means of countering the element of rationalisation in the objection, which arguably sprang from disapproval of the woman's extravagant devotion to Jesus rather than from any real concern for the poor? We do not always state our real objections! Was it simply a rebuke to meanness of spirit? In what ways does the text suggest what the narrator had in mind? All such questions are part of the process of interpretation. One question we have not raised: was Jesus simply indifferent to the poor? From the many texts that witness to his deep concern for the poor, we know that this was not so: the possibility can be eliminated. Interpreting a text thus means reading it closely in itself, critically assessing possible meanings, and relating it to other texts. We have to be open to its 'word' (or '*parole*' in technical discussion): the particular statement of value – or 'point' – conveyed by a given text. Sometimes its 'word' is particular to the given context. As readers with a moral interest, we have to relate the value found in one text to the broader ground of value evident in the Bible as a whole.

Diversity   Finally, one must be aware that the Bible contains not simply one account of God's ways with his creation but multiple accounts. There are even two or more versions of the ten commandments. All this speaks of a lively teaching tradition spanning the centuries and reinterpreting the will of God for new circumstances. We have to deal not with a static but with a dynamic process of understanding the divine will. The most dramatic series of reinterpretations is found in the New Testament itself, which sets the older scriptures of Israel in the perspective of faith in Jesus as the Christ (and vice versa). Christian readings of the Old Testament today will reproduce this kind of perspective to good effect: for example, in relation to the treatment of enemies, where Jesus' teaching may be held to bring the issue to full expression. But it is also important, at least on occasion, to study the Old Testament in its historical context in order to appreciate not only the extent to which the New Testament draws on its resources but also the profound moral insights which the Old Testament itself contains. As we shall presently seek to show, the fundamental ground of value in the Bible derives from the Old Testament.

(iv) *The Word and the words*

Some secular critics scoff at the idea that an ancient book such as the Bible can throw any light on the moral issues of today. Moral discussion is nothing if not contemporary, they maintain. Ancient lore has nothing to offer. Others of a different persuasion insist that because the Bible is the scripture of the Christian church, it overrules any human reflection on morality. Christian discipleship is about hearing God's Word and obeying it: but can the Bible override human reflection on morality – precisely when it is read in the context of moral concern? 'Will not the Judge of all the earth do what is right?' (Gen. 18:25).

The first criticism ignores the fact that, when the Bible is read today, it becomes a contemporary book. It becomes a factor in moral debate – not in the sense of giving instant answers, like a railway timetable, but rather as a primary resource in decision making. Iris Murdoch once observed that 'the argument for looking outward at Christ and not inward at Reason is that self is such a dazzling object that if one looks *there*, one may see nothing else.'[5] The Bible brings a distinctive dimension into ethical discussion: the dimension of one of the world's great religio-moral traditions, shared in part by Judaism and Christianity and liberally exploited by the Western moral tradition. It comes into our moral reckoning in various ways: it enjoins basic moral requirements, as in the ten commandments; it offers concrete models, including Jesus himself; it opens up moral situations, as in Paul's ministry or some of Jesus' parables, so that we can see

[5] I. Murdoch, *The Sovereignty of the Good* (1970).

how to resolve moral dilemmas in love; it suggests that there are deeper values than mere prudence and self-interest (however disguised); and it puts human existence *sub specie aeternitatis*, so that we are made aware of our own limitations and illusions.

To read the Bible as a contemporary book means participating in its meaning. Just as our knowledge of our own world illumines the biblical text so that we can enter more deeply into its world, so the situations in the Bible can, by analogy, illumine our own world by their powerful moral insights – or, occasionally, by the demonstration of the human limitations of the characters they depict. Care must be taken to ensure that the analogy is appropriate.[6] Placing more weight on the narrative element, we could say that the biblical story, with the values it enshrines, intersects with our life-story, and questions and transforms it. The moral possibilities opened up in the text qualify all our efforts and enrich our vision. The horizons of our world are extended by the new ground of value encapsulated in the text and made present with us through the act of reading.

The Word of God comes to us precisely through this kind of engagement. Words can only be read, heard or spoken. In the case of written scripture, the process of reading adumbrated above is central to the engagement. The ministry of the Word in worship (reading, hearing, exposition and proclamation, response and action) also presupposes engagement. Hence the Word that comes through words is not a surface communication nor a message set in concrete (nor in print!), but an encounter with the transcendent reality to whom the words bear witness. Often the witness may be indirect, employing story, parable, metaphor or likeness, since divine truth in its completeness transcends the comprehension of the finite; and sometimes when the communication appears direct, the form of the passage ('God said...'; 'God repented...'; 'God veiled his face') is in

---

[6] Cf. the 'correspondence in relationships' model developed in liberation theology: L. Boff, *Theology and Praxis* (1987), pp. 147–9.

fact an accommodation to human weakness. The essential point is that through the witness of the words the Wisdom of God and the Spirit of Christ can be conveyed to us. In them we find the ground of moral value.

2 *Reading the commandments*

Does the above discussion over-emphasise the *indirect* nature of the ground of biblical morality? Surely the ten commandments are direct, explicit, categorical, unmediated: carved in stone! Surely here we find moral foundations and universal standards, grounded in divine law and secure against undermining by the shifting sands of cultural relativism? But is this what we find when we *read* the text?[7]

Consider the manner in which the 'ten words' are introduced:

> God spoke all these words:
> I am the Lord your God who brought you out of Egypt, out of the land of slavery. (Ex. 20:1–2, *REB*)

The moral teaching presupposes the story of the Exodus from Egypt and of God's gracious relationship with the people he has chosen. God identifies himself by his story! The 'ten words' describe the obligations which this relationship imposes on his people. The so-called 'first tablet' defines its exclusive nature: one God alone, no likeness on earth, no invoking of God's name to underwrite false testimony, and no work on the sabbath. The fact that the commandments tended to be expanded in the course of teaching is readily seen by comparing the Exodus and Deuteronomic versions. The sabbath commandment, for example, which is related to the creation story in Ex. 20:11, is made to refer to the Exodus story in Deut. 5:15 – possibly the earlier form, even though Deuteronomy has perhaps a more developed covenant theology than Exodus.

[7] For an introduction to 'Reader-Response Criticism', see the article by M. Davies in Coggins and Houlden (eds), *A Dictionary of Biblical Interpretation* (1990), pp. 578–80.

Interpretation is also evident in the 'moral' commandments (the division is artificial: all the commandments presuppose the unity of religion and morality). The commandment to 'honour' your parents (to care for them in old age, not to 'dishonour' them through neglect) reflects both the sociological unit of the clan or extended family and a primitive theology of blessing for oneself (cf. Deut. 5:16); the intention is to demonstrate the way of *shalom*, peace and wellbeing. The form of the tenth commandment reflects a patriarchal society in which a household is personified by its male head (Ex. 20:17, Deut. 5:21). Thus, reading identifies the context of the commandments in the story of God's relationship with Israel, and therefore in Israel's memory; it identifies also their context in the teaching of Israel, through which they were interpreted, extended and, in a minor way, diversified; and it identifies the factor of socio-historical conditioning. Much more could be said along similar lines. The incomparability of Yahweh, God of Israel, and his moral sovereignty may well be asserted over against foreign religious cultures and the totalitarian claims of monarchs external to but also eventually within Israel, and the moral ethos they promoted.[8]

However, when all this has been said (and it is important to say it), are we not left with a hard core of moral imperatives as the basis of a universal morality? Yes and no! The moral imperatives are there: indeed, the form of the 'ten words' has often been described as 'apodeictic' – categorical statements of sovereign will, such as those issued by a monarch to his people. And here the monarch is Yahweh, God of Israel, creator of heaven and earth, making known his will to Israel, his covenanted people: the 'ten words' present the parameters within which Israel's life must move. The concept of covenant is particularly strong in the Deuteronomic version: 'The Lord our God made a covenant at Horeb. It was not with our forefathers that the Lord made this covenant, but with us, all of us who are alive and are here this day' (Deut. 5:2–3).

---

[8] Cf. N. K. Gottwald, *The Tribes of Yahweh* (1979).

Succeeding generations in Israel appropriated the story with its religious and moral obligations. These were written not in stone but in the hearts and minds of the people (Deut. 6:6), and were to be put into practice as the expression of their love for their God (Deut. 6:5). And they are part of a much wider body of divine teaching – religious, moral and cultic – which came to be known as *torah*. Israel affirmed it in its totality. It became incumbent on prophets to remind the people and their leaders of priorities within it, and on the scribes of the 'wisdom' tradition to relate its general obligations to the practicalities of daily life.

Is it nevertheless possible to affirm in the 'ten words' a universal ground of morality which transcends the particularities of its Jewish setting? This question can be addressed at several levels. Behind the 'ten words' one can discern, at least at some points, the values of immemorial tribal custom and affirm a dimension of 'natural law' that was morally binding on all. By locating the ground of morality in the will of God as revealed in historical experience, the 'ten words' insisted that the *basis* of morality was not a human product but was a given, a *datum*, and this *datum* had to be expressed in experience and in society. The particularities of the story ensured that the 'ten words' were, in practice, the moral parameters of God's people, Israel. Some requirements, for example sabbath observance, were not expected of non-Jews, although it was always accepted that God was concerned for all humankind (as in the covenant with Noah), and the so-called Noachian precepts prescribed the level of conduct Jews required of Gentiles, at least when living and working in a Jewish environment.[9]

A possible conclusion is that the quest of a universal set of values is a chimera, and that the best we as humans can have is a culturally or religiously conditioned statement of supreme moral value. It is possible, of course, to translate specific

[9] Its provisions related negatively to meat (not idolatrous, non-kosher, nor ensnared and killed); to forbidden degrees of marriage and unchastity; to blasphemy, robbery and bloodshedding; and positively to justice.

commands into ideas and principles, and claim general validity for them. Thus the command to 'honour your father and your mother' expresses filial duty; the prohibition of killing expresses respect for human life; and others affirm truthfulness and respect for neighbour. No one would argue about the moral worth of such principles in general, but they are precisely that: generalisations from the specifics of the moral tradition. They do not in themselves constitute the ground of moral value nor experience, and could easily be built into a moral structure alien to the genius of the Hebrew moral perception. Even when the prophets were driven to use summative terms for the moral requirements of Israel's God – an exercise in moral discernment – their use of terms such as 'justice' and 'mercy' was qualified by the covenantal relationship, as the third term, 'walking humbly with your God', demonstrates (Micah 6:8). Morality has a transcendent horizon. It is not given to mere humans to eat of the tree of the knowledge of good and evil.

3 *The first of all the commandments*

When we look at the ministry of Jesus, socio-historical perspectives claim attention. We find a ministry performed in the socio-economic and religio-political environment of late ancient Judaism; a central figure who resisted typecasting but who had affinities with his Pharisaic contemporaries in particular, however sharply he disagreed with them at times; a leader whose significance was much canvassed, not least in his own group of disciples, and who focused on the deeper values of religion rather than on conventional accommodations; a teller of parables, who picked up familiar images to elucidate religious themes such as the Kingdom of God and somehow gave them immediacy for his hearers. We find him *giving performance* to the Kingdom in the historical setting of his ministry:[10] bringing the 'beyond' into the midst of life and so giving actuality to eschatological hope; expressing a dynamic for peace and healing in the midst of a violent and suffering

[10] Cf. B. Chilton and J. I. H. McDonald, *Jesus and the Ethics of the Kingdom* (1987), pp. 110–31.

world, and so creating a social ethic through his disciple community.[11]

When the question of the ground of moral value was raised with Jesus, the nature of the issue lends it an equal immediacy for the modern reader. The question arose in the context of the reading of the scriptures. He is reported as responding to a questioner with the words, 'What is written in the law? What is your reading of it?' (Luke 10:26). Significantly, in Mark 12:28–34, where a Jewish scribe enters into discussion with Jesus about the 'first of all the commandments', Jesus begins his answer with a citation of the *Shema*: 'Hear, O Israel: the Lord our God is the one Lord' (Deut. 6:4). Moral and religious truth begins with the recognition of the sovereign will of God. The primary requirements of God's people are love to God and neighbour; and the scribe volunteers the comment that these mean far more than all the burnt offerings and sacrifices put together. This has the hallmark of genuine dialogue: real questions and answers, and agreement in evaluation. How far the audience was scandalised we are not told, although Mark adds the standard if cryptic editorial comment that nobody dared to put any more questions to Jesus. But Jesus and the scribe are in accord in thus elevating the transcendent and the moral above the cultic; 'you are not far from (i.e., truly a sharer in) the Kingdom of God'. Here is a critique of moral value from within the biblical tradition, designed to recall the tradition to its own deepest vocation.[12] Jesus tended to be hard on those who were always appealing to laws, standards or conventional patterns of religious morality. The ground of value is obscured in such appeals by a variety of other considerations, not least self-righteousness and judgementalism.[13]

[11] Cf. S. Hauerwas, *A Community of Character* (1981), pp. 40–44; *The Peaceable Kingdom* (1984).

[12] For a fuller discussion, cf. J. I. H. McDonald, 'The Great Commandment and the Golden Rule', in A. G. Auld (ed), *Understanding Poets and Prophets* (1993), pp. 213–26.

[13] Cf. the story of Jesus and the adulteress (usually printed as John 8:1–11, although its textual history is complex), especially Jesus' refusal to pass judgement.

Like the leading rabbis of the day,[14] Jesus did not devalue the *torah* by his search for its ground of value, but he was clearly deeply involved in presenting a 'critique from within' in terms of faithfulness to the 'leading commandments' and the divine will. One may discern, beyond the ostensible terms of the dialogue, an important common denominator: the rhetoric of all parties is concerned, directly or indirectly, with 'the other'. Love to God defines a relation to 'the Other', the Transcendent One. Love to neighbour concerns the other person. Jesus, taking his cue from the scriptural prohibition of vengeance, extended 'neighbour' to include the outsider, the alienated, the 'enemy'. There is an intrinsic link between the two forms: God's covenant love for us is love for the other. As Jesus became the focus of the Christian story, the love of God was expressed not only in his teaching but in the totality of his ministry and suffering. God's love was seen in the midst of alienation: the most radical statement of 'other-regarding love'. This concrete expression of the divine love in ministry is one of the most creative elements in the gospel story.

Sometimes it is suggested that, while Judaism required study of the whole vast apparatus of the *torah* and its interpretation, Jesus dispensed with all commentary and focused radically on *agape* alone. This is misleading. Jesus and the scribe both presupposed the story of God's people Israel, within which his love for his people is revealed. The suggestion that 'all you need is love' is shallow sentimentality, while the notion that *agape* can be treated as a philosophical principle is sterile. In Jesus' teaching, love is wholly contextualised in the story of God's people. This commentary is essential. It points to the motivating factor, namely the prior love of God for his people,

---

[14] There is a well known story about the response of rabbis Hillel and Shamai to summarising the law. When challenged by an enquirer to state the whole law while he (the enquirer) stood on one foot, R. Shammai drove him away with his rod. How dare he suggest that the *torah* in all its magnificence could suffer any such reduction! R. Hillel made the point in a different way. He offered the 'golden rule' as a response to the demand, but added: 'The rest is commentary. Go and learn it.' The acceptance of a summary formula does not detract from the centrality of *torah*.

and to the quality and scope of love. 'If God thus loved us...we also must love one another' (1 John 4:11)

4. *The justice of God*

It is hazardous to attempt to specify the biblical ground of morality under one single heading. The richness and variety of the Bible resist superimposed structures. If we can point to an inherently unitive concept in Old and New Testaments, it is *the justice of God*.[15] Such a claim carries the implication that the ground of value in Christian ethics is properly expressed in theological rather than philosophical terms. It also requires that such a concept be subjected to the disciplined process of interpretation outlined above.

As we have seen, the Bible does its theology primarily through narrative. Biblical narratives are designed to show how God, the sovereign Lord of the universe, made known his righteous nature and will through the complexities of Israel's experience (or the experiences with which the Israelites identified): above all, through their memory of the Exodus and covenant at Sinai. God's justice or righteousness is thus made known through the *relationship* which he established with his people. Justice in this tradition was therefore not simply a harmony of the parts nor a distributive or retributive process in society as in Graeco–Roman thinking, but a creative relationship which sought the good of the other party. It therefore involved the protection of the weak and vulnerable. It comprehends not only the norms or laws or commandments governing Israel's expected behaviour but God's graciousness, faithfulness and constancy towards his people; also, his disciplining of them when erring, and his readiness to heal the breach and overcome alienation. God's covenant is therefore the model for understanding his justice; Israel's moral practice must be shaped by it. Justice thus involves the responsibilities that arise out of social relationships. As already noted, when the prophets recalled Israel to God's righteousness, they

---

[15] Cf. J. D. G. Dunn and A. M. Suggate, *The Justice of God* (1993).

spoke in terms of doing justice, loving mercy and walking humbly with their God.

Covenants not only *include*: they also serve to *exclude*. Three comments need to be made here. Israel's unfaithfulness to God's covenant is a constant theme of the prophets. Within the covenant, the cult gave liturgical expression to the renewal of the relationship. However, as the prophets always insisted, liturgical practice alone could not sustain the covenant, for it subsisted in righteousness. Unrighteousness therefore excludes. Yet God never finally rejected disobedient Israel, although the relationship was strained to breaking point. God's justice is thus far more than his requirement of obedience: it is also the goodness that makes for reconciliation and healing. Here is an important aspect of the biblical ground of value.

The second point recapitulates the notion of God's justice as reaching out to the other: as inclusive rather than exclusive. There were times when Israel believed that God was leading it into a kind of *laager* mentality, but this was always challenged, sooner or later, by a wider concern. And in the *torah*, the distillation of God's teaching, there was a clear duty towards the outsider: to allocate a part of the harvest to the needy, the outcast, the stranger in the midst, in short, to care for those who had no means of subsistence of their own (cf. Leviticus 19). God's justice is thus inseparable from social concern: it does not sponsor an individualistic ethic. The ground of value is thus further defined.

The third point takes this wider concern further. The Sinai covenant, made with Israel, is only one of the covenants of which the Hebrew scriptures tell. They entertain the belief that Israel will be a means of blessing to the whole world. Other covenants, especially that made with Noah, emphasise that God's justice is exercised on behalf of all creation. For that reason, the narrative theology of Israel began with the creation theme and looked to the ingathering of the nations. The ground of value is a universal justice.

All this throws light on the New Testament view of justice. For Jesus, the moral obligation was to neighbour rather than self, to the outsider rather than to neighbour narrowly conceived, and to the enemy rather than simply to one's friend or kinsman. For Jesus, healing took precedence over formal observance, and reconciliation over liturgical act. And his followers believed that his faithfulness to this pattern of ministry in life and death had universal moral and religious significance, channelling the forgiveness of God to all who entered into the covenant of faith (cf. Acts 10:43).

Finally, Paul's celebrated doctrine of justification by faith affirms that God's justice brings the Gentiles within the covenant of faith. To understand what Paul is saying we need to read afresh what Paul says of his own calling. Paul's 'conversion' was the moment of truth when he saw Jesus as the divine instrument in overturning the false narrowness and particularism of the Judaism he had known and revealing the grace and justice of God to all the nations. This understanding lay at the heart of Paul's vocation as apostle to the Gentiles. Henceforth his message was God's gracious acceptance of the Gentiles into the covenant of faith: in line with the full biblical understanding of justice and covenant, God 'justifies' them by his grace and brings them into the orbit of faith. Here, through Christ, is the fulfilment of God's covenant with all creatures; here is the long awaited bringing of the light to the Gentiles, who are now called in that light to live out the justice of God. Thus, although Paul rejected the notion that salvation depended on moral achievement, moral practice was the expression of responsiveness to God: 'faith active in love'. Hence, he can readily carry over moral teaching from the Hebrew scriptures in so far as it depicted the just ways which God requires of all.

To claim *the justice of God* as ground of moral value is indeed to affirm the interdependence of ethics and religion in the Christian tradition and thus to claim that two distinct 'realms of meaning' (religion and ethics) ultimately cohere. From the standpoint of ethics, the ground of moral value is transcendent: it is not *our* creation. Human beings do not define nor do they invent 'good' and 'evil' but find themselves participating in moral reality as a realm of meaning which transcends them but which they can explore rationally and experientially. Moral reality exists before us and beyond us and, in some sense, comes to meet us. We learn how to respond to it – or fail to do so to our cost. This is the reality which religion and ethics attempt to interpret. In religious or theological discourse, we speak of the grace and justice of God, of resurrection and new life, of heaven and eternal life, while the negative side is expressed in terms of estrangement, of entrapment in evil or sin, and of hell and judgement. In ethics, we speak of obligation and responsibility, of motivation and response, of the education of the moral sense, of the reality of alienation and moral degradation, and of the primacy of love, justice, mercy, reconciliation and transformation. Both realms speak of deep realities of the human condition. Christian ethics acknowledges that religious and moral concerns ultimately merge in the justice of God, which is no dire super-ego crushing the life out of the ego but a vibrant, liberating reality enfolding humanity in its covenant of promise.

The living reality of the divine justice – its vital, creative nature – means that we must think in terms of moral energy and dynamic, rather than in terms of specific actions that are intrinsically right or wrong. Parameters and rules have their place, but they subserve a greater moral reality. A parallel of sorts may be drawn with modern science, where steady-state views of the universe and the rigidity of physical laws have had to yield to much more fluid and dynamic concepts. In the science of Christian ethics, the basic reality is a creative moral force which defies reduction to immutable laws or intrinsically wrong acts. That would be a 'steady-state' view of moral reality. The Bible witnesses to a righteous transforming power which constantly surprises the conventionally minded by the risks it takes to create wholeness and blessing.

5 *Ethics and biblical motifs*

Finally and briefly, we indicate twelve ways in which this divine dynamic has been imaginatively grasped and expressed in biblical motifs, and note the implications for ethics.

creation   The earth as a gift; respect for and oneness with creation; the ethics of ecology (e.g., McDonagh).

disorder	Moral and spiritual confusion and physical disorder in a created order at odds with itself and its destiny; cumulative power of evil; moral realism (e.g., R. Niebuhr).
deliverance	The exodus motif: deliverance from oppression; realisation of destiny; freedom for the future (e.g., liberation theology: Guttierez).
instruction	*Torah* as God's instruction for his people, in the context of covenant and including commandments (e.g., Muilenburg); *wisdom* as pragmatic ethics within the constraints of worldly structures, but expressing the wisdom of God as enlightened tradition knows it (e.g., Crenshaw).
incarnation	Identification with others in their humanness; participation in the life of the world; ministry (e.g., Temple).
reign of God	The sovereign reign of God, powerfully presented in Christ's ministry; repentance (turning to God), obedience and renewal; *shalom*, the peace of God; acting in peace (e.g., Martin Luther King; Yoder).
suffering	The atonement motif: suffering as a consequence of and as engagement with the fallen order; suffering as self-giving for others; suffering as birth pangs of a new order; compassion and healing; fellowship of suffering (e.g., Hauerwas).
transfiguration	The new order envisioned in Christ; participation in the new order (Lehmann).
resurrection	Death and resurrection of Christ as symbol of new order; dying and rising as moral and spiritual possibility (e.g., Bonhoeffer, O'Donovan).
justification	The outworking of the justice of God; divine acceptance as a universal reality; faith active in love; justice as righteousness (e.g., Häring, Dunn/Suggate).

community/ connectedness	Restored human community; inter-dependent and connected; overcoming barriers of race, gender, economic status and all symbols and expressions of patriarchy; understanding sexuality in the context of relationships (feminism: e.g., Ruether, Jantzen).
consummation	Eschatological vision of completion: hope amid incompletion (e.g., Pannenberg, Moltmann).

CHAPTER 2

PERSONAL AND SOCIAL VALUES

It is easy to become impatient with rules, principles, goals and consequences. It all seems so abstract: far removed from the human experience it is describing and analysing. Surely Christian values hinge on *the kind of person one is* rather than on one's actions considered in isolation: on 'being good' rather than simply 'doing good'? After all, does one not express one's core values primarily in relationship with others: in personal moral growth and growth in community?

To take this line is to adopt the position often described as 'personalist', but some disclaimers must be entered. To emphasise personal and social values does not dissolve human reality into mere relationships (as if there was nothing else to the self), nor does it equate the person and the individual (as if the self was self-sufficient and self-contained). The personal is interwoven with the social, the moral and the religious, and even the political. Christian values are discovered and lived out in the world we inhabit.

While actions, it must be said, also have their importance (sometimes critical importance), the focus of concern in this chapter is on the agent. Personal growth presupposes moral development, which is inseparable from growth in moral awareness and sensitivity towards others. The agent is seen to be much more than a thinking machine: she or he is a person who feels, is capable of empathy, exercises willpower and takes responsibility for actions. The relational frame of reference posits a rounded view of the human person as a social being. Yet a picture of an 'ideal person' would also be untrue to human experience. Personal and social relationships are liable to strain and fracture. Alienation is a fact of life. Reconciliation is a personal, social and religious need.

I *Four Case Studies (Una Stewart)*

We begin with four brief case studies, exemplifying four different situations all of which relate to broken relationships: (i) where reconciliation is wholly lacking, and there is no appreciation of the need for it; (ii) where it is again absent but there is an awareness of the need for it; (iii) where it is offered by one party but rejected by the other; and (iv) where it becomes a reality. In view of the nature of this theme, the discussion of Christian values overlaps with pastoral ethics.

CASE STUDY 1

Mrs A, widowed when in her forties, brought up her family of three children and in her sixties met and married a man considered by her family as 'beneath' her in social status, education and financial standing. In order to express their disapproval of the match the 'children', all married with families of their own, refused to visit the new husband or to invite him to their homes. Words were exchanged and a rift developed in the family. Some years later the husband died and Mrs A, who had become embittered by her children's attitude, refused to have them at the funeral and when they attempted to approach her with a view to re-establishing contact at the scattering of the ashes, there was an unpleasant exchange. From that day Mrs A had no further contact with her children or grandchildren and died a few years later a lonely, bitter, proud old lady.

Divisions and splits within families can occur for many reasons. Often they begin with apparent expressions of loving care and concern, as in this case. The 'children' had great respect and admiration for their mother and for the job she had done in raising them. They repeatedly stated that they only desired what was best for her; that they only had her interests at heart; and that this man was not 'worthy' of her. As is so often the case they failed to realise their mother's loneliness, her need for someone for whom to care and her desire for companionship.

The conflict arose for a number of reasons:

lack of understanding on both sides;

lack of communication: people made statements instead of asking questions and listening to one another;

pride on both sides and determination not to 'give in';

a lack of unconditional love;

a refusal to forgive or forget.

When both sides put themselves and their feelings first, there can be no room for reconciliation. Vulnerability, open love, forgiveness and acceptance were never truly present. Consequently the 'children' as well as the mother were changed by the experience: a sense of hostility, regret and dissatisfaction permeated their relationships and affected even the grandchildren. Had faith been a reality to any of those involved rather than a social convention, there would have been a starting point for the process of reconciliation. As the situation progressed attitudes hardened and the willingness to concede any ground disappeared, thus making reconciliation more difficult. Justice in the form of personal rights or the demand for apologies is not a precondition of reconciliation. Both sides were so concerned with being in the 'right' that they failed to appreciate that the sacrifice of putting the other first could have led to a deeper 'rightness' and to a real freedom and love on both sides. Their attitude was, and remains to this day, that the other party alone was the cause of the injury. For the future, the 'children' need to be reconciled to the past, because the guilt of the past affects the present and interferes with the future and only by accepting their own brokenness can they come to a situation where they can go forward with freedom from the past guilt and openness to a new beginning.

Case study 2

B is a well respected man, much loved in the community. Nothing is ever too much trouble for him and he is always willing to do that little bit extra for others. His sensitivity, cheerfulness and apparent selflessness combine to enable him to bring comfort and sunshine into the lives of many of the elderly in the community. However, during the Second World War while on active service abroad he witnessed an incident involving several enemy soldiers and was so enraged by what he saw that he lost control and took revenge, causing the horrific deaths of those involved. Prior to this he had been a practicing RC, but he has never set foot in a church since his return except for baptisms and funerals. He is so revolted by what he did that he has hardly shared it with anyone, including his wife who died recently. He had talked to a priest on a couple of occasions in the past, but refused adamantly to believe that God could forgive what he had done. He believes he is therefore outside both God's love and the church. His whole life is, in his view, an attempt to make amends for what he did – almost an unending penance, with no final forgiveness. He refuses to accept that he can ever be reconciled to God, while at the same time longing for it.

B is unable to be reconciled to himself. His feeling of having stepped outside the bounds of acceptable human behaviour has led to self-alienation and because his understanding of God is too small and based on a God of judgement, the love and forgiveness offered by grace are not realities: he identifies Christ with condemnation and judgement.

The case is a good example of the fact that an ethical problem may also be fundamentally a religious problem. B must learn that there are other and truer ways of understanding Christ: particularly, the Christ who gave himself that others might have new life. Forgiveness is a transformation, not an abolition, of the past. The hope for the future is B's awareness of his need for forgiveness. His guilt over the past has to be faced and allowed some form of ritualistic expression of repentance and absolution, so that he may come to accept and respect himself again. A sensitive priest and the rituals of the RC Church provide a context for his reconciliation to the condition of his existence. His pain, grief and shame must not be minimised but acknowledged and given due importance, within the context of the greater love of God for him.

CASE STUDY 3

C and D met and married while at university. Highly intelligent people but both from homes of family breakdown, they had an inability to display or share emotion. After the birth of two attractive and very intelligent children, they had a Down's Syndrome child. Both coped internally and alone, not even allowing outsiders (e.g., doctor, minister, friends) to help them discuss their feelings. Eventually the strain proved too much and one day in an unemotional rational manner C explained that she was moving out of their home and taking the children with her. She left that weekend. D accepted her intention in the same unemotional rational manner and made plans for her and the children's financial security. While both had been church attenders, D had been slowly moving towards religious experience from intellectual assent and his self-understanding changed accordingly. He explored, with help and support, the emotions he now felt free to express and sought to be reconciled with his wife. She unemotionally refused all attempts and offers, stating that she wished neither a divorce nor a reconciliation.

D's remarkable spiritual awakening did not necessarily make the situation more capable of solution. He realised that the old relationship was finished; could a new one begin? His enthusiasm to communicate his new-found feelings was in fact frightening to his wife, who now viewed him as a total stranger. D saw himself as first reconciled to God and then with his wife: why shouldn't his wife respond? Further opportunities for him to talk through how he felt and to begin to see it in context helped him to view the situation from his wife's perspective. He began to see how threatening was his desire to communicate his long pent-up feelings, despite his good intentions, and slowly the awareness grew that reconciliation was not an immediate prospect. He finally decided to try gently to come into dialogue with C, and to attempt to understand her inhibitions and fears. Despite there having been no actual reconciliation, D is sufficiently at peace to allow himself to fulfil his life in other ways. C, on the other hand, remains withdrawn and remote. She will have no contact at all with the church and refuses to discuss the situation even with close friends. The best hope for a future reconciliation (neither wish a divorce) is D's continued gentle approach, in the knowledge that reconciliation is not an easy nor automatic process.

CASE STUDY 4

> Corrie ten Boom was brought up in a family home in Holland
> where the Bible was central and prayers and the practical
> outworking of the faith were taken for granted as normal behaviour.
> As an extension of this practical outworking she had become
> involved, along with other members of her family, in hiding and
> smuggling Jews. Finally she and her much loved sister Betsie were
> arrested and after many hardships ended in Ravensbruck
> Concentration Camp. Their faith sustained them and gave them
> vision for the future, despite the brutality of their day to day
> existence. Betsie, however, was not strong and she died just before
> Christmas 1944. Corrie was released the following month and
> returned home, where she determined after recovering her
> strength to put the vision she and Betsie had shared into practice
> – a home where those who had been damaged and hurt by the war
> could learn to live again. All were to be welcomed, victim,
> perpetrators and collaborators. She travelled extensively to realise
> her vision, including going back to Germany. There she met for
> the first time one of her former SS guards who was attending a
> church service she was addressing. He held out his hand and she
> found all the anger and vengeance which she thought she had
> eradicated welling up in her and knew, although it was sinful, she
> could not shake his hand. She prayed, 'Jesus, I cannot forgive him.
> Give me your forgiveness.' When her hand was taken in his she
> knew a rush of love for him which almost overwhelmed her and at
> the same time knew that God had given her the love and the
> freedom which true reconciliation brings.[1]

Despite her forgiving and reconciling actions up to meeting
her former guard, it was only when confronted by one of
those who had caused her much loved sister pain and
humiliation that the true depths of alienation became clear
to Corrie. When faced with the cause, not only of our own
pain, but that of someone whom we love, forgiveness is not
easy. Corrie realised the necessity for that reconciliation and
also knew that in her own strength she was unable to
accomplish it. The cost was too great for her to pay alone.
Through the inspiration of Christ, she was able to transcend

---

[1] Cf. Corrie ten Boom, *The Hiding Place* (1976).

the boundaries of hate and anger and to make the final desperately difficult response.

The theme of reconciliation thus takes us across the frontiers of ethics and theology, and is central to both. It has much to say about the deep alienation and damage which occur in human life, and the need for pastoral help: the above cases could well be classified as pastoral ethics. Barriers to reconciliation include fear of losing face, pride, self-justification, and lack of openness to the transforming possibilities of faith. Reconciliation is a kind of healing which takes place not least in the depths of our own being; and that requires a new awareness of the ground of moral being. When this becomes a vital awareness through the intersection of our story and the Christian story, new possibilities are created which one can realise only through faith and love; yet not all these possibilities will be realised in practice, for alienation is hard to overcome. That is the story of the Cross!

II *Moral Attributes, Moral Persons*

We now need to stand back a little further from particular cases to consider some of the theoretical aspects of the human reality we have been surveying. Needless to say, philosophers and ethicists have long been concerned with such moral issues. In our discussion of theory, we shall try to keep in touch with recognisable human experiences.

1 *Virtue*

'Virtue' has come to the fore again in recent discussions of ethics.[1] Discussion of the subject, however, goes back to Aristotle. As we have already noted, Aristotle held a teleological view of existence. He pinpointed *eudaimonia* as the 'end in itself': 'happiness', 'wellbeing', but in an active sense: it is that which is actively sought by rational beings. They cannot pursue it in isolation but with 'parents and children and wife, and friends and fellow citizens as a whole, since the human being is naturally involved with others'.[2] This life-long quest, carried out in community with others, is undertaken 'in accordance with virtue, or if there is a plurality of virtues, in accordance with the best and most complete of them'.

What then is virtue? Virtue (Gk *arete*) denotes excellence, the power to fulfil the proper function of the organism. As a rule of thumb, Aristotle takes what people praise or blame as an indication of virtues, which may be intellectual (wisdom, understanding, prudence) or more strictly moral (openness or liberality, moderation or self-control). Intellectual excellence is produced and enhanced by instruction, but moral virtue is the product of habit and practice. We become just by practising justice, self-controlled by exercising self-control, brave by doing brave acts. We must therefore regulate our life-style,

---

[1] E.g., S. Hauerwas, 'I am trying to suggest the recognition of the historic character of human existence demands an appreciation of narrative which shapes an ethics of virtue': *A Community of Character* (1981), p. 5.

[2] Aristotle, *Nicomachean Ethics*, II.

since our character is shaped by the quality of what we do. Moral education is therefore very important. Thus we learn to exercise moral choice, perception and responsibility.

Characteristically, Aristotle defines virtue as the mean between two extremes, one of excess and one of defect. For example, there are the primitive and powerful feelings of fear, pleasure and anger. In relation to the first, courage is the mean between rashness or foolhardiness (the excess) and cowardice (the defect). In relation to pleasure, self-control is the mean between between profligacy (the excess) and insensitivity to pleasure (a defect which, says Aristotle, is seldom found). In relation to anger, the mean may be termed gentleness, the excess irascibility and the defect spiritlessness. He gives other examples, many from the realm of human relations and converse. Truthfulness is the mean between boastful exaggeration and self-depreciation or mock modesty. Genuine wittiness is the mean between buffoonery (the excess) and boorishness (the deficiency); and genuine friendliness the mean between obsequiousness and sulkiness. The overall pattern of excess, mean and defect can be set out diagrammatically, and it is possible that Aristotle himself did so. In practice, we must avoid the extreme that is most opposed to the mean; and we must recognise the errors to which we ourselves are most prone and push ourselves in the opposite direction, being aware in particular of how our propensity to pleasure can cloud our judgement.

There is much to be said in favour of Aristotle's mean. We can speak of someone as a 'balanced' person. The whole system reflects the need for judgement and sensitivity. There may be occasions in public or professional life where the middle course is the appropriate way. The notion coheres with Aristotle's teleological approach; but if one were following a different criterion, one might be more sceptical of his general position. It is not only the situationist who will point out that one's judgement of the mean is affected by the context and question at issue. In a monastery, celibacy, fasting, penance and mortification of the flesh were included in the 'monkish virtues' attacked by David Hume. Hence, 'the very plurality of different notions of virtue indicates that any account of the virtues is context-dependent'.[3] The deontologist will say we should opt for the right rule or our sense of duty, as Ramsey and Kant did respectively. We do not always seek the middle way in order to know how to act: as W. D. Ross put it, 'we recognise what is too much or too little by recognising what is right'.[4] And Aristotle's 'excesses' or 'deficiencies' do not admit of a mean: they suggest wrong actions. Besides, the quantitative tabulation creates the illusion (which Aristotle did not recognise as such) that the opposite vices are more opposed to each other than to the virtue which represents the mean between them. As Kant indicated, this leaves out the question of motive. The profligate and the miser are both deficient in the stewardship of money. Aristotle's tabulations often present only the external relationships. W. D. Ross observed: 'It seems to be an accident, but a very frequent accident, of right action that it should be intermediate between extremes.'[5]

While the tradition of moral theology has been influenced by Aristotle both in its treatment of virtue and in its teleological perspectives, Christian ethics has attempted more recently to recover a neglected emphasis on virtue, character and conscience. Arguably, the Bible and the New Testament in particular have laid emphasis on virtues as 'the fruit of the Spirit' or growing 'in Christ': 'love, joy, peace, patience, kindness, goodness, fidelity, gentleness, and self-control' (Gal. 5:22, *REB*). They cohere in the moral dynamic of the Christian life. Good acts proceed from good persons (Mark 7:14–15). Virtues, as Aristotle emphasised, are fostered in community, the context of moral education. Theological and philosophical emphases were responsible for directing attention elsewhere,[6]

---

[3] S. Hauerwas, *A Community of Character*, ch. 6.

[4] W. D. Ross, *Essays on Bioethics* (1993), p. 196.

[5] Ross, p. 195.

[6] Dialectical theology (the theology of the Word) questioned ethical discourse in general as a piece of human pretentiousness. Hence, Barth's engagement with moral issues resembles 'act deontology' (cf. also Bonhoeffer: cf. n. 17 on p. 64). More typically, the emphasis on revelation in neo-Calvinism and the 'biblical theology' movement favoured a normative ethics of rules and principles: Paul Ramsey is an example, especially in his earlier

for example to duty or divine command. The issue, however, is not that norms should be rejected in favour of virtues but rather that the clarification of norms, though an important part of moral discourse, does not adequately represent the scope of Christian ethics. Emphasis is now on the quality of personal being and the matching emphasis on participation in community. Such changes represent a redressing of balance rather than revolution. The leading moral virtues often correspond to leading principles and rules: thus, honesty relates to truth telling, kindness to benevolence, courage to constancy, integrity in personal and professional matters to respect for persons, and fair-mindedness to justice. They also correlate to one's notion of the ground of value or existence.[7]

A cautionary note should be sounded. It is not enough simply to list virtues. Virtues like courage and self-control might be found in an immoral person; and there is no agreement about what qualifies as a virtue in any case. Virtues are meaningful only when they are fully integrated into the life of a person and thus related to questions of motive and character. These matters are taken up below.

2 *Motive*

It is not just in detective fiction that weight is placed on motive. It has always been an important strand in moral reflection and Christian self-understanding.[8] The New Testament evokes powerful images of rebirth and renewal, of inner transformation, and of the 'heart'; good thoughts and actions

work. Even Häring, in *The Law of Christ*, placed more emphasis on norms than in his later work, *Free and Faithful in Christ*, where his concern for virtue and the person is evident. One reaction to rules ethics was to place weight on situation, as in Joseph Fletcher; but while this might have drawn attention to the moral agent, situation ethics focused on decision in the given context. The re-emergence of virtue, for example in the work of Gustafson and Hauerwas, threatened to replace the misplaced antagonism between norm and context with an equally misguided opposition of virtue and obligation, but happily discussion took a more positive form.

[7] Cf. E. LeRoy Long, *A Survey of Recent Christian Ethics* (1982), ch. 7.
[8] Cf. Fairweather and McDonald, *The Quest*, ch. 3.

proceed from within. In discussing the commandment, 'Thou shalt not kill', Jesus draws attention to the uncontrolled anger which prompts actions of this kind.

No-one denies that motive is important; but can it be the sole criterion of moral action? Is an action right simply because it is done with a good motive? If we say 'Yes', we adopt the *strong form* of the theory. We then have to face the question: on what grounds do we call the motive 'good'? Are we not presupposing some measure other than motive by which motives are judged good or bad? Besides, we can do the 'right' thing from the 'wrong' motive, and vice versa. Well motivated people can make bad decisions. We need to affirm that right motives and right actions go together. The writer of the Epistle of James made the same point about faith: it must find expression in good acts. 'You will know them by their fruits' (Matt. 7.16). The strong form of the theory – that motive is the sole criterion – cannot be sustained.

It is possible to hold a *modified* or *weaker* form of the proposal: motive is an important, but not the only, criterion of morality. Kant, for example, combined two criteria: actions are right (i) when they conform to the moral law (deontology); and (ii) when they are done *because* they conform to the moral law (right motive). Motive can, of course, make a difference to the moral assessment of the act: for example, telling a lie. Mendacity or not telling the truth is certainly a 'disvalue'. It may be classified as 'wrong in itself', but subject to casuistry in difficult situations; or it may be held to be wrong when it attempts to deceive or to inflict harm or to excuse the agent in some way. Teleological dimensions or questions of purpose are relevant to the moral assessment. Thus a situation may arise where the objectives and motives are of a different order. We may disguise the truth – a euphemism for not telling the whole truth or for not telling the truth at all – not to deceive or cause harm or for defensive reasons but for the sake of someone's welfare, or in the interests of security, for example. This is a grey area and needs close scrutiny. Sometimes we may be patronising in assuming that another person cannot bear the truth; and politicians or senior civil servants who have been

'economical with the truth' on occasions have found it difficult
to retain credibility. Such cases, however, turn on considerations
of motive, intention or aim, as well as the general moral
obligation to be truthful. Or we might put it thus: the action
must be compatible with being a truthful person; and acting as
a truthful person includes motive and other moral criteria as
appropriate.[9]

In Kant's view, we should do 'duty for duty's sake', and act
out of good will. Good will, he believed, is good without
qualification; and we should 'act only on that maxim which we
can will to become a universal law'. Is 'duty' adequate as the
fundamental motive? This takes us back, of course, to our
discussion of the ground of value. One point to be emphasised
here is that duty requires to be internalised. In this way we
portray to ourselves the notion of the self we want to be. We
build up an ego-ideal; we are guided by self-praise and self-
blame. However, in taking this line, we are in danger of
adopting a purely cognitive view of ethics, which presupposes
the moral ideal of the 'autonomous, rational being'. In personal
as well as Christian terms, the unbalanced nature of such a view
is evident. Emotions, intentions, motivation, will, disposition,
virtue, character: such terms point to a much more rounded
and inclusive view of the person. When New Testament tradition
endorses the moral law, which it identifies with the will of God,
and suggests *agape* as fundamental motive, it presupposes an
inter-personal, interactive, caring realm of discourse,
articulated above all in the teaching of Jesus and the story of
Jesus' ministry. This type of view is not only more appropriate
to Christian ethics in terms of biblical teaching, but it is also
more true to life as human beings know it.

3 *Character*

'Character' has also to do with personalistic understanding. It
embraces virtues and habits as characteristic of a person and
thus implies consistency in moral practice. Thus Stuart

[9] See chapter 1, pp. 7–8.

Hampshire took character to be the established pattern of one's habits of action.[10] Interaction with one's world may also be made the focus of character definition. R. O. Johann described character as 'the personal achievement of a stable and fruitful relationship with one's natural and social environment':[11] a definition which helpfully underlines the range of one's personal operations and responsibilities. S. Hauerwas, relating character to the growth of the self in virtue, emphasises its narrative nature: it relates to 'my' story as a human being.[12] 'My' story begins with the gift of life – given to me by others and supremely by 'the Other' (the symbolism of baptism is suggestive here). 'My' story is thus enriched and redirected as it comes into vital contact with other stories and – specifically in Christian ethics – with the Christian story, transmitted by others' example and teaching. The task is to appropriate the moral convictions of the communities to which we belong – family and church being cardinal in moral and spiritual terms – and I in turn contribute to their stories. Such communities provide the conditions for the agent to grow towards fulfilment.

The notion of character is not without its paradoxes. We praise constancy and consistency of character, but character is always in the process of formation, always growing and becoming: 'not that I have attained, but I press on...' (Phil. 3:12). Consistency lies in maintaining quality of character as growth takes place. The notion of 'fulfilment' also needs clarification. It refers not simply to personal autonomy (as in 'autonomous rationality') but to relating to others and, above all, to the Other who is the ground of our being.

Another problem is that of over-simplification. The older I become, the more complex is the narrative of my life, with conflicting loyalties and roles that have to be held together. I may try to unite them through my understanding of my identity or ego-ideal, or through the notion of creative justice,

---

[10] Stuart Hampshire, *Two Theories of Morality* (1977), p. 44.
[11] R. O. Johann, *The Meaning of Love* (1966), pp. 79–80; quoted in Long, pp. 105–6.
[12] Cf. Hauerwas, *Community of Character*, pp. 145–52.

one of my core values, but elements of compromise creep in as necessary adjustments. Is my character thereby enriched or impaired? At all events, the case is by no means simple. A possible solution is to appeal to moral integrity, understood in this context not as a static principle but as 'more usefully linked with a narrative sufficient to guide us through the many valid and often incompatible duties and virtues that form our selves'.[13]

Several further paradoxes have been noted by Hauerwas in particular. Strength of character involves openness to others and the Other, by which we are ourselves changed, yet through such transformations we find ourselves and our character: by losing our life we find it! Character growth involves appropriating virtues, yet as soon as we claim them as ours we have lost them (the 'Pharisee and the publican' presents a relevant picture). It also involves struggle: against the temptation to deny our true story, to lose out in the 'war that is in our members'; and against complacency and self-deception, which retard and undermine moral growth. We thus presuppose receiving the skills 'to recognise the ambiguity of our moral achievements and the necessity of continued growth'.[14]

4 *Conscience*

Conscience represents something of a battlefield in modern debate. In Freudian terms, it is central to the Superego – the 'big brother' which operates within us as censor and thus suppresses or sublimates our basic desires and drives. In sociological terms, the conscience is a social product: it is our response to the social forces which have shaped us. It would not be useful to attempt to controvert such hypotheses here, in whole or part; nor even to engage in dialogue on grounds dictated by these social sciences. Useful insights accrue from them, but if they were to be regarded as definitive accounts of

[13] Cf. Hauerwas, ch. 6.
[14] Cf. Hauerwas, ch. 7.

moral reality, they would incur the charge of reductionism: that is, of reducing the moral dimension to a single perspective. Here we wish to look at the phenomenon of conscience as it relates to persons acting as moral agents.

Familiar in everyday speech as in Christian ethics, conscience has a cognitive, an intuitive, a prescriptive and an affective side. It should not be described as a 'faculty', as if it were a separate organ or identifiable segment of the brain. It is rather to be conceived in an integrative way as the operation of the whole person in the moral realm. At this point, however, difficulties begin.

Positive views can be of several types. Conscience was described by Aquinas as 'the human mind making moral judgements'.[15] Some have identified an intuitive as well as an intellectual side to conscience: 'it sees directly the rightness and wrongness of actions rather than discovers them by reasoning processes'.[16] As a result, conscience came to play a notable part in certain kinds of Protestant thinking, since it provided an alternative to prescriptive views of morality reinforced by ecclesiastical authority. Yet it is necessary to enquire closely into the content and authenticity of the intuition. A Reformed critique of conscience can be quite negative. Thus Bonhoeffer:

> Conscience pretends to be the voice of God and the standard for relation to other men…. Man has become the origin of good and evil. He does not deny his evil; but in conscience man summons himself, who has become evil, back to his proper, better self, to good. This good, which consists in the unity of man with himself, is now to be the origin of all good…. Bearing within himself the knowledge of good and evil, man has become judge over God and men, just as he is judge over himself.[17]

[15] Aquinas spoke of *synderesis*, suggesting the grasp of moral principles that enables one to do right and avoid evil; but equally, he was thinking of the disposition of the morally mature person which prompts morally good actions and the avoidance of evil ones.

[16] Cf. Lillie, *An Introduction to Ethics*, London 1957, p. 81.

[17] D. Bonhoeffer, *Ethics* (1958), pp. 3–6.

Finally, there is the modern defiant assertion of the role of conscience in values creation. Don Cupitt writes:

> So I just contrast worthlessness and value, by way of stressing that it is all up to us, that valuation is just human and that we cannot any longer look for support to an imaginary cosmic Foundation and Duplicate of our ideas.'[18]

There is a measure of agreement between Bonhoeffer and Cupitt about human creativity in matters of conscience, but they evaluate it in different ways. In response to Bonhoeffer, it is necessary to emphasise the social context of conscience formation and the role of the faithful moral community in mediating to us the ground of moral value, particularly in scripture. Christian ethics underlines, rather than denies, the importance of upbringing and Christian moral education, not least in the broad context of life in a secularised society where there are many conflicts of value. In response to Cupitt, one must affirm God, not as a duplicate of our ideas but as the voice of the Other, calling us to true humanity. It is important not to capitulate to modern secularism, with its spurious openness and determined reductionism in relation to all things religious.[19]

Conscience is indeed, as Aquinas said, the human mind making moral judgements, but in Christian terms it does so in the light of one's knowledge of God and in the Spirit of Christ. Conscience is not simply enlightened rationality. Its emotional ramifications arise from the fact that while we may know what ought to be done, we may be drawn towards performing that action or we may feel an aversion to it. We may even represent to ourselves that our aversion is morally justified: rationalisation thus enters the equation. In Christian ethics, therefore, we not only recognise a duty to obey conscience but also to develop a degree of self-knowledge which enables us to recognise our

---

[18] D. Cupitt, *The New Christian Ethics* (1988), pp. 133–4.

[19] There are dangers in rampant individualism, which makes the self master of all it surveys in the moral realm; also in overlooking the importance of moral tradition, which may be critically appropriated from generation to generation but not discounted.

rationalisations and prejudices and take appropriate action to control them. Yet Christian experience – with its openness to the dimension of 'otherness' – testifies that the greater one's moral insight the less at ease one's conscience may be.

The task of rightly divining true value is part of the development of a critical consciousness which is essential to Christian ethics and practice in the modern age. It is part of what may be described as growth in virtue, or as the internalising of taught norms. It is integrally related to what some moral theologians have called the 'fundamental option': that is, one's total moral disposition, the core of the person, which is expressed in decisions about individual actions.

The question of morality is larger than any of us: it has, even in this limited sense, a transcendent quality. The Christian tradition, as we have seen, points to a ground of value which is not in any way our creation and which is mediated to us through moral community, story and scripture. At times there may come to an individual a powerful 'moving of the Spirit', which conveys direct intuition of moral truth. Without impugning the intensity or sincerity of such intuitions, it must be pointed out that even in the New Testament the spirits must be tested to see whether they are of God; and the criteria adopted in such issues are precisely whether the intuition is in accord with confession of Jesus as the Christ and therefore with his story. Once again, we are directed to the tradition of the moral community and the ground of value to which it testifies.

III   *Personal Formation*

1 *The 'whole person'*

Personhood is a unitive or holistic concept, but what is a 'whole person'? Schizophrenia – divided personhood – is a pathological condition. Instability – contradictory or inconsistent behaviour, for example – suggests moral immaturity or damaged personality. Language such as 'whole person' presupposes a unitive concept of the self, as well as coherence and balance in relation to the world of people and things. Such is the groundwork of moral maturity.

The root of this holism is much debated. Traditional Christian thought made use of the Greek concept of the soul, but modern discourse is more at ease with a metaphorical rather than a metaphysical interpretation of this term. More recently, theologians have tended towards the notion of the shaping of 'the total self' within the Christian community by the grace of God (or the 'humanising action' of God), and have thus given renewed emphasis to the formation of conscience.

Personal growth is thus growth in community. In this respect, the self is not a static state but a social product. It grows and develops – for good or ill. Christian ethics has sometimes borrowed from social psychology in order to illumine this dimension. Our dependence on others limits personal freedom in important respects. So great can be the alienation and deprivation of love that there are many who may be considered to have had no chance in life.

The fear/distrust/hate reaction becomes a syndrome – directed not just at some people or some section of society, but at all people, whether we know them or not. It becomes an archetype by which we interpret all our experience. *All* people are feared, distrusted or hated. This is a typical example of the stunting of personal growth. People thus affected are never capable of accepting other people and trusting them – or so it seems. There is, however, always the possibility that they will have their 'moment of truth' when

they 'find' themselves as they encounter others who treat
them as having worth and give them a measure of self-
esteem. For the Christian, it is never true that 'human
nature does not change' or that some people are
'irredeemable'.[1]

Lack of freedom is thus a leading factor in much of life. We are
conditioned by our culture and constrained by our environment
– in some cases, to the point of personal disintegration or
destruction – and 'there but for the grace of God go I' is more
than a pious sentiment. It would be a false step at this point to
divide humanity into the sheep and the goats, the elect and the
unregenerate – notwithstanding the imagery of the Last
Judgement (which is in God's hands). *All* have sinned...; and
all human beings, religious or unbelievers, experience the
alienation that mars and disables humanity. But there is a
moral counter-force, a dynamic for good, which is also
embodied within the cosmos. It is proclaimed in Christian
story and vision; it is embodied in truly moral people. It is the
force which is expressed in authentic community – whether
that occurs, fleetingly or frequently, in family, church, school,
political group, 'grass roots' community or revolutionary cell
– and which is morally creative and spiritually liberating. It is
the dynamic of moral growth and transformation, which
matures the person and creates space for relatively free moral
choice and action. It is, in theological terms, the power of the
Holy Spirit, which indeed 'bloweth where it listeth' and which
is realised through openness to the transcendent, however
effected. It witnesses to the fact that goodness is always given
– never created by us, though we respond to it and it is created
in us.

2 *Gender*

Gender plays a vital role in personal formation and in the
shaping of values. Patriarchy has given *carte blanche* to male
dominance and aggressiveness. Deontological and teleological

---

[1] Fairweather and McDonald, *The Quest*, ch. 10.

values typically presuppose an adversarial and competitive view of human nature, with violent and even murderous propensities. In consequence, Luther spoke of the law as a 'dyke against sin'; and Calvin underlined the role of government in restraining violence and disorder. While grace is prominent in their religious or theological outlook, it did not form the bottom line of their ethics. Appeals to justice and utility are similarly made in the context of competition for the desired goods and thus establish corresponding rights or duties. Indeed, as Grace Jantzen has put it, from the time of John Locke onwards,

> this possessive individualism has become the anthropological model for morality, with its view of competing egos joined in a social contract to protect and advance their own interests as far as possible.[2]

The 'autonomus, rational man' (*sic*) is thus lonely and estranged in his atomised view of human existence. Even Kohlberg's influential interpretation of moral education, which was based on a study of 84 boys, has been shown by Carol Gilligan to have presupposed the male competitive model, to the disadvantage of women with whom comparison was made.[3]

In a radical re-visioning of society, feminism has questioned the legitimation of this model by ethics. To institutionalise rather than challenge the adversarial view in political and economic structures is to reinforce alienation.[4] In its place, a 'connectedness' model is advocated. As we have suggested above, personhood is properly understood in terms of a web of relationships, by which we may be humanised or even dehumanised. Emphasis now falls on caring relationships, on commitment to one another and to the community, and on sensitivity towards advancing the welfare of the community.

---

[2] G. Jantzen, 'Connection or competition: identity and personhood in Christian ethics', *Studies in Christian Ethics*, 5.1.1992, p. 11.

[3] Cf. C. Gilligan, *In a Different Voice: Psychological Theory and Women's Development* (1982).

[4] Jantzen, p. 4.

Here is a decided gravitational shift in the basis of morality. The reinterpretation of human reality in woman's perspective requires a radical reorientation towards connectedness, which presupposes moral learning and character development. We must respect and accept other people as they are, in their *difference* from us, not simply because of their similarity. At a stroke, evils such as racism, sexism, homophobia and the like are seen for what they are. In recognising the place of the emotion (as in caring), this view avoids the insensitivity and moral blindness that can be engendered by a stance of detachment. Connectedness implies working for reconciliation where alienation occurs, and rights and obligations are set in a new context. 'The isolated, autonomous individual clinging to his or her rights and impartially performing his or her duties is, from the connectedness perspective, a good picture of hell.'[5]

It must be evident that such proposals are in line with the personal and social model outlined in this chapter. They encounter, of course, some of the problems of revolutionary programmes. They present an attractive and compelling ideal, but while they may arguably reflect the *ius naturale* (at least on the basis of feminine perceptions of it), they run counter to the *ius gentium*, with its adulation of competition and market forces.[6] Some women affirm the *ius gentium*, whether in their careers or their personal life. How frequently we pass on our oppression to others! Nevertheless, the connectedness model represents a valid call to humankind, an affirmation of personal and social value transcending and challenging the *status quo*. It interprets the work of caring professions far better than traditional ethics, but it will encounter much resistance, even derision, from the power brokers. Yet it is not a stance from which Christian ethics can stand aloof. Whatever it draws from Christian ethics, it illumines many of its fundamental features. Its call is valid.

[5] Jantzen, p. 11.
[6] See above, on 'natural law'.

3 *Alienation and reconciliation*

Estrangement – hostility, separation from one's true being – affects every aspect of life: one's personal being, religious awareness, relationships and experiences of families, gender, race, and economic and political structures. Its pervasiveness questions and invalidates every over-optimistic interpretation of the human condition – whether in moralistic, humanistic or political guise.

It is all too easy to give a partial response to the problem. Prohibitions and rules hold its worst features in check and act as negative markers of a better way. Principles seem to offer more. Being general and universal, they can be readily brought together in a kind of federation or hierarchy to describe a moral world view and, as in theological and political liberalism, to portray a community of interest between Christian values on the one hand (equality under God, love, brotherhood, social concern, spiritual freedom), and enlightened societal values on the other (justice, liberty, rationality, equality under the law, democracy, enterprise). Although this kind of liberalism has its noble side (it is hard not to respect a disciplined Christian liberalism) and retains validity in certain contexts, it does less than justice to the radical nature of alienation. Deontology and teleology are all too easy to manipulate, rationalise and domesticate. Again, natural law may be used not only to categorise certain classes of actions as evil (and thereby reduce morality to the doing or avoiding of certain actions) but also to sanction socio-political structures and the ideology which supports them, with apparent disregard for their alienating role. Some scholars locate evil primarily in the exercise of oppressive power, whether of the state (as in liberation theology) or of patriarchy (as in feminism), both of which claim justification in 'natural law'.

The wellsprings of human being and action – the fundamental orientation of the person, questions of motive and character, human interaction and experience of life – have to be brought into the picture before one approaches the heart of the matter. Childhood is the cradle of character. Experiences of acceptance or rejection, understanding or guilt, achievement or failure, are important factors, as is the question of identity and self-acceptance. Moral growth and development takes place through the totality of social experience. Sometimes fear and hostility indicate immaturity, and sometimes deeper disturbance. Pathological conditions may emerge. Some are too aggressive; some too dependent and easily led. All reap the benefits or become the victims of their upbringing and experiences. The unfairness of life can wound. Some find little to stimulate: stagnation and despair may be the outcome.[7]

In face of the realities of life, Christian ethics finds its primary baseline not in rules, acts, standards or even principles, and not in judgementalism, but in the promotion of 'wholeness', both personal and social. It is concerned with understanding and accepting, with caring for the victims of life's harshness, with conciliation and reconciliation. It is concerned to promote community and, in particular, supportive community. It is concerned also with the injustices in society: again not simply to condemn, but to work for the conditions which will support meaningful life and hope.

In taking this line, Christian ethics embodies the principal symbols of the Christian faith. The Incarnation is a symbol of sharing and identification: God with us. Jesus and his disciple community symbolise a community of loving service. Love is a bridging of barriers, a healing of the alienated, a concern for others' welfare and thus the basis of a creative justice.[8] The Cross is a symbol of healing, hope and peace in the midst of hostility, rejection and death: only a love which is open to suffering can offer reconciliation, open the way to forgiveness, and provide the basis for a new human solidarity.[9] The Trinity signifies divine community, interdependent, supportive and

[7] Cf. Erik Erikson's classic study of emotional development: *Childhood and Society* (1950); on moral education, cf. John Wilson et al., *Introduction to Moral Education*; William Kay, *Moral Education* (1974); *Moral Development* (1975).

[8] P. Tillich, *Love, Power and Justice*, pp. 62–71.

[9] E. Käsemann, 'Some thoughts on the theme "The Doctrine of Reconciliation in the New Testament"', in J. M. Robinson (ed), *The Future of Our Religious Past*.

reaching out to others.[10] Acceptance and reconciliation is the gospel characterisation of God's approach to an alienated and divided world. Only in the *eschaton* will reconciliation be complete: here we live and act by faith.

Christian ethics thus recognises that personal formation embraces not only the entire range of relationships and life experiences but also the deep questions of life. There comes a point at which answers must come from a level beyond that at which the conventional criteria and moral markers operate. How does one come to terms with oneself and one's past? How can one break free from the shackles of sin (the theological term in all its seriousness suggests the gravity of the question)? Here, there are no glib answers. Self-acceptance is hard to achieve when one is condemned by one's past. The symbols in which the Christian faith is so rich testify to a reality which obtains even in the face of the most horrendous evil: the reality of reconciliation with God, the availability of forgiveness, the possibility of transformation, the offer of new life. All these are devalued if presented glibly or merely as an academic exercise. The context in which they can most readily be brought to life is that of the faithful moral community, where the reality of acceptance and forgiveness can be demonstrated and the relation of resurrection to moral life can be sympathetically explored.[11]

---

[10] Cf. J. Moltmann, *The Trinity and the Kingdom of God* (Eng. tr. 1981).
[11] O. O'Donovan, *Resurrection and Moral Order* (1986).

CHAPTER 3

FAMILY VALUES

As we have already noted, there is a close relationship between the personal and the social realms. Their interdependence is beyond question. Apart from biological dependence, one grows as a person through interacting with others. Socialisation is a fundamental factor in moral growth. One learns to speak, act, play, learn, achieve, gain self-worth and much more through life in community. The form of community into which we are born is the family. Whatever shape it may take, it is the crucible of personal growth. If there is a crisis in the family, its repercussions will be felt throughout society, as well as in the impoverishment of the personal realm.

Suggestions of 'crisis' arise when some shocking event – such as murder committed by children – shatters complacency and produces a hysterical public reaction. What is happening to our families? What are we doing to our children? Where were the parents/teachers/social workers/churches/police? Panic reaction looks for scapegoats: videos, the media, working mothers, unemployment, one parent families.... These comments, even if valid, simply describe a particular aspect of the problem and are invariably partial. The problem is much more deep-rooted and disconcerting. It springs from widespread perceptions about the nature of human life itself. For this reason, theological perspectives are specifically evoked by the problematic nature of the empirical reality.

The first step is clearly to focus on the family in society today, and to form some notion of the pressures upon it.

I *The Family and Social Value*

The entire picture is not so bleak as first appearances may suggest. The family has been described as 'the strongest and most highly valued basis of social attachment' in most countries today.[1] Most young people want to get married and have children. Many children get on well with their parents and say that their parents understand them. However, within the continuity of the family unit, changes constantly occur – rapidly, in the second half of the twentieth century. One could cite the incidence of cohabitation, divorce, and one parent families as major indications of change; even more disconcerting is the incidence of violence within families, although this is not new. A factor of a different kind is longevity: four generation families are not uncommon. And, of course, there is the variable of affluence and hardship.

Also very significant is the marked change in roles within families: the husband is not necessarily the principal income earner, nor is the wife's role simply to look after husband and children. Changes in sexual practice, such as birth control, have had far-reaching consequences for the understanding of marriage. Indeed, since the economic groundwork has shifted and sexual relations are increasingly controlled by the female partner, we can even distinguish between a 'traditional role' model of marriage, a 'companionship' model and a 'loving intimacy' model. It may be that such developments make for a less stable family unit. If so, the contribution of a supportive community becomes important.

Yet the contribution which society makes to family life is highly ambivalent. As we have noted, families are not insulated from the wider life of society. They are part of the warp and woof of society itself: open to the stresses of employment and unemployment, advantage and disadvantage, education and ideology, peer pressure and identity crises, war and peace....

---

[1] P. Abrams, 'Social facts and sociological analysis', in P. Abrams (ed), *Work, Urbanism and Inequality* (1978), p. 10; cited in E. Craven, L. Rimmer and M. Wicks, *Family Issues and Public Policy* (1982), p. 11.

The family, the crucible of personal and social value, is thus itself subject to social and economic pressure, ideological change in society, and gradual re-evaluation. Historically, the family has shown itself resilient to the challenge of social and political change. In recent centuries, for example, it coped with the propaganda of the French Revolution and Marxism, and with the massive dislocations of the industial revolution; just as today it is coming to terms with the modern technological revolution and contemporary ideologies. Flexibility is required in the way the family operates and understands its function if it is to provide stability for its members and inculcate personal and social values in a perplexing and changing world. It is not surprising if some families fail in the face of circumstances. What is seldom appreciated is the extent to which families are undermined by values given currency within the very society which looks to the family for stability and a sense of values! Freedom and fulfilment, the cult of the individual, the values of the market place, the drive for power, prestige and success, democracy itself, all possess a degree of ambivalence or error which can be destructive. We must get used to the idea that value is expressed not merely in the invoking of a moral concept but in the manner in which the concept is understood and applied.

At this point, it may be helpful to look at several distinctive perspectives on the family which represent responses to this scenario.

1 *The traditional view*

The so-called 'traditional' or 'conservative' view of the family implicitly acknowledges the moral battlefield on which the family plays out its role. The typical version suggests the values it cherishes and the disvalues it seeks to counteract. The family is seen:

(i) *As a champion of freedom* against the encroachment of the state. On this view, the state is seen as a centralising, bureaucratic monster, and family, church, guild and club as intermediate, countervailing groups. The bottom line is personal freedom and initiative. Implicit moral values are self-reliance and independence, industry and personal responsibility.

(ii) *As the seat of authority*, especially paternal authority, from which stems its role in disciplining its offspring and affording a stable and secure base for healthy personal growth. Firm parameters are themselves the product of loving concern, and within them children can successfully negotiate the stages of moral and social development. Disruption of this stable pattern causes anxiety and may lead to disturbed and anti-social behaviour. There is a tendency among those who hold to this view to ascribe social evils such as juvenile crime, hooliganism and sexual licence to the erosion of parental authority.

(iii) *As interactive community* It is a cohesive group, resting on kinship, inculcating loyalty, and placing emphasis on duties rather than rights, and on obligations to others rather than on what is owed to oneself. The upbringing of the young, like the care of the elderly and dependants, are priorities which devolve particularly on some members of the group, especially female members. Within the ethos of this caring group, personal and social values are minted.

A feature of the traditionalist stance is its unequivocal endorsement of the family as the crucible of values formation. It claims, and its proponents usually expect, the endorsement of Christian bodies. It can appeal to the moral structure of reality, as in the 'natural law' tradition, as well as to the moral basis of duty and to criteria of personal and social value. But there are weaknesses which must be of concern to the Christian ethicist. These may be summarised as follows:

(i) *It tends to present an oversimplified view*: for example, in relation to authority and the breakdown of discipline. It tends not to recognise the complexity of modern society and the extent to which family life is governed by it. The family is thought of as an island haven in a stormy sea: it is more like a storm tossed ship! Families in nineteenth-century industrial society, brutalised by poverty and low wages, contrast not only with middle class families, geared to private property and economic advantage, but also with better paid mid twentieth-century working class families with their consumer orientation. Corresponding values and disvalues are generated. Hence it is inadequate to think of families as primary groups in isolation from economic and other social factors which largely determine their ethos and moral practice.

(ii) *Its view of authority is top-down and repressive* Thus in a patriarchal family love comes to be linked with power, and obedience with punishment; such families may seem geared to control rather than love. The peculiar forms of socialisation which this system may encourage, many suggest, tend to generate non-assertiveness in the female and aggressiveness in boys. It has therefore engendered violence within families, a factor often concealed. Role changes within the family, as well as changing ideas of education and nurture (which are in turn targeted for criticism by traditionalists), have eroded the credibility of this aspect of the model.

(iii) *It reproduces stereotypes,* which are blind to the proper claims of people within the family. It admirably stresses the caring functions, but attributes such duties to certain members with a notable lack of care for their welfare. This is particularly true of its stereotypical view of women's roles. It is also true of class structures which impose on each his/her proper station!

(iv) *It can be in-turned and self-regarding* As such, its moral stature is compromised. This criticism is levelled particularly at the so-called 'nuclear' family, itself the product of industrialisation and the individualism it fostered. If the family is a unit of self-interest, it is open to manipulation by political, economic and commercial forces. An in-turned ethos may fail to check racism, chauvinism or appeals to extreme nationalism.

Such criticisms are certainly sufficient to make one think twice about an unequivocal endorsement of the traditional view, although many families will recognise the dangers and take counter-measures. If it is to realise its full potential for nurture, the family must generate a moral vision which affirms all that is truly humane in its nature while recognising its own weaknesses and temptations. It needs to develop the capacity to reappraise the roles performed by its members, especially if there is the suggestion of stereotype about them. And it needs to develop a critical consciousness of those influences which contradict, erode or undermine such values within families. Thus, families need the support of perceptive moral communities if they are to realise their own potential as moral communities. Some influences are undoubtedly insidious: modern society, with its individualistic, materialistic and at times depraved hedonism, mounts a constant attack on the values its leaders wish to preserve but often singularly fail to support. Propaganda is another matter. Most Western citizens have been bombarded with rhetorical attacks on 'scroungers' and have heard state 'interference' castigated as an intolerable intrusion on family prerogatives (it costs money!). The question of disadvantage in society is thus side-stepped and deprived of its urgency. Many families urgently need material support. The much trumpeted return to 'good old-fashioned values' is a reaffirmation of the traditional model accompanied by a seemingly wilful blindness to its proven weaknesses.

2 *Alternatives to traditional patterns?*

Are there convincing alternatives to traditional patterns?

(i) *Feminist perspectives* Modern feminist perspectives present a radical critique of the family unit, especially in its 'nuclear' form. The demise of the patriarchal family would be a matter for celebration, for one of its most oppressive features is the transmission of traditional gender stereotypes, evident in widely held views of marriage, child care, care of the elderly, and domestic drudgery within the family. Such conditioning subordinates women and girls and inhibits economic independence and career prospects. It is reinforced, at least in part, by traditional biases within schools, the business world and job market, and even churches. Within the family and outside it in the labour force, women are made to subserve the interests of a still patriarchal capitalistic system. Feminist objectives include control over fertility, economic independence, and the overthrowing of oppressive gender stereotypes. 'Can we accept that many people fleeing the nuclear family are doing so for valid reasons?' asks Shere Hite.[2] No doubt they are, but it is often difficult to find in such critiques of the family any clear pointer to alternative structures.

As always, rumours of the death of the family are greatly exaggerated. It has shown itself capable at least of modifying its ethos, even if the degree of change appears to many to be modest. Accordingly, a more positive view is also found in feminism. Some feminists view the family as a possible instrument of change as it develops critical consciousness and reflects feminist critiques of traditional practice. The feminist revolution can begin within the family itself as it gives more adequate expression to mutuality and inter-dependence: to the 'connectedness' model discussed in the previous chapter. An implication of true connectedness is that the interests of all members of the family must be safeguarded if personal formation and humane values are truly part of the scene. Thus it can become a new locus of moral learning, which will in turn produce an effective critique of values in society.

(ii) *Socio-economic perspectives*   Socio-economic factors arguably provide a definitive context for families, which relate to the socio-economic system in different ways according to class and social context.[3] Family values have thus influenced and been

---

[2] Cf. Shere Hite, *The Hite Report on the Family* (1994). The quote is from Joan McAlpine, 'Hand that rocks society', *The Scotsman*, 23.2.1994.

[3] In nineteenth-century Britain, urban working class families were trapped in a cycle of low wages, long hours, poor working conditions and poor housing, leading to demoralisation. Children were valued as economic assets and treated accordingly. This was the seed-bed of socialism. Middle class families, who secured their social status through entrepreneurial activities and the acquisition of property to be passed on within the family, related to the values of the ruling class. In the twentieth century, the general improvement in housing, wages and conditions enabled working class families to become

influenced by political perspectives. A century or more of socialist thinking has evinced remarkable ambivalence towards the family. On the one hand, the family is seen negatively as the tool of the capitalist system, which exploited it for its labour resources; and on the other, it is valued for its emphasis on human values which transcend market norms. With the perceived failure of certain types of socialist policy – whether the Eastern European variety or, for all their evident social benefits, post-war British policies – capitalism has been widely reaffirmed as an autonomous self-regulating system, and many people see no alternative but to affirm the *status quo*. 'Of itself', Charles Davis comments, 'it deploys a purely functional and means–end rationality, closed to any ethical or religious considerations such as the solidarity of all persons.'[4] Nevertheless, Michael Novak has come to see it as the bedrock of democratic and liberal values, although capitalism need not be liberal (nor has it always been so) and Novak himself sees limitations to the unfettered working of market forces, particularly in the area of human values and welfare.[5] Changing interpretations have an influence on family values. Families may be more than the tools of the system; they may nurture 'achievers' within it. Other families may be deeply demoralised. Morally, capitalism is by no means neutral. Its spin-off can hardly be other than selfishness and materialism, and its aggressive attempts at refuting criticism sponsored by Christian ethics do nothing to reaffirm 'basic values'. The upshot of the economic history of the West may well be that some people

oriented to the acquisition of consumer goods and to be less consciously 'working class' – until, later in the century, unemployment or redundancy changed the picture. Even then, state support – minimal though it was – prevented a simple return to the deprivations of the thirties. Middle class families consolidated their position mainly through education and cultural acquisitions. As the technological revolution registered its pervasive effects, the need for education and training came to be recognised more widely across the barriers of class, but the gap between rich and poor became as wide as ever.

[4] Charles Davis, *Religion and the Making of Society* (1994), p. 173.

[5] Michael Novak, *Will It Liberate? Questions About Liberation Theology* (1986), p. 215; *The Spirit of Democratic Capitalism* (1982); Davis, pp. 173–87.

here are suffering 'from a morally apathetic and fearful seeking for a safe niche in our present predatory society'.[6] Little wonder if families find themselves the moral casualties of socio-economic and political developments.

(iii) *Other forms of community* The two broad alternatives to the 'traditional' view outlined above have been presented in such a way as to preserve the focus on the family, with whatever reservations. The family itself is not a fixed unit. It can vary from the extended, multi-generational unit that has its origins deep in history to the much quoted 'nuclear' family of modern times. Other forms of community are, of course, possible. There are many examples of religious communities throughout the ages, whose *raison d'être* is derived from vocation and common purpose. The *kibbutzim* in Israel provide a contemporary example. There are other groups of various types, often of a supportive nature, and sometimes of one gender. Frequently, such groups bear witness to the failure of family life in some way – often because of violence.

(iv) *Cohabitation* There can be no question about the widespread practice of cohabitation. Several generations of people of marriageable age have increasingly opted for this kind of relationship. It is undoubtedly a response to the problematic nature of marriage and family life in a mobile and disturbed age, and to the relational possibilities which modern control of sexuality opens up. An element of judgementalism can creep into the assessment of reasons for the trend. Some point to 'the scandalous examples of impermanence among many of the famous in the land and the opinion-formers'; the erosion of moral values – 'deviation at one point is apt to lead to deviation at other points'; 'widespread ignorance about the profound significance of human sexuality'; 'general revolt against established norms and also the unwillingness to make serious commitments'.[7] Others simply lament the decline in the influence of the churches.

[6] Davis, p. 187.
[7] Cf. Kenneth Greet in *Epworth Review*, 20.3.1993, p. 51.

It is easy to criticise this practice from a traditional stance within Christian ethics. G. Jenkins identifies six areas which he believes he derives from scripture - permanence, love, sex, community, children and freedom - and finds cohabitation relationships to be deficient in at least two: permanence and community.[8] It is well to remember, however, that cohabitation is prompted by a variety of motives, ranging from short term convenience to long-term commitment. And the bases on which the traditional case rests are not always as firm as their exponents represent. A particular notion of marriage – often of the 'nuclear' type – is smuggled into 'natural law' or declared to be 'scriptural'. Both claims are disputable. As we have seen, 'natural law' is valid only in general terms: specific injunctions exceed its remit. Biblical perspectives emphasise the relationship between male and female (Gen. 1:27) as well as implying marriage (Gen. 2:24) and fidelity within it (Mark 19:7–9). Jesus also points to a vocation that transcends marriage (Mark 3:31–35). A literalist, non-contextual view would also require us not only to subordinate the female partner but also to endorse household slavery (cf. Eph. 5:22, 6:5–8). There is no short cut to an unqualified endorsement of a traditional stance over against the less formal relationships under discussion; and to speak of 'norms' may be the wrong way to go about it.

A view of Christian ethics which places emphasis on personal and social value – a relational view, in other words – cannot but accept that cohabitation can be validated in these terms. What matters is the quality of the relationship. The outsider can sometimes see this more clearly than some champions of traditional views. One journalist writes:

> You have to wonder too at those who declare that sex is unacceptable outside marriage. Have they convinced themselves that a legal contract confers some status on a union which automatically renders a bad, loveless marriage

[8] G. Jenkins, *Cohabitation: A Biblical Perspective* (1992); 'Cohabitation and the local church', *Epworth Review*, 20.3.1993, pp. 47–50.

inherently superior to a loving commitment where the partners have dispensed with formal recognition?'[9]

A loving commitment is a loving commitment! To be sure, one would wish to enquire why the partners have dispensed with formal recognition: it may be a lack of commitment for the future (as opposed to the present). Any loving relationship implies permanence (love is never provisional or divided) as well as fidelity and constancy. Children, in particular, need stability in the family context. Hence, in terms of Christian ethics, it is not a matter of condemning cohabitation as 'wrong' in favour of marriage which is 'right'. Rather, the former is a relationship which may well be moral (there are risks, in this as in all relationships) while the latter represents the call of God to an avowed commitment for the future, with all that that implies. As well as a public and legal statement, it could also be interpreted in a specifically Christian context as signifying the availability of a supportive moral and pastoral community.

Family values and disvalues are generated within the complexity and contradictions of human relations and of society itself. In the next section we take a very particular look at aspects of the broad scene: the fracturing of family relationships and its consequences.

---

[9] Ruth Wishart in a review of the General Assembly of the Church of Scotland, in *The Scotsman*, May 1994. See also below.

II *Fractured Families – Broken Children?*
(Elizabeth Spence)[1]

'For the husband is head of the wife.' (Ephesians 5:22)

The history of the family from ancient times is that of a patriarchal system. The letters of Paul present conflicting pictures of it: in one place he lays the emphasis on male headship (Eph. 5:22–23), just after he had affirmed reciprocity in relationships (Eph. 5:21), while elsewhere he suggests equality and freedom under Christ (Gal. 3:26–29). In the Gospels, Jesus affirms the permanence of marriage according to the Creator's purpose, but agrees that the Law of Moses permitted divorce 'for the hardness of your hearts' (cf. Mark 10:1–9): the factor of human alienation affects practice. Clearly, the New Testament, let alone the Hebrew scriptures, can be read in such a way as to give support to widely differing interpretations. This diversity is also found in the traditional views of marriage. It is therefore difficult to hold that there is one central, unchanging view of Christian marriage, although certain emphases are clearly important.

'His banner over me is love.' (Song of Songs 2:4)

Perhaps one of the most significant changes in the understanding of the family is the reason for marriage in the first instance.[2] It had been seen as a union to create children and as a social institution. But from the romantic era onwards, marriage became linked with ideas of love and fulfilment. People now married for love and companionship, and the family began to be a vehicle for self expression. This has resulted in a conflict between society's demands of marriage and individual need for a good experience within the family.

Two or more contrasting models of marriage emerge. The older model saw marriage as a contract of necessity. A marriage partner was often selected by the senior member of the

---

[1] This section is largely based on the work of Elisabeth Spence.
[2] See below.

household, or at least such members had a strong influence on the event – the ultimate goal being that of an 'acceptable' marriage. In the newer, contemporary marriage models a partner is found for personal and romantic reasons and all other qualities are secondary. The two partners make decisions on their own behalf.

If it seems to the contemporary mind that the arranged marriage violates individual freedom, it may also be said that there has been a romanticizing of the role of love in marriage. In the old model of marriage love was understood in terms of the agreed roles of the husband and wife. A husband loved his wife by working hard and looking after the welfare of his home. She loved him if she looked after the family and was faithful to him. In the newer models it is bound up with feelings and emotions. In terms of Christian perspective, love (*agape*) may be taken to mean that when another's security and wellbeing become as significant to a person as one's own, the state of love exists.

'*Keep that which I commit to you.*' (2 Timothy 1:12)

Today, marriage is not seen as the only way two persons may declare their commitment to each other. As was noted above, there is a greater sexual freedom in today's world and living together has become socially acceptable. Indeed there is often considerable pressure on couples to adopt this course.

The reasons for people choosing to live together rather than marry are varied. Some think that marriage is outdated and that it has no particular relevance to their lives. Church authority has been eroded. Other reasons include the high financial cost of 'getting married', the 'bad risk' element which is often in the minds of those who have already suffered a broken relationship, and the need for a preparation for the 'real thing' – in 1989 half of the couples married had chosen this avenue. Although some of these reasons are not altogether lacking in cogency, the churches have been reluctant to endorse this trend. Nevertheless, the issue is now being actively debated.[3] The issue of cohabitation is complicated when the

[3] See above, p. 83f.

question of sexual relationships outside marriage is raised, and further complicated when one of the partners is already married.

In spite of the changing ethos, marriage remains popular: over 90 per cent of people in Britain eventually choose to marry. However, statistics also show the other side of the picture. In the early 1970s there was a peak where 70 per cent of Scottish women were married; the figure for the early 1990s is 55 per cent. In face of the challenge of the times, churches tend to reaffirm the traditional ideal:

> One man and one woman freely give themselves to each other in the life long commitment of marriage, making promises before God and other people. They express their love for each other in action, caring for one another and helping each other to continue to mature.[4]

The call is clear; the problem lies in implementing it.

'*I will make a covenant for them.*' (Hosea 3:18)

What elements could be said to make a Christian marriage different from others? What understanding of marriage sets it apart from other views? The idea of marriage as a *covenant* reflects an idea of relationship and commitment without excluding emotional content. Covenant implies a spiritual foundation, a relationship with God that is brought to a personal level. Marriage is 'a reflection of the loving covenant uniting Christ with the Church and a participation in that covenant'.[5] The use of the image of marriage partnership in the Hebrew scriptures describes the relationship between Yahweh and Israel (Hos. 2:17–20): it is in Malachi that the term 'covenant' is first applied to marriage among the Israelites (Mal. 2:14). Prophets extolled God's love for Israel in terms of covenantal love. God is seen as a husband, a redeemer to Israel. In the New Testament, Paul describes Christ's redemptive work in terms of a husband's love for his wife.

---

[4] The Church of Scotland Board of Social Responsibility, *The Future of the Family* (1992), p. 7.
[5] A. V. Campbell (ed.), *A Dictionary of Pastoral Care* (1987), p. 618.

Covenant is seen as a more biblical term than the word 'contract' but it is this word which has been more often used to describe marriage. Although contract talks of personal agreement it has a harsher tone to it and does not encompass the idea of inclusion within the community which covenant seems to imply. Our modern understanding of contract is more legal and clinical than covenant. Contracts are secular, deal with things, are made for a specific length of time, can be broken, can be made by children who understand the value of money, and so on. Covenants, on the other hand, are sacred, deal with people, are forever, if violated can result in personal heartbreak, and can only be made by those emotionally, mentally and spiritually mature. The most significant difference between contract and covenant is that contracts are witnessed by people while in covenants God is called on as witness.[6] Even if theologically a Christian does not believe marriage to be a sacrament there needs to be some understanding of marriage as a covenant.

'*Your people will be my people*' (Ruth 1:16)

But what of the modern day family at the end of the twentieth century? In times past there were identifiable ties that linked a family: one set of ties to the extended family, another to the wider community, while the final set of ties held it both to its past history and to future generations. In its journey into the modern world these ties have been broken.

As Stanley Hauerwas sees it, the family was once part of the establishment of society in which morals were determined and expressed but is now regarded as a private realm where the accent is on the emotions: 'Family is not characterised by how many people are living under the same roof but by the privileged emotional climate that must be protected from outside intrusion.' [7] Family life has become a private domain

---

[6] Nevertheless, in so far as a contract is a promise, the binding nature of the promise is underlined in the third commandment and reinforced by Jesus' teaching in the Sermon on the Mount.

[7] S. Hauerwas, *A Community of Character* (1981), p. 159.

which keeps its own secrets. It is no longer to be seen as the main contributor to society's make up but a tight-knit unit of individuals. The nuclear family has become the familiar way of families. No longer do grandparents live in the same street. Many families are fragmented geographically in that members may not even be in the same country. There is much more of a trend for people to 'keep to themselves': to do other is to interfere. But even in the nuclear family roles have changed. Father is not always in the role of breadwinner and mother in that of child carer.

Families today are called upon to provide a sense of meaning and worth. In today's world of high unemployment people can no longer depend on work to give them status and worth in society. Since it has become apparent in these times that work is not guaranteed, there is a greater need than ever to generate and foster a sense of personal worth. The task falls primarily on the family. It is also within the family that a sense of authority and control has to be developed. What is learnt in the home about controls is then manifest in the community. If children are not taught how to live responsibly within the home, the effects will be felt in society. The crisis that has befallen many institutions in society has meant that traditional supportive agencies such as school and church have been rendered impotent, at least as far as the neediest children are concerned. The gap left is a serious one.

Many of the children I lived and worked with in 'Dean', a residential community for children with emotional and social difficulties, had had very little guidance or control from parents. They had a very shallow idea of 'right and wrong': their ideas were mainly determined by the outcome for themselves. One of the most significant contributions adults could offer these children was a role model for another way of living and thinking: one that included ideas of morality and fairness in a wider concept. I would go so far as to say that many of the children had displayed anti-social behaviour because of their parents' shallow concept of morality and their inability to discipline their children.

The function of the family in modern times is thus to provide care and protection, to give meaning and worth to its individuals, to offer scope to exercise responsibility and to motivate. Such a function is socially requisite and theologically significant. And it has to carry out this function in face of the changing roles within the family itself. So great is the responsibility that it is hardly surprising that some families fracture and fail.

'*Fathers, do not provoke your children.*' (Colossians 3:21)

The family is a powerful institution. Hauerwas describes it as the only remaining 'natural' institution capable of commanding complete loyalty. Consequently, there is as much potential in it for destruction as for sustaining a healthy environment.

> Family life can be a source of deep, rich emotion but it can also be a place of tyranny and repression, where a parent takes advantage of the children, where a spouse can use sexuality as a bribe or reward for getting their own way.[8]

In the lives of many children the negative power of a family can be very real. One boy who was at 'Dean' was encouraged by his father to steal the school's VCR. In times past this would not have been any problem for him as he had a background of theft but things had changed for 'Robin' since being in the school. He had invested in the adults around him and, more importantly perhaps, they had invested in him. His loyalties were severely tested. Would the knowledge that what he was being asked to do was wrong and would affect people he now loved prove stronger than the need to please his father and the hope that he would thus gain his father's love? His father won.

The power of family ties can also be seen in another youngster who had been in care for almost all his life. He had been fostered at the age of ten by a particular family. There had always been discussions about the possibility of 'Roger' being adopted by the family, and he himself was keen on the idea. Only a few days before the papers were to be signed 'Roger' could not go through with the adoption. Although he

---

[8] *The Future of the Family*, p. 56.

knew his chances of being able to have any real contact with his mother were slight, he could not give up the small chance that it might be so.

Loyalty to family members is a very strong emotion. Even when things are at their worst, when every avenue to patch up a relationship seems to have been explored, family members will continue to persevere. For the Christian, this parental love is an imitation of God's love – it is unconditional. The longing for the reconciliation of the estranged members comes from the deeper levels of human existence. But family loyalty needs to be directed not simply to healing breaches when they have occurred but to maintaining stability and coherence in the family unit. On the basis of a questionnaire answered by professionals involved in work with families, Dolores Curran drew up a check list of elements for a healthy family. The main elements were:

> Communication
> Affirming and supporting
> Respecting and trusting each other
> Sharing time together
> Fostering responsibility
> Teaching morals
> Enjoying traditions
> Sharing religion
> Respecting privacy
> Seeking support and help.[9]

It is possible to have a healthy family and not necessarily be able to tick off ALL of these elements! The healthy family is a goal or target: challenge enough for families with two functioning parents and stable employment for at least one breadwinner. What of those families who may not be in this position?

For the remainder of this study I would like to look at families who are fractured by divorce and to concentrate on the consequences for the children in particular.

---

[9] Dolores Curran, *Traits of a Healthy Family* (1983), p. 124.

'*He has sent me to bind up the broken-hearted.*' (Isaiah 61:1)

The general trend of divorce in the Western world is well known. In Britain in 1988 one in five men in their 40s and one fifth of women in their 30s and 40s had been divorced. Britain has the second highest divorce rate in the European Community with 12,272 divorces in 1990. This statistic leads to another – that of lone parenting. In 1990 lone parents made up 19 per cent of families. The vast majority of lone parents are women with only 2 per cent of one parent families headed by a father. Of the total number of lone parents, 60 per cent result from divorce and 30 per cent have never married.

People who have suffered marital breakdown and divorce often talk in terms of death and bereavement. As Kevin Kelly states, the death–resurrection paradigm is central to Christian living. This paradigm may be helpful in relation to divorce. For the Christian who finds him/herself in the situation of divorce there may be an added sense of failure, of having let God down by breaking the covenant. However, Kelly argues that from this 'death' will come new life. Any theology of marriage which is sensitive to the death–resurrection paradigm should 'be able to speak a positive word of hope to men and women who have been through the "dying" experience of the failure of their marriage'.[10]

Divorce and fractured families are on the increase. It is no longer a secret taboo of society and people are able to talk openly of their difficulties and pain. Yet, as Ruth Spinnanger observes, 'The fact that divorce has become so common that it is no longer regarded as a shame or a disgrace, in no way nullifies the effect on the children.'[11] Children also will be experiencing loss and pain but their feelings may often be sidelined. In the trauma this can often be forgotten. When an adult is in pain it is easy to forget that children notice the change in atmosphere. 'When the tension is not discussed or

---

[10] Kevin Kelly, 'Looking beyond failure – life after divorce', *The Tablet*, Aug. 1991, p. 937.

[11] Ruth Spinnanger, *Better than Divorce* (1978), p. 33.

even acknowledged by the parents, the children tend to become more fearful and anxious.'[12]

Children even begin to feel responsible for the fact that the family is fractured. They imagine that it must have been something they have done and that if they loved daddy more he would stay. Young ears overhear adults living out their pain and the arrows that were intended to damage the partner in fact also hit the children. A wife saying, 'if you really loved the kids you would spend more time with them' may be interpreted by the child as 'Daddy doesn't love us any more'.

Gary Richmond outlines four points that parents should aim to keep in focus once a family is fractured by divorce.

(i)   Children will begin to feel that their world is uncertain and unpredictable.

(ii)   Divorce robs children of their hope that 'everyone will be happy ever after'.

(iii)   The process of divorce produces a steady chain of painful events for children.

(iv)   Parents at this time are feeling such pain that they are often unable to help others. The effect of this on children is that they wonder if anybody loves them.[13]

As point four indicates, divorce is a traumatic time. Parents who lose contact with their children may never be able to pick up from where they were before it occurred. Divorce can leave children with a negative view of themselves. They see themselves as worthless, hopeless and in need of punishment. The only people who can really change their view of themselves is their parents: by reassuring them and affirming that they are not responsible for the divorce.

'*Let the little children come to me.*' (Mark 10:14)

The future for children of fractured families can look bleak. They are more susceptible to getting involved in delinquent behaviour; they are more likely to commit suicide; their school

---

[12] Campbell (ed., 1987), p. 296.
[13] Gary Richmond, *Successful Single Parenting* (1990), p. 116.

work can suffer; they may become involved in drug addictions. There is no one factor to which these findings can be attributed, but some features have obvious relevance. Children may be left unsupervised at periods of the day, perhaps the few hours between finishing school and mother coming home from work. Such children, and boys in particular, lean more heavily on their peer group, and this can be where their value system is formed. For an already disturbed child this is rarely good news.

Children may also feel that they have to take on the adult role now vacated. This can put pressure on a youngster which propels them into adulthood too quickly. Bobby at 'Dean' was on a weekend leave and did not return to school on Monday. His mother, who had just separated from her husband, said that Bobby was ill with stomach pains. Two days passed and still he had not returned to school. On visiting I found a healthy-looking thirteen year old playing video games. In talking with me he said he couldn't return to school because he had to stay at home since his young brother was giving trouble and his dad would normally have dealt with it. Bobby had assumed the father's role in spite of the fact that he had many difficulties of his own to address.

For the divorced parent this may well sound like depressing reading which does nothing for their feelings of guilt, but there is reassurance from Richmond:

> Your job is not to heal your children. Only God can do that. But you can provide them with the tools to cope with life. They are wounded lambs and they have been injured in many areas.[14]

In an attempt to find out more of what the children thought, I used a simple questionnaire designed only to reflect the thoughts and concerns of a particular group of children. There were, in fact, 35 children, aged 10–13 years, in the sample; and the groups were taken from a comprehensive school in Edinburgh, a Christian youth group in Hamilton,

[14] Richmond (1990), p. 11.

Lanarkshire, and the school we have called 'Dean' in the north of Scotland. The breakdown of the sample was as follows: twenty of the children lived with both parents; nine lived in a 'step' family; and six lived with mother only.

In the first part of the questionnaire ('Describe your family'), children were asked to comment on particular statements about their family. This was done by numbering the statement using the scale below:

1	2	3	4	5
Almost never	Once in a while	Sometimes	Often	Always

Many of the responses showed little difference between those children who had both natural parents at home and those whose family had suffered fracture.

> *Q.3* 'I have some say in any punishment I get for doing something wrong.'

All children in the sample responded with *Almost never*.

> *Q.9* 'We eat together as a family at least once a week.'

All the responses were either *Almost never* or *Once in a while*, perhaps illustrating the situation for many modern families of eating round the TV and not the table.

Where differences did show up was in questions about interaction in the family.

> *Q.6* 'I help make decisions about where to go on holiday and help with other family decisions.'

Most children responded *Once in a while* or *Sometimes*. Children from lone families either responded *Often* or *Always*. This may suggest that because of the lack of a partner, parents were more inclined to discuss such things with their children.

> *Q.7* 'There is always someone home when I come home from school.'

Most of the sample responded *Always*. Seven children responded *Sometimes* – five of these children were older, attending secondary school, and from lone parents. This would seem to corroborate the suggestion that children from lone families are more likely to have unsupervised free time and therefore have a higher risk of getting involved in deviant behaviour.

Q.12 'Mum and dad raise their voices in our house.'

The children from 'step' families responded either *Sometimes* or *Often*. Children with lone parents responded *Often* or *Always*. This perhaps indicated the stress involved in having sole responsibility for the children. Interestingly, in the sample of children with both natural parents at home there was no consensus and the responses were across the board.

The second part of the questionnaire ('Thinking about your family') was intended to allow the children to write in more depth. I kept it within the realm of their experience by asking about family, friends and teachers.

Q.1 'If you could choose one person with whom to go to Disneyland, who would it be?'

Most of the children thought they would take their mother or their best friend. This is probably an indication of the typical view of children of this age. Two of the children from lone families stated that they would take their fathers.

Q.3 'What would you wish for if you had one magic wish?'

Again answers were a reflection of the age range – have a big house, lots of money, flash car. One child from a 'step' family and three from lone families said that they would wish for a happy family. *Q.4* was a question asking what they would change about particular people. It made amusing reading to discover that nearly all the sample wanted to change their teachers' propensity to shouting! Mothers and fathers were fairly unanimously asked to change from being too strict. One child from a lone family wanted her mother to talk more about what was making her sad. Another child from a lone family stated that he would want his father to be closer to him so that he could see him more. *Qs. 5, 6, 7* asked the children to suggest what people found best about them. Most of the responses were as might be expected:

Best friend   - personality, fun to be with
Teacher   - industrious in class, well behaved
Parents   - good school work

Qs. 8, 9 asked what those people would want to change in them. The answers revolved around family life – help more, go to bed early, not to be so cheeky.

In the third part ('Where do you fit in your family?'), the children seemed to feel more free to write what they were really feeling. A large part of this section was given over to how children in lone and 'step' families felt. *Q. 2* asked how often children saw the parent they did not live with.

Monthly or more   - 6
School holidays only   - 4
Yearly   - 2
Not at all   - 3

Q. 3 asked if this was enough. With the exception of three of the children who saw their father monthly or more this was not enough. It was not the job of the questionnaire to discover the reasons for the access levels but it may well be tied in with the mother's need for a 'clean break' with her husband and with the thought that it would be better for the children. I would only reflect that children stated a need to see their fathers more. *Q. 4* 'Do you ever feel guilty that your mum and dad are not living together?' Twelve children said that they sometimes felt guilty. Six expressed the feeling that they never got a satisfactory explanation about why it had happened. Four felt that if they had not been so much trouble at the time Dad would have stayed. These real feelings from children underline the well known claim that children often shoulder the blame for their parents' marriage breakdown. *Qs. 5, 6* asked the children to evaluate the happiness or sadness in their family. Most of the children thought their family was happy most of the time but two children from lone families thought their mother still missed their father a great deal.

In response to the question 'What makes you sad about your family?', there was a high consensus that arguing or family disharmony was the biggest problem. Five children from lone families said the fact that their father was not there was the saddest thing; one said her mother was crying all the time. One of the children in a 'step' family said that what made him unhappy was his mother and stepfather arguing about his natural father. Often because of the emotional state they find themselves in, parents may not always give enough attention to the effect family events are having on their children. As some of the answers in this very limited questionnaire show, children *do* pick up the atmosphere of the home. They *see* the unhappy faces of adults; they *hear* the tense conversations of angry adults and, perhaps more importantly, they *feel* the pain and hurt of those they love dearly.

'*The power of His resurrection and the fellowship of His suffering.*' (Philippians 3:10)

Divorce, with the consequent fracturing of the family, is not an easy road to take. There will be times when one feels isolated from other adults, and guilty for having made a 'selfish' decision. There will probably be constant juggling to make the family accounts work and a degree of worry about the effect on the children. Is it possible to have a 'healthy' fractured family, as Dolores Curran has suggested? To achieve such a family would be a challenge for anyone, yet once the acute pain and upheaval of divorce is passed, many families may well address the challenge with a measure of success.

In Christian terms, the paradigm of death and resurrection points the way to an answer. This theme was also used by a single Christian mother when addressing a group of lone parents:

> The people who have let God resurrect them from their pain are the people who carry the fragrance of the Risen Christ everywhere they go. The unmistakable peace and presence of the living God surrounds them.[15]

Jesus brought the good news to the afflicted; he was sent to bind up the broken-hearted, to proclaim liberty to the captives

[15] Richmond (1990), p. 161.

and set the prisoners free. He comforts *all* who mourn. He is the companion of our suffering. Divorce is 'man made', but the people – both adult and children – who feel its pain are God's children. To use Richmond's image, *all* are wounded lambs and *all* need the healing touch of God to give their lives purpose and direction.

III *Vision and Values*

The family is of immense social significance, transmitting its peculiar mixture of values and disvalues to its members, yet providing nurtural possibilities unparalleled elsewhere in society. For this reason, when family values appear to be undermined, alarm bells ring and calls for reinforcement are made. But valid calls also emanate from those who want to see changes. Feminism is rightly conscious of the oppression, violence and alienation that can be generated within families: points frequently underlined by social and economic analyses. Every right minded person is concerned with the casualties of the system: the broken lives and frustrated hopes. That reorientation and healing are required – an injection of new vision, rather as an ailing business requires an injection of new capital – seems an inevitable conclusion. Since so much fragmentation and fracturing occurs, a concern for conciliation and reconciliation – by which we do not mean simply patching things up – is a further requisite. Our closing section thus emphasises certain aspects of a Christian approach to marriage today.

1 *Marriage as vocation*

The Christian ideal of marriage is a life-long relationship which far transcends notions of romantic love but is based on *agape* and requires all the qualities indicated in 1 Corinthians 13. It presupposes a relationship that turns on the kind of person one is, or rather the kind of people we can become together: yet not in our own strength but through the discovery of resources that are realisable in our lives. True marriage is sustained not by mere determination to maintain the semblance of unity but by accepting the call to grow together and enhance the tie: not keeping before one the possibility of dissolving it if things go wrong (a form of negative thinking) but believing that we are always called to be more than we are. Marriage is a journey undertaken in faith, hope and love. One needs to look beyond our immediate horizon, for marriage, as Hauerwas has remarked, is not merely about 'happiness'.

> The Hebrew–Christian tradition helps sustain the virtue of hope in a world which rarely provides evidence that such hope is justified. There may be a secular analogue to such hope, but for those of us who identify with Judaism or Christianity, our continuing formation of families witnesses to our belief that the falseness of this world is finally bounded by a more profound truth.[1]

2 *Marriage as 'koinonia'*

Families involve relationships, the dynamic of community. They constitute special kinds of community, for younger members are born into them. They have no choice but to belong. The situation is open to the exercise of power and authority, moral leadership, modelling, persuasion – and disobedience, rebellion and growing apart. The need is to interpret family life in terms of genuine interdependence, of sharing in community, in the context of faith, hope and love. The root meaning of *koinonia*, which is not a synonym for the church, implies a sharing partnership, an interdependent unity. Christian perspectives reinforce the concept. 'Be subject to one another out of reverence for Christ' (Eph. 4:21).

Hauerwas has identified two assumptions which undermine the family in modern society. One is the moral ideal of the 'autonomous, self-sufficient, free person'. 'Autonomy', he says, 'has been taken to mean that we are not and should not be dependent on the past or upon others.'[2] It happens that this attitude suits an economic policy that tells people to 'get on their bikes': in other words, become part of a mobile workforce. The second assumption is the notion of self-fulfilment, which is the accompaniment to autonomy. It is as if marriage is designed primarily as a means towards individual fulfilment.[3]

---

[1] S. Hauerwas (1981), p. 174.
[2] Hauerwas (1981), p. 171.
[3] Hauerwas (1981), p. 172.

But marriage puts different demands on people. It changes them. It requires that partners build a new life together: it is a mutuality, or a power-sharing partnership. Hauerwas therefore argues that the moral presuppositions for sustaining the family are frequently missing in modern societies. The fixation with autonomy and self-fulfilment means that we are conditioned to regard one another as strangers rather than brothers or sisters: as having 'rights' over against each other, instead of the ties of family and friendship.

To these points we would add a third. The materialism of modern culture is also a distorting influence. Material prosperity has brought blessed relief from poverty to many families, although many are the victims of changing economic times. But materialism is also a corroding influence, confusing the notion of 'the good' with 'having goods', as in the pathetic cry of the parent of a child who has gone badly wrong: 'It's not our fault: we gave him everything he wanted!' Except, perhaps, what he most needed!

All of this points to the need for the family to be part of a wider community in which the values and aspirations of its members may be challenged or seen in a new light. And the church would seem to be in a good position to supply this need. This presupposes that the church is able to relate to families and at the same time present a counter-culture which offers new vision. It must not be simply an extension of the family, for then it would simply reproduce the limited visions which families have of themselves. Worship, the fellowship of the church and opportunities for giving of oneself to others are potentially creative experiences.

3 *Conciliation and reconciliation*

Attention has been directed above to the fact that Christian marriage, with its commitment to a life-long vocation, entails the need for a supportive, moral community. Such support is offered conventionally in the form of instruction on the meaning of Christian marriage and may perhaps include an element of pre-marital counselling. This is valuable, especially if it is done in a personal way rather than as part of an instructional course. It should be offered rather than imposed. Ethical concern focuses on the relationships involved. No amount of exhortation on the meaning of the marriage vows or the permanence of marriage can be a substitute for genuine openness to the people concerned.

Remedial counselling may involve reference to specialist consultants. However, there is much value in pastoral counselling at the local level where the person concerned feels sufficiently free to tell his or her own story, in the knowledge that it will be heard and discussed in an open, non-judgemental way. The primary values are acceptance and supportiveness, a readiness to share in the reality of people's lives 'where they are', and a willingness to challenge as appropriate. The greatest disvalue in this situation is any attempt by the counsellor to short circuit the discussion by intruding religious or moral 'solutions'. Other disvalues, such as failure of the parties to communicate their feelings adequately or sensibly, can be tackled by a variety of counselling skills.[4] The immediate objective is to foster a meaningful dialogue which reveals blind spots, discovers a degree of leverage on the situation, explores possibilities of advance and moves towards commitment to a new course of action. The process is concerned to give the partners space to clarify their own view of the relationship, to find solutions to their own problems, and thus to move towards and sustain a better quality of life for themselves.

All this is part of the ethics of relationships. As we saw in the last chapter, reconciliation is the positive response to alienation, but it takes a variety of forms. Not every attempt at remedial counselling will lead to full reconciliation between the partners. There is no guaranteed happy ending of this type. To suppose otherwise is gravely to underestimate the factor of alienation in human lives. Another outcome is reconciliation between partners who decide to divorce: thus helping them cope with the situation and the pain it occasions. Another form is helping individuals to come to terms with their own feelings of guilt or inadequacy: to be reconciled with themselves and God.

[4] Cf. G. Egan, *The Skilled Helper* (1975).

CHAPTER 4

THE ETHICS OF SEXUAL ORIENTATION AND PREFERENCE

A CASE TO PONDER

By all accounts, the two Hensons were kind and quiet, with a track record of good works: running a free pantry for the poor in St Louis; teaching illiterates to read; and offering their farm near Ovett, Mississippi, as a women's retreat. And that was where the difficulties began. The Hensons were lesbians who opted to share the same name. That meant they were not only outsiders, they were 'different': too different for the liking of the conservative community of Ovett. The women received threats by mail and phone, and a campaign of harassment was waged against them. The local Baptist minister was quoted as saying, 'We are being invaded by activists with a radical agenda.' The strongest objection was taken to people who were seen as a threat to 'our way of life'. In the growing hostility, compromise became impossible. The upshot was that the Federal authorities had to act. The Attorney General (Janet Reno), recognising the threat of violence to be real, declared that the intolerance and bigotry encountered by the Hensons should have no place in the country. Federal mediators were dispatched to try to heal the breach. As the journalist Michael Pye observed, the Federal government was for the first time treating the harassment of gay people as a serious issue.[1]

There is much to ponder in this situation. The life-style to which objection was taken on Christian grounds seems to have

---

[1] Michael Pye, 'In God's name, hate thy neighbour', *The Scotsman*, 21.2.1994.

been Christian enough, while not conventional. The New Testament advocacy of love towards the outsider, or people who are 'different', is far stronger than any reservations it may entertain about same-sex relationships. Intolerance and bigotry are categorically anti-Christian. Any objection advanced on moral grounds must be expressed in moral ways and loses credibility if it is not. 'Love your enemy' – even supposing any should be regarded as 'enemy' – is close to a categorical imperative in the teaching of Jesus; but the newspaper article on which the above excerpt is based was headed, 'In God's name, hate thy neighbour', and claimed that 'persecution of homosexuals by religious fanatics in the US has reached sickening levels' – although the problem is far from being confined to North America. A community is certainly entitled to its way of life, but so also are others who come to live within it. Uniformity cannot be imposed without intolerance. To be sure, the 'sojourner in the midst' has also a duty to relate to the host community: that was expected in ancient Israel, and St Paul respected the principle on his visits to Jerusalem. Where alienation exists, value attaches primarily, not to condemnation and rejection, but to moves towards reconciliation and mutual understanding.

Apart from the broad band of churches who regard it as their duty to affirm traditional stances, it is hardly an overstatement to claim that even those churches which have been commendably active on the AIDS question have been hesitant to tackle the moral issue of homosexuality in an open way.[2] This reluctance probably stems from the fact that, in order to understand homosexuality, the nature of all human sexuality has to be questioned. As this affects everyone of us as sexual beings, to open up the question can be uncomfortable. This, however, provides the starting point for the present essay. It will attempt to set the issue of homosexuality within the wider context of human sexuality and consider the problems raised for the churches as moral communities.

[2] See below, n. 8, p. 125.

In this chapter, the term 'homosexuality' is taken to refer to men and women whose sexual orientation is for their own gender. It denotes not sexual activity but orientation and preference.[3] In some form or other, the problem has always been with the churches.

[3] In Britain it is an offence for *men* to engage in sexual relations with another male under the age of eighteen. There is no legislation regarding women. It is illegal for anyone to practise buggery (anal intercourse). Recent local government legislation prohibits any overt encouragement or propagation of homosexuality (Clause 28).

I *Human sexuality and the Church (Sharon Kyle)*

1 *The purpose of sex*

As early as the fifth century, Augustine set out his views on sexuality, based it must be remembered on his own particular struggle. By translating his views into doctrine the church has been left with a legacy which inhibits rather than encourages open discussion. The legacy includes the belief that sexual activity is solely for the procreation of children, and it is the means by which original sin is transmitted to all people before they are born. It would be bad enough to believe that sexual activity was purely functional and not for pleasure, but to be saddled with the guilt of responsibility for the pollution of one's children by original sin is the extreme act of double jeopardy. If we add to this equation the comment in Genesis 3 about women bearing children in pain as a result of the Fall, we have completed a cheerless scenario of sex and childbirth that continues to influence Christian belief. Despite all the sociological, psychological and medical advances made in 2,000 years and also the real, daily experiences of men and women, there is still a level of fear and guilt about sex that takes the subject out of all proportion to other concerns within the church. Jesus' teaching notwithstanding, sexual sins are still in effect regarded as much more serious than other sins.

In view of this kind of legacy, it is hardly surprising that homosexuality, in which there is no possibility of procreation, immediately causes a problem. Homosexuality makes us face what we already know: sex is a need which is a fundamental part of the human make-up, and it is not primarily a need to have children but to have sex. This does not sit easily with the church's teaching, neither is there an easy way out by turning to the Bible for guidance, for remarkably little is said there about sexual activity. There are warnings against fornication and adultery, but that is to do with relationships rather than sexuality as such. The exception to all this is the wonderful and inspired inclusion in the canon of scripture of the Song of

Solomon: a description of lovers' passion and sexuality that leaves you in no doubt of their enjoyment.

For too long the church has gone along with a view of sex as being about genital activity rather than accepting the fact that we are all sexual beings whose interaction with each other in all circumstances has a sexual element. Our sexuality is not something we can turn on and off but is rather part of our whole being whether or not we are always conscious of it. Like all that God has created, sexuality is capable of being used for good and for bad, but in giving it to us it is surely first and foremost a gift for our enhancement and enjoyment, individually and corporately. The church has been slow to celebrate the gift of sexuality that we all have and share. If we apply this argument to the specific issue of homosexuality we can begin to see ways in which the barriers between 'straight' and 'gay' can be broken down by affirming the shared enjoyment of sexuality rather than concentrating on genital activity as the only expression of sexuality. As Christians we have inherited a very deep-seated fear of owning our sexuality and this has proved a barrier not just to homosexuals but to the single, the widowed, the disabled, all of whom need their sexuality affirmed in an appropriate way within a caring environment – namely the church.

2 *Sexual deviance – reality or myth?*

This is not a phrase I like or would generally use, but it serves to highlight the questions that the subject of homosexuality raises in respect of why it produces so much disquiet among people. Our culture and heritage in Western Europe have resulted in an expectation of sexual behaviour which is called 'normal' but which in fact means acceptable to the majority. Heterosexual behaviour is therefore classed as normal and homosexual as deviant and consequently generally unacceptable. What we must remember is that same-sex relationships have been found in some form in every society world-wide, but that acceptance of them has depended on tradition and the local culture – including the impact of

Christianity. The phenomenon of homosexuality is not therefore the result of any one culture (it would then be localised), but its acceptance in societies is dependent on their history and culture. In Britain, for example, the legacy of Christian teaching and Puritan and Victorian morality has played a large part in producing a conservative and emotionally and physically restrained society in which physical contact is limited and governed by strict rules – for example, the taboo on men touching other men in an affectionate way (an obstacle that has been overcome largely by a passion for contact sports where all sorts of physical and emotional needs are given legitimate expression). Another cultural feature that is very significant is the emphasis on the importance of the nuclear family as the traditional and correct social unit in society; in turn the importance of marriage and children is implicit in this idea.[1] The result is that people outside these norms are all too easily labelled and marginalised.

3 *The cause of homosexuality*

Much debate has raged on over the years between scientists, psychologists, doctors, theologians and all interested parties about what it is that causes someone to be sexually attracted to their own gender. Current theories include the possibility of a genetic cause – with much research being done to establish whether this is in fact the case. It has to be said that the homosexual community is divided on the merits of such work because of the fear that if a genetic cause is found then there may be a 'cure'. And yet many homosexuals would welcome scientific proof of what they have believed all along, that they were born homosexual and cannot recall ever having felt differently: a view backed up by my own conversations with homosexual men but less so with homosexual women. By far the most popular theories concern the psychological development of the individual. This includes the theory that natural development is retarded or stuck in some way at a stage in which it is normal to be dependent on one's own gender –

[1] See Chapter 3.

most people can recall a phase in adolescence where they were attracted to their own sex, often an older person in a position of authority. Other theories rely on sociological factors in a person's development – the absence of one or other parent, the desire of a parent to have had a child of the opposite gender, the influence of single sex schooling, and so the list goes on.

In the last decade the whole area of child abuse and incest has become a recognised part of the lives of many people – much more than was previously imagined or acknowledged. It has always been accepted that child abuse – sexual, emotional and physical – has been the experience of many homosexuals. But it is only as people become aware of the extent of child abuse and the capacity that people have to eradicate any memory of it from the conscious mind, that the full extent of its prevalence among homosexuals as a prime cause of their homosexuality is seriously considered. It takes little imagination to understand why a little girl raped by her father or a little boy introduced to sexual gratification at a very young age by another man then grows up to be homosexual.

Whatever the causes of homosexuality are, a distinction should be made between sexual preference and sexual orientation. The problem with these terms is that the latter term implies a fixed or given position whereas the former term implies a choice. I would suggest that in reality there are many homosexuals whose instinct is unquestionably for their own gender but who are acting subconsciously out of preference in the interests of their own safety – victims of abuse would obviously come into this category. We cannot ignore the very basic need we all have to make safe relationships.

II *Homosexuality and Ethical Considerations (Sharon Kyle)*

While there are many aspects that could be considered here, I have selected four broad headings which follow on from each other: the biblical perspective; then the question of homosexuality and the family; homosexual behaviour and life-style; and finally homosexuality and the church.

1 *Homosexuality – biblical perspectives*

If one of the differences between secular ethics and Christian ethics is that the latter is in line with the teachings of Christ, then the biblical evidence has to be taken into account, if necessarily in brief compass.

Several texts appear to condemn homosexuality or homosexual activity, although the term 'homosexual' was not in use at the time when the Old Testament was written. In it (Lev. 18:22), we find: 'you shall not lie with a man as with a woman; it is an abomination'. This would appear to be clear enough, though some have taken it to refer to prohibiting anal intercourse – especially as the following verse prohibits sexual activity with animals. Its context is that of rules for purification during the time the people of Israel wandered in the desert and settled in the promised land. It can be argued that the laws were specifically to do with preventing disease and illness and were peculiar to that time. In any case, we are selective today in what laws from Leviticus we keep.[1] If we are prepared to accept only some of the laws as relevant now, we need to be very clear why and have sufficient supporting evidence for those we retain.

In Genesis the tragic story of Lot and the visitors from Sodom is perhaps the most commonly cited scriptural

---

[1] For example, the law about refraining from intercourse with a menstruating woman is not given any priority today nor are many of the laws about what food we eat or the mixtures of fabric in our clothes – all of which were spelt out along with the verse quoted.

injunction against homosexuality. Undoubtedly a key part of the story was the incident of homosexual rape – an action done in preference to the offer of sex with Lot's daughters. The many further references in scripture to the events of this story indicate that it was a very serious event from which many lessons should be learned – consequently it is held up as a frequent reminder of an evil to avoid. It is too easy to limit the lesson learned, however, to a warning against homosexuality, when in fact there were many sinful aspects to the story, not least of which was the abuse of hospitality, which in the culture of the time was very serious.

It is only in the writings attributed to Paul that we find specific references (cf. Romans 1 and 1 Tim. 1:9–12). It cannot go without note that homosexuality is not a subject mentioned by Jesus in what we find recorded in the Gospels. Different people draw very differing conclusions from this lack of comment. However, Paul's references to it are clear enough and certainly indicate that homosexual acts are evil and sinful. But again, this is true if read at face value; put into a cultural context the picture emerges of homosexual acts being a feature of pagan worship at that time, and some would suggest that it is this wider context that Paul was concerned with – the lure of idolatry and of defilement by association with pagan worship (Rom. 1: 25–27, 1 Cor. 6:18–20). Whatever truth there is in this it is difficult to ascribe to the Bible the view that homosexuality as we have defined it is wrong; but certain homosexual acts – buggery and sodomy – are clearly defined as wrong.

John Spong endorsed the view that David and Jonathan, and possibly Ruth and Naomi, are biblical examples of homosexual love: certainly the remark by David of Jonathan, 'his love was wonderful, surpassing that of women', is highly ambiguous. Spong also held that Paul's 'thorn in the flesh' was a reference to his unfulfilled homosexuality. However, it is not sufficient simply to draw conclusions from what is not overtly stated. Likewise it is just as foolish and partial to draw conclusions from what is said without reference to context and culture, ancient and modern. Homosexuality as an issue in Christian ethics has to be understood within the context of the Bible as a whole and in relation to what we understand is being said about sexuality, sexual behaviour, social and family concerns, and Christian obedience and discipleship.

2 *Homosexuality and the family*

For many people homosexuality is to be feared because it is a threat to the family unit and family life. It is condemned because it isn't 'natural' – in other words, it can't produce children. Yet when homosexual couples try to adopt children there is an even greater outcry. Some fear that to allow homosexuality marks a significant point in the breakdown of society: parallels are drawn with Greek civilisation and its demise. Among Christians there is the belief that any sexual union outside of marriage is fundamentally wrong.

In the New Testament, and in particular the teaching of Jesus, there is consistent support for the family unit. Marriage should be honoured and monogamous; adultery and fornication are wrong, and divorce highly undesirable. To this teaching we can also add the many injunctions to be aware of the danger of unguarded sexual behaviour, of the use of sex as an idol that can take the place of God in our affections, and of the need to lead balanced lives motivated by love rather than passion and lust. There is also teaching on the place of restraint from sexual activity for a while, or more permanently in celibate lives. The teaching is by no means negative; husband and wife are to give themselves to one another, and this surely implies enjoyment and satisfaction that can be given as well as received. In complete contrast to the views of Augustine, the view of sex and sexuality in the scriptures is of something precious and gifted by God, of something sacred and pure for enjoyment – our bodies are temples of the Holy Spirit.

It is perhaps all too easy for Christians to stop at this understanding of the biblical ideal of sexuality and family life, and traditionally this has been the case. After all, Genesis tells us that it was God himself who made male and female in his own image but that woman was given to the man to provide companionship, and that man should leave his father and his

mother to become one flesh with his wife. Within this ideal scenario there is no place for an understanding to be formed on real issues and events such as contraception, abortion, broken marriages, child abuse, marital violence, and there is certainly no place for homosexuality. What is missing are the aspects of the culture and context of today that we have already identified – and which have been used to considerable effect in the whole debate about the role of women in the church and in society. More significant is an understanding of the breadth of the teaching of Jesus, where the priority is in bringing each of us into relationship with God and with each other, and so becoming a whole person – the person God created within us at conception. The question is, given the evidence of the experience of homosexual people, whether wholeness always means that they ought to be heterosexual or whether there are some for whom wholeness is not within this parameter. This is not to suggest that we open the floodgates to the idea that 'Jesus loves me, therefore anything goes'. This brings us to consider the behaviour and life-style of homosexuals.

3 *Homosexual behaviour and life-style*

This is one of the most contentious areas in the discussion about homosexuality. There is a widespread belief that homosexuals are a threat to society because they actively seek to promote and encourage others to be homosexual. For men particularly there is a fear of being thought of as homosexual if they don't behave in a fairly stereotyped way. Western society and certainly British society seems to want men to be 'macho' and aggressive as proof of their virility and heterosexual orientation. This pressure to conform to such role models not only alienates many men but inevitably produces an equally strong polarisation among homosexuals to be a 'camp' stereotype or in the case of women a 'butch' female. Much has been written about the sociological and psychological causes and effects at work in these stereotyped images, but for our purpose it serves to highlight that there is a recognisable image and life-style associated with homosexuality. One can easily understand the need of a minority group to express its strength

and defiance by a corporate identity. But since it is our purpose to set homosexuality within the context of Christian ethics, I would suggest that the church should have no part in reinforcing such unhelpful stereotypes but instead should be working to break down barriers and, if it values wholeness and the concept of the whole body of Christ, it should be welcoming those who bring a different dimension of gifts and characteristics with them. We need the ability to recognise and welcome the feminine within the masculine: gentleness and creativity. We cannot ignore that the church has always attracted to its ordained ranks a high proportion of homosexual people. There is something about the combination of caring and sensual stimulation that is so much a part of worship that many homosexuals find themselves suited to and at ease with it – unlike much of competitive society. As I see it the church has to decide what priorities it has in its ethical construction: nurturing wholeness and acceptance in the body of Christ, or putting traditional notions of family and sexuality first.

One of the features of homosexual life-style that causes greatest concern within the church is the degree of promiscuity among homosexuals. Statistics continue to support the fact that homosexual men have a far higher number of partners than heterosexual men, and this despite the fear of AIDS. Yet being homosexual does not make one promiscuous. There is, however, pressure to be sexually active, if you wish to be accepted by other homosexuals. A further pressure that I became aware of in conversation with homosexuals is that society's failure to acknowledge partnerships is a major factor in their failure. It is a feature of human nature that we look for support and affirmation of our relationships and that this acts as a cement for them. The fact that the churches seldom allow this to happen at an informal or formal liturgical level again raises questions about the type of ethic being employed. In this respect the recent publication, *Daring to Speak Love's Name*, is a major step forward.[2]

---

[2] Elizabeth Stuart, *Daring to Speak Love's Name: A Gay and Lesbian Prayerbook* (1992).

One of my observations of the way churches approach the issue of homosexuality is that too often they fail to make the connection between the ethical aspect of homosexuality and the pastoral. They will preach about homosexuality as sin – something for which healing should be sought – and promote heterosexuality as the only acceptable form of sexual expression; but at the same time they promote a pastoral approach that encourages everyone to believe that God loves and accepts them just as they are. The obvious dissonance between these approaches is a result of the failure to link ethics with pastoral work.

The reason for this prevalent dissonance is, I believe, rooted in the argument I have put forward above: that the issue of homosexuality cannot be dealt with separately from the issue of human sexuality. To try to provide a different ethic to govern the behaviour of homosexuals and heterosexuals brings conflict and consequently pastoral confusion. In turn, to produce sexual ethics for today based entirely on biblical evidence without taking into consideration culture, history and experience is equally foolish but the easy way out. The more radical and risky approach is to try to find an ethical framework that takes account of the whole teaching and purpose of Christ, along with all these other factors.

III   *Case Study (Sharon Kyle)*

THE GAY AND LESBIAN SUPPORT GROUP AT ST PAUL'S AND ST GEORGE'S
EPISCOPAL CHURCH, EDINBURGH

This group was set up in early 1991 with the agreement and support of the church of St Paul's and St George's. Prior to the group being founded, I had instigated and edited a discussion paper for the church called, 'Gender and sexuality: Issues for the church today'. The paper contained a series of articles written by people in the church on traditionally taboo subjects such as masturbation, sexual abuse and homosexuality. All the articles were printed anonymously for obvious reasons. The paper raised considerable interest and, among other things, brought me into contact with a wide range of homosexual people in the congregation – almost all of whom felt unable to be open about their homosexuality. From those involved in counselling in the church I also became aware of the extent of the problem and that the church had nothing to offer them. St Paul's and St George's is a church in the evangelical tradition with a large number of students and younger people. Its conservative emphasis acted as a restraint on homosexual people and in time some left the church because of the conflict of interests. Not least of these was the most frequently expressed concern of homosexual Christians, that in order to be acceptable to the church they lived a lie, and that deceit was a routine part of their life.

With the consent of the vestry and clergy, the support group began. I had spoken to the local community organisation across the road from the church knowing that they dealt with a lot of homosexual people; the area attracts a large number of homosexuals because of the presence of the headquarters of the Scottish Minorities Group. Both these organisations had reservations about what we were trying to do, fearing that it would be with an emphasis on healing or prevention – this had been their only experience of church involvement to date. After discussion they were pleasantly surprised and supportive. We also had the support of the local Gay and Lesbian Christian group.

1 *Aims and objectives of the group*

From the start the principal aim of the group was to offer support to people (men and women) at the point at which they are. We recognised that for some this would be at the stage of not being sure of their preference; for others it would be in the process of coming out; some would be struggling with relationships, and others fearing HIV tests and the consequences; and probably all would be wrestling with the dilemma created by being both homosexual and Christian. A further objective was to offer prayer support, as appropriate, for one another. The second main aim was to become better informed within the group of the Christian and biblical position and to feed back into the church the findings and feelings of the group.

2 *Group format*

From the start the group has involved two heterosexual people in whose homes it has regularly met. They are both members of the church, one male, one female, and one of them is the pastoral counsellor in the church. It was agreed that their presence would stop the group becoming too introspective and would prevent it from being wrongly labelled as a gay meeting group. They do not organise or run the group but are members on the same basis as everyone else. From the beginning the group agreed a code of confidentiality so that anyone could attend with confidence that what was said stayed within the group, and that no one outside the group knew who attended. The group was advertised in the church's literature but not the details of time and place; all enquiries were fed through the pastoral counsellor. Her position does not imply that the group has a counselling role; if people require counselling, this is dealt with separately from the group.

The group was open to men and women, though no more than six women have been involved against 20–25 men over the first two years. At most meetings about eight to ten people were present, except for the social evenings when there were more.... There were two particular things that the group did not do. First, it was purely for support and had no campaigning function. Second, there was no pressure put on people to conform to a particular form of Christianity. Within the group there has always been a mixture of Christians at different stages of their journey, some non-Christians and some seeking but unsure. It was made clear to everyone that the group was principally a forum for the meeting of Christianity and homosexuality, and how this could be worked out in people's lives. Prayer was a part of the support offered.

3 *The first two years' progress*

I revisited the group recently, having been away from it for about fifteen months during my training for the ministry. It was a real delight to be back with the group and to see that it was still going strong. My question was, how had the group progressed in two years?

In fact there is no simple answer to the question and it appears that after all this time the group is still trying to decide how to proceed. It soon became obvious that it was impossible to meet the needs of all the people involved at any one time, and so the group has tended to concentrate on one or two people's particular concerns at each meeting. This seems to have provided the support needed at the time even if in the end individuals realise that this is not the right group for them – it has at least helped them be clearer about their current requirements. It is hard to address the needs of a homosexual person who believes their homosexuality to be wrong, along with a homosexual person struggling with a choice between partners. But this has been the reality of the task the group has faced. Meetings have been marked by a great deal of honesty and openness; people I have spoken to tell of feeling able to say things in the group that they couldn't say anywhere else. The whole atmosphere has remained very supportive, loving and caring – often shown in practical ways outside of the times the group meets. Group members support each other between the monthly meetings. Others I have spoken to tell of how they used the group for support as they 'came out' to friends and family, and sometimes to themselves. It has been harder to keep discussion of the Christian faith as a regular priority set against individual needs, but the group has recently reaffirmed the need to redress this balance.

Among the specific practical problems the group has encountered are: (i) the problem of not being accepted by either the local Christians because you are homosexual or by the homosexual community because your personal belief does not let you take a partner – let alone partners; this double rejection causes great problems of identity; (ii) the prevalence of sado-masochistic practices, which are common in homosexual relationships; this has caused much debate on the ethical problems raised for Christians; (iii) the almost complete lack of any acknowledgement of the existence of homosexuals, let alone their relationships, within the life and prayers and liturgy of the church, apart from negative references to sin and evil. These are some of the real issues for the group at present.

Perhaps, for me, what is most gratifying is that the group is still running and obviously meeting a need. While it can't be said to have blazed a trail for the future, I firmly believe that a group such as this within a church is at least a first step in facing the issue of homosexuality. In my experience nobody is more aware of the need for forgiveness and the reality of the love of God than Christians struggling with homosexuality, and consequently they have much to share with the church at large. I will always be grateful for what I have learnt about the love of God, and the pain and struggle and the desire for personal wholeness in Christ, from the fellow members of this group and my many homosexual friends within the Christian church.

IV *Liturgy as a Pastoral Response* (*Ruth Harvey*)

How far can the worship and liturgy of the church respond to the pastoral needs of homosexuals?

1 *Worship, community and liberation*

The church, as a faith community with a strong moral concern, finds a focus of its life and work in worship. Worship is an action which takes us beyond ourselves. It affirms our uniqueness in the eyes of God and reminds us that despite the oppression which we suffer there is meaning and purpose beyond our visions. Worship is highly political, motivating us to action in the world: action for justice and peace. Above all, worship is a space in which to give praise and thanks to God for the gifts of life.

Worship is therefore a supreme expression of the liberation and reconciling love which are the hallmarks of the Bible and thus of Christian faith. Reconciliation, liberation and love should be the key words in expressing a single ethic of respect for all, whether heterosexual or homosexual. I believe that it is through worship that we can best understand the meaning of respect and reconciliation. But are the churches ready to extend such respect and reconciliation to homosexual minorities?

The 1960s in Western Europe and America saw much discussion about the rate of divorce, sex before marriage, promiscuity and homosexuality. The churches took part in this debate. In 1963 the Society of Friends published *Towards a Quaker View of Sex*,[1] which spoke of moral values in general rather than condemning any particular sexual acts. In 1968 the Universal Fellowship of Metropolitan Community Churches was founded by the Revd Troy Perry in the USA as a church open to all but with a particular focus on lesbian and gay Christians. Both of these events the mainstream churches

---

[1] *Towards a Quaker View of Sex*, London: Friends Home Service Committee, 1964.

largely ignored. Nevertheless, many churches and denominations have produced reports and instituted widespread study of the matter.[2] Conferences have been held with representatives of the homosexual community.[3] The number of pastoral groups working with homosexuals is also increasing.

Gay men and lesbians have not waited for the sanction of bishops or of committees. Indeed they have often gone ahead explicitly *against* the wishes of such authorities.[4] The

[2] In Britain, the Church of England Gloucester Report commissioned in 1974 was not discussed beyond the structural committee level; the Osborne Report, commissioned in 1986 but never published, talked of the recognition that 'homosexual people can live responsibly in settled partnerships', condemned a deontological approach to sexual ethics and concluded that the Church needs 'to affirm the value and richness of same-sex friendships, and consider ways in which support and structures can be provided to enable friendships to flourish'. This radical statement could have begun a movement in the Church of England away from analysis to pastoral action. In the event the 1991 Bishop's Report which took its place was much more conservative. The Methodist Church (1990) affirms the 'joy of human sexuality' (p. 3) and invites the churches to continue exploring issues of sexuality. The United Reformed Church largely coincides with the Methodist position in emphasising love and quality of relationships, and strong pastoral concern. While the Roman Catholic Church of the 1970s was still focusing on genital sex and adopting the 'love-the-sinner-hate-the-sin' approach, the Catholic Theological Society of America (1977) concluded that 'Christian homosexuals have the same needs and rights to the sacraments as heterosexuals'. Here we come across a church dealing with the issue of human sexuality on the level of the sacraments for the first time. It is, however, in the context of who should legally be admitted to the sacraments that the discussion takes place, rather than sacrament as healing. Vatican II remained silent on the issue of homosexuality, thus reaffirming the official Roman Catholic line that homosexual activity is as objectionable as contraception because neither are even potentially reproductive (A. Hastings, *Modern Catholicism* (1991), p. 279). Finally, the Church of Scotland reported to the General Assembly in 1968, 1983 and again in 1994. The 1994 report was much more radical: it provoked controversy and was sent down to lower courts and congregations for study.

[3] The Pitlochry and Dunblane conferences of 1980 and 1990, which brought together representatives from the churches, the Scottish Homosexual Rights group and the Institute for the Study of Christianity and Sexuality among others, ensured that pastoral approaches among lesbian and gay people stayed on the agenda of the churches.

[4] E. Stuart, p. xii.

homosexual community is worshipping, praying, celebrating and finding a language and a style which speaks with and for their needs.

2 *Loving our neighbour: worship as pastoral care*

Our whole life ... is a search for wholeness.
Of ourselves we cannot make this happen.
We cannot make ourselves whole
any more than we can make ourselves happy or good.
By grace we are to structure our lives,
both individually and together, in obedience to the
vision that God has given us of what wholeness is like,
primarily through the life,
death and resurrection of Jesus Christ.
So on Iona, we are committed to the belief
that worship is everything we do,
both inside and outside the church.[5]

Worship is about wholeness. It is about integrating prayer and politics, action and stillness. It is a search for the common bonds which unite us to each other and to God. 'Precisely because it engages the whole personality, worship has a role to play in the integration of the personality.'[6] Yet this integration can only be felt, worship can only be reconciling, when the words and styles and forms used relate to the whole spectrum of those personalities found in God's creation.

Many groups have felt excluded by patriarchal, male-dominated and judgemental worship. Women no longer feel easy referring to God solely as He, Father, Lord, King. God is now addressed as counsellor, friend, lover, nourisher, Mother. The feminist movement has seen a huge increase in the amount of literature reflecting women's needs in worship. In their book *Women Included* members of the St Hilda Community write of the anger and frustration at being excluded as women

---

[5] *Iona Community Worship Book* (1988), p. 7
[6] D. B. Forrester, J. I. H. McDonald and G. Tellini, *Encounter with God* (1983), p. 150.

from celebrating the sacrament of the Eucharist. Prayers and litanies reflect this anger and use inclusive language and imagery which affirm the feminine. There is still much uneasiness with this transition but inclusive language is becoming more commonplace.

Bread of Tomorrow by Janet Morley is a book of prayers, liturgies and songs reflecting the experience of the world's poorest. Using the words of the poor rather than talking about them is becoming more commonplace. Only recently has the gay and lesbian community begun to speak out in a similar way. The publication in 1992 of Elizabeth Stuart's book *Daring to Speak Love's Name*, a gay and lesbian prayer book, was a landmark. Its publication was controversial. Liturgy is still regarded as dangerous.[7]

It is evident from the stories of gay and lesbian people that church worship does more than ignore them in its prayer, hymns, wedding ceremonies, confirmation, funerals. It positively excludes them by denying their need to worship day by day and to mark the significant moments in life with inclusive, sensitive liturgy. It can be seen from the survey of church reports[8] that far from grappling with the issue of inclusive liturgy, the churches are still debating whether or not homosexuals are 'allowed'.

Stuart's book goes beyond this debate. It acknowledges the pain and hurt that still exists, but states boldly that lesbian and gay people need a language with which to worship. And so it includes ceremonies for 'coming out', for 'housewarmings', for 'blessings' of gay couples, for 'partings', and for those who live with HIV/AIDS. By daring to speak out in this way it is part

---

[7] Initially commissioned by SPCK, the book was finally published by Hamish Hamilton. The SPCK committee had taken its reservations to the Archbishop of Canterbury, president of the SPCK, who contended that the book included prayers for people living with HIV/AIDS alongside those affirming gay and lesbian relationships and might encourage the myth that homosexuality and AIDS were integrally linked. The initial commissioning had been a sign that 'the pastoral needs of lesbian and gay people were beginning to be taken seriously' (Stuart, p. xi). The controversy that followed suggested a certain fear of the power of liturgy if given over to a minority group.

[8] See above, n. 2, p. 123.

of the creation of a gay and lesbian Christian ethic. It goes beyond a heterosexual ethic in that it does not mirror, for example, a marriage ceremony in the section on celebrating lesbian and gay relationships. Rather it states that the needs of lesbian and gay couples are different from heterosexual couples and so the liturgy must reflect this difference.

Neither are the liturgies exclusive to homosexual couples. They could equally well be used by individuals or groups of any sexual orientation wishing to express themselves in all-inclusive worship.

Jim Cotter in a pamphlet produced by the Gay Christian Movement of Bristol talks of the model of friendship being basic to the expression of commitment between a same-sex couple.[9] What is offered is simply a form for expressing a covenant of friendship between two people who honour and respect each other and want to affirm this publicly. The pamphlet also outlines in more detail services of blessing for a couple. These services again include all types of relationships. They simply do not talk in heterosexual terms.

From the work of Cotter and Stuart we can see that the lesbian and gay movement, far from corrupting or distorting our image of relationship, is widening the meaning of relationship immensely. By offering models for partings, blessings, housewarmings, coming out, these two liturgists are among the increasing number who are saying that lesbian and gay relationships are blessed by God. These models are offered to the whole worshipping community as nourishment for our worship. They also offer acceptance, form and understanding to a group of worshippers previously excluded from worship.

> Worship is not just a kind of ... corporate pastoral counselling, but ... plays an important part in the process of healing, restoring, reconciling, purifying, growing and forming fellowship.[10]

---

[9] John Ferguson, *Moral Values in the Ancient World* (1958), observed: 'it is surprising that the Christian tradition has not made more of the value of friendship' (p. 75).

[10] Forrester, McDonald, Tellini (1983), p. 145.

If worship is about healing, about forgiveness, about reconciliation, about justice, then the liturgical revolution of the 1990s can only be an enhancement of the Kingdom. God's 'Yes' is a yes to all who worship through Christ Jesus (2 Cor. 1:17, 20). God's 'Yes' is a yes to loving friendships (1 Corinthians 13, Rom. 12:9–10, John 15:12–17). God's 'Yes' is a yes to new life (John 11:33–44). We need to use all our creative and imaginative skills to find ways of saying 'Yes' in worship to all of God's people.

V   *Case Study (Ruth Harvey)*

THE METROPOLITAN COMMUNITY CHURCH

In 1968 the Revd Troy Perry in a gay bar heard someone cry 'Nobody loves me'. Perry's response was 'Jesus loves you' and thus the base was laid for the founding of the Universal Fellowship of Metropolitan Community Churches. Ordaining their own pastors and bishops, and having congregations throughout North America and Europe, MCC has become universally accepted as a safe and liberating church for lesbian and gay worship.

In 1988 I first met Bill, a campaigning and 'out' gay, when I was appointed as 'Gay Rights Officer' of the Students Representative Council of Aberdeen University. Bill taught me something of the pain in the lives of many homosexuals who are both gay and Christian. A student of theology, he had been told that his sexual orientation was incompatible with ordination.

It was in 1991 that Bill and I met up again, this time following his invitation to lead a worship workshop with some friends of his from the MCC in the north of England. They were coming to Glasgow in an attempt to establish an MCC group in Scotland and wanted a colleague and myself to facilitate a workshop on worship. Rather than looking at worship *for* gays and lesbians, we guided the group in terms of their good and bad experiences of worship, focusing on the good and developing, through imagination exercises, a framework for holistic, healing, celebratory worship.

Having been asked to lead a second workshop in Newcastle we were then contacted by Paul Whiting of MCC Europe to help with a series of workshops he was planning to run in Scotland in the Spring of 1993. We were to join the workshops and provide worship relating to each theme.

In the event only three workshops took place, and we provided worship at only two. Three of us spent two evenings before the workshops discussing the forthcoming theme and creating a framework for the worship which would then be filled out by the participants themselves. While we were keen that the worship reflected participants' experiences and feelings, we were also aware that a certain amount of planning was needed.

Workshop 1

The first workshop was a basic introduction to lesbian and gay sexuality and the Christian faith. With ten participants and four leaders the group relaxed quite quickly after a couple of brief warm-up and getting-to-know-you games. Two of the leaders, both employed by MCC as outreach workers, led us through some of the history of ideas about gay love: what the Bible has to say about homosexuality and sex and God. The purpose of the workshop was to affirm homosexuality, and to offer a space for gay and lesbian people to share their sense of self.

Taking for the theme of this worship 'Held in the palm of God's hand', we were keen to focus on acceptance: acceptance by God despite the rejection of society. The opening responses reflected our coming together as a group before God, and included the use of three candles to symbolise light for the world in the midst of darkness. The first prayer reflected diversity, chaos, creation and uncertainty: all being clasped close to God as part of the pattern of life. This prayer affirmed all that may seem random in our lives as being real.

Reading from Isaiah we affirmed our acceptance by God and the promise he made that despite all the troubles of life we will never be forgotten for we are 'graven on the palm of God's hand'. To confirm this symbolically we then each wrote the name of our neighbour on the palm of his or her hand. We need each other to help us to understand that we are never forgotten by God. And we need constant stark reminders that individually we are accepted by God.

The worship ended with a song of offering: offering all that we are and all that we have to God. Offering to God our friendships, our tiredness, our regrets, our fears, our talents and our skills: offering all, yet asking that in the end while our whole life is God's, I am still 'me'. The final blessing from

Ireland sent us out from worship 'held in the palm of God's hand'.

All the participants in the workshop helped to lead the worship. Comments at the end were very positive: one woman said that it was the most affirming worship she had ever attended.

Workshop 2

The second workshop focused more specifically on what the churches have said about lesbian and gay relationships. Participants were given the opportunity in small groups to talk about their own experiences of being 'out' in the church, Most related bad experiences of rejection and total misunderstanding. Some talked of the value of MCC, although a running theme was how to integrate homosexuality into the mainstream churches rather than set up a separate church. Opinions on this were varied, but the general consensus was that until the mainstream churches act more positively towards gay and lesbians, not only in worship but in ordination, marriage and so on, there is a need for a church for gays and lesbians.

In this worship we used drama to convey the sense of confusion about 'appropriate' worship in 'appropriate' churches. Jesus told Peter that on him he would build the church. But he gave Peter no blueprint for how that should happen, what should happen in church, who should lead, what kind of music there should be, far less whether homosexuals were to be included or not.

Using prayers and songs from around the world widened our focus. We then put together a meditation based on the stories of the participants as told in the small groups. As a symbol of our interwovenness despite our diversity we each wrote words of hope on a coloured strip of paper and wove them together to form a banner.

The final prayer reflected the anger and frustration expressed by participants towards the church, offering these feelings to God in the hope that they could be used positively.

A final blessing continued the weaving theme so clearly summed up in the symbol of the Trinity, three woven into one. We are part of the fabric of the church whether it or we like it or not.

VI   *An Ethic of Reconciliation (Ruth Harvey)*

> Come, Hope of unity
> make us one body,
> come, O Lord Jesus,
> reconcile all nations.

Liturgy is dangerous. It can subvert the established order and threaten those in power. Elizabeth Stuart discovered this in her attempts to have *Daring to Speak Love's Name* published. What is it about a book of prayers and liturgies that can be so controversial?

When we touch on issues of identity, sexuality and minority groups in daily life and in worship we are bound to use the language of liberation, of love, of justice, of action. These words, symbols, movements, songs speak from the heart of experiences of rejection and pain. So they will be 'gutsy' words which may hit 'established' nerves.

In discussing issues of human sexuality and homosexuality the churches are dealing with peoples' lives at their most sensitive level. Yet the churches cannot hope to respond pastorally until they convert their statements and reports into life-giving, risky worship. By repenting, by listening, by celebrating, by blessing in worshipping communities, the churches can join the movement for the renewal of worship which is already on the move.

I believe that through the lesbian and gay community the churches are being offered a gift of grace, of freedom. That gift comes in the form not of statements and declarations and study guides alone, but in the form of healing, forgiving, respectful, reconciling worship.

CHAPTER 5

SOCIAL VALUES AND PUBLIC POLICY

Introduction: Christian Values and Society

On the face of it, there is no reason why Christian ethics should be in difficulty when addressing values in society. The world is God's creation, inhabited by his creatures – some of them confessing their faith in him, others not, but all exhibiting that curious mixture of values and disvalues which characterise the human race. There is thus no reason why *the world* should not be the locus of Christian ethics, nor why Christian ethics should not be at home in 'secular worlds'.[1] Indeed, it might even be held that such a perspective represents a rediscovery of its true nature, or at least of a lost emphasis within it.

The reason that public moral debate frequently marginalises Christian ethics is found in the *extrinsic* reference which Christian ethics, not unreasonably, is perceived to have. In other words, Christian ethics frequently appears tangential to the concerns of the world. We might profitably explore a little further the distinction between *extrinsic* and *intrinsic* expressions of Christian value.

In the first case, moral value is explicitly related to the Christian community itself. It is widely recognised that Western society is in a post-Constantinian, if not post-Christian, phase and that churches and Christians cannot effectively speak *ex cathedra* about social values: they are ignored or regarded as impossibly conservative if they try to do so. Nevertheless,

---

[1] Cf. R. Gill, *Christian Ethics and Secular Worlds* (1991).

133

churches embody and express within their own communities the insights into right and wrong, good and evil, given within their own tradition – indeed, the distinctive life-style or way of life to which their faith and worship lead them. But too often, Christian values are located *tout court* within this community, either as authoritarian 'natural law' or as 'objective' biblical revelation. There then follows the problem of 'application' to the worldly situation. While church members try to bear witness to Christian values in their daily avocations, most have some awareness that the context is quite different from that of their churches and that faith and values must therefore be expressed in a different key or even separated altogether. Luther, for example, distinguished sharply between personal responsibilities and duties toward the state. The danger here is of a 'two worlds' view, in which the worlds are separate and irreconcilable. The church is increasingly marginal to society; society and the business world effectively claim moral autonomy, and morality is virtually dissolved into relativism. Even the life-style of believers may be fashioned as much by the world as by the church. Some find church teaching out of step even with the realities of family life today.

In the second case, value – like wisdom – is not seen to be the monopoly of the churches. As in 'natural law', a structure of value is seen to be inherent in the human situation – even if it is as general as the 'moral sense' of humankind or the 'fiduciary foundations' of human communities. Values emerge in different forms in different situations. There are business, professional, trade union and consumers' values. All of them are subject to critical examination, and all require to be related to the wider (or deeper) human scene. This interpretive process has many dimensions: political, philosophical, social and religious. To attempt to impose moral solutions from outside the situation is to invalidate, or at least marginalise, one's contribution. Churches (or Christians) may feel the need to emphasise certain human values, but this must be done from within the organic process of the moral development of the group, profession or industry in question. It must be *implicit* in the context. We may draw a parallel here with the 'wisdom' tradition in Israel, which was grounded in the professional awareness and prudential experience of the scribal coterie while remaining faithful to the insights of the religious tradition of Israel.

In terms of social ethics, the second approach appears particularly apposite. It is the kind of approach which was advocated, *in extremis*, by Dietrich Bonhoeffer when he spoke of 'worldly holiness';[2] by Dag Hammarskjöld when he said, 'In our era, the road to holiness necessarily passes through the world of action';[3] and by Nicholas Berdyaev when he called for 'a new type of saint who will take upon himself the burden of the complex world'.[4] We are thus not speaking here simply of commending the Christian life-style or extending church influence. We are speaking about discovering value in the midst of life, although such 'discovery' is vouchsafed only to those who are open to moral values and recognise the demands it places on themselves. The risks are evident. The possibilities of distortion are very great, and the insights of the Christian tradition – indeed, the values of Christians themselves – may die the death of a thousand worldly qualifications. Collusion in disvalues may be the result.

Arising from these prefatory remarks is the need to consider the moral significance of churches and, subsequently, the nature of their relationship to society.

1 *The moral significance of churches*

Certain features of church life are *implicitly* related to social value. In terms of Christian ethics, the church is important in at least five senses, as set out below:

(i) *The church as community*
For our purposes here, the church is neither an authoritarian power structure nor the repository of dogma: it is the community

---

[2] D. Bonhoeffer, *Letters and Papers from Prison* (1953), pp. 164–6; *The Cost of Discipleship* (1959), pp. 250–2.
[3] Dag Hammarskjöld, *Markings* (1964), p. 108.
[4] Nicholas Berdyaev, *Spirit and Reality* (1939), p. 99.

of people in whom the gospel or the Spirit of Christ dwells. A community may be described as: 'A group of people who are socially interdependent, who participate together in discussion and decision-making, and who share certain practices that both define the community and are nurtured by it.'[5] But the church as community, while falling short of this definition in some respects, exceeds it in others. In particular, its nature as *koinonia* signifies a sharing in a reality that transcends the remit of social science. Whether we speak of gospel, or the faith, or Christian values, the significant factor is that any such focalisation is *enfleshed*: it is expressed in people. To proceed thus is to be incarnational in one's thinking, for what matters in terms of ethics is not primarily the nuances of ancient christological debate nor the vacuity of much modern debate about the 'virgin birth', but the insight that the Word became flesh in Christ and becomes flesh in the community of faith. A peculiar qualification attaches to this concept. Central to it is the *calling* of the church to be the people of God: as a community, it has constantly to answer that call. At any given moment, it may fail to do so. The church is only truly the church when in its *koinonia* it points beyond itself as it witnesses to the truth, as happens in worship, word and sacrament, and in caring ministry.

(ii) *The church as moral community*

As the church points beyond itself, it discloses the 'fiduciary foundations' of Christian morality; and in so far as the *koinonia* builds on such foundations it is *de facto* a moral community. Again, the disclaimers are important: at any given point, it may not act thus. It can therefore never adopt a position of moral superiority. It is a community that confesses its sins, itself an act of moral significance. And it is a community that is called to translate the gospel into loving action. How the community expresses such action in the world, other than through personal witness and local church initiatives, is a real question. Churches have various mechanisms for doing so, all of them subject to

---

[5] Cf. R. Bellah and others, *Habits of the Heart: Middle America Observed* (1985), pp. 333–5; also, R. Gill, *Secular Worlds*, p. 16.

critical reservation. As Paul Ramsey put it, 'Who speaks for the Church?'[6] Nevertheless, from bodies as diverse as the Society of Friends and the US Catholic Bishops there have emerged influential and challenging moral studies. Duncan Forrester has observed:

> A new kind of quality of reflection on public policy is becoming possible in churches which are realistic about their own situations, theologically serious, cogent in argumentation, attentive to the facts, and willing to pioneer.[7]

(iii) *The church as worshipping community*

Worship is a corporate action in which the worshippers offer themselves to God and open themselves to receive his Word and presence. It is morally significant as a community act, an act performed together; as an act of humility, of shared fellowship in which all are equal before God and all are in need of God's grace and healing; and an act of moral and spiritual discovery, in which all are open to gospel and Spirit, in Word and sacrament; an act of sharing peace. Of course, while corporate worship – hamstrung as it is by convention and torn between traditional form and experimental shapelessness – retains its place as the gathered embodiment of the worshipping community, it may well be defective in some of the aspects with which we are directly concerned here. Sometimes, groups within its fellowship may be more effective. Yet for all its ambiguity, it does have moral and therapeutic potential, which is explored below. As Robin Gill comments:

> Worshipping communities act as such moral harbingers, whether they realise this or not, and then spill these values more widely into society at large, again whether they realise this or not. Indeed the very moral judgements so frequently offered by the media of Christian communities may act as an important reminder that Christian values are already scattered in society at large.[8]

[6] Paul Ramsey, *Who Speaks for the Church?* (1967).
[7] D. B. Forrester, *Beliefs, Values and Policies* (1989), p. 97.
[8] Gill, *Secular Worlds*, p. 17.

(iv) *The church as community of story and vision*
Undergirding the church's life and faith is the witness to God's grace in the historic experience of Israel, in Christ and in the lives of faithful people: and the witness begets hope and a vision of new possibilities. It takes narrative form because it is revealed in history and human experience. It is also heard and received as a historical happening, in the context of human experience. Each intersection of the church's story and our story is an explosion of meaning, a transforming possibility sustained in the continuing worship and fellowship of the church. It is a renewal of hope, a call to new possibilities and revitalised action: hence, a 'new song', a 'new story' making new history.[9]

(v) *The church as critically conscious community*
The church's faith is concerned with truth, reality - that is, the truth about life. The intersecting of the church's story with our story is the means by which we are enabled to discern truth: to receive revelation not as a prefabricated set of propositions but as insight into the way things are – with us and with the world. Hence, a critical function is involved: a heightening of awareness which new vision brings, the development of a critical consciousness. This is invalidated if it becomes a judgemental act, as it frequently does when revelation is interpreted as an authoritarian *datum*, whether based on Bible or church. The critical process includes self-awareness, awareness of one's own limitations, moral and cognitive. What is given is an awareness of that to which we are called: a clearing of vision. The moral and spiritual task is a sharing of that vision, which is not done by condemnation. 'Judge not – that you be not judged!' Truth is not seen unless it is discerned in love, nor will it be communicated unless the stances people adopt, and people themselves, are respected and understood.[10]

[9] On narrative theology in general, cf. G. W. Stroup, *The Promise of Narrative Theology* (1984); S. Hauerwas, *A Community of Character* (1981), pp. 9–12, 15–16, 18–23; T. H. Groome, *Christian Religious Education* (1980).

[10] On critical consciousness, cf. Paulo Freire, *Pedagogy of the Oppressed* (1972), especially ch. 3.

As a final comment here, the marginality of the church in modern society is a two-edged phenomenon. Putting aside laments about church decline, we could invoke the familiar image of Hebrews 13 – 'here we have no lasting city but seek for the city that is to come' (13:14) – and argue that the place of the church is at the margins, outside the camp: 'the place of discernment and of redemption, the place to which Christians are called to keep company with their Lord'.[11] Events in South Africa, and perhaps in Poland, Russia and elsewhere, give a degree of contemporary validation to this perspective. But it does depend on what churches are doing 'outside the camp'! Are they the remnants of Christendom or the harbingers of a new age? We pursue the question by considering how churches relate, or may relate, to society.

2 *Churches and society*

Churches do not relate to society in the same ways. The 'sect' type is a smaller community defined sharply over against the outside world. Such groups commonly, but not invariably, assert an 'ethics of conviction', often conservative or traditional and not designed primarily for dialogue with 'worldly' positions. The larger associational type of church faces both ways: it identifies sacramentally and nurturally with the family, but opens out upon the world in which vocation and witness are located. While members are free to work out their own solutions to the problem of relating personal and vocational or social stances, the leadership of the churches will attempt some kind of mediation between church and state, and will characteristically espouse social ethics.

How then are we to assess the *function* churches may perform in relation to values which society itself may endorse or confront? How far can Christian values influence general morality? Three sociological models may help to shed light on the problem:

---

[11] Forrester, *Beliefs, Values and Policies*, p. 97.

(i) *The structural–functional view* (Talcott Parsons)[12]

This view stresses the need for equilibrium in society, which depends on widely shared values and norms fostered by institutions such as church and school. Adaptive change is held to be essential, otherwise deviance results. On this view, religion is regarded as a kind of social glue. Consequently, when there is a breakdown in moral standards, politicians blame the churches for being ineffective. It is a role which is most readily thrust upon national or established churches, and to that extent is a hangover from 'Christendom'. The nearest counterpart to it in the New Testament is found perhaps in the *Haustafeln* or lists of family duties which occur in many of the letters. The social convention of the Graeco-Roman household structure is adopted and 'christianised'. St Paul is also anxious that the Roman Christians should be dutiful citizens of the Empire, for those who preserve law and order are instruments of God. A very different view is found in Revelation.

Both conservative and liberal theological positions have colluded with this view: the first, because priority is given to preserving the pattern of belief and religious practce in the context of traditional social mores (their attitudes to issues such as marriage and homosexuality are generally predictable); and the second, because Christian values are reduced to sets of first or second order principles with which the secular establishment is relatively at ease. However, when politics and society move away from a 'consensus' view and 'conviction' politics or 'economic positivism' hold sway, Parson's 'social glue' model begins to lack credibility. Conservatives sharpen their social awareness; liberal ideology acquires a much more critical edge, and cries of betrayal or derision begin to emerge from the secular establishment. There are at least two sides to the puzzle: one is that there is an element of truth in the 'social glue' contention: Christian expressions of love, care and hope, as well as emphases on moral norms, do help to provide equilibrium; the other is that churches – and, to some extent,

---

[12] Talcott Parsons, *The Social System* (1952).

schools and professions – are bound to resist domestication to the state in order to be true to their own vocations.

(ii) *The conflict model* (Festinger)[13]

This view interprets society as engaged in constant tensions, struggle and conflict between competing groups within itself. Change is effected through disequilibrium and cognitive dissonance: that is, the need for change is pressed by interested groups through various stages of stress and upheaval until the justice of the claim is more widely accepted and change is effected. This scenario assumes contradictory values, often asserted by opposing groups. In so far as liberation ethics is of this type, it presupposes that the values of oppressive power groups must be deconstructed so that their real nature is revealed. Religion acts here as a counter-force, advancing the cause of creative justice. It fosters a critical consciousness and assumes a critical role for Christian ethics. In Western society, this type of approach is associated with prophetic religion and is usually advanced by highly motivated groups within churches or by charismatic individuals, often at times of perceived crisis.

It is a mistake, however, to regard the prophetic task as restricted to individuals, particularly when recognition is given to the importance of community for values.[14] The role of the prophet is primarily to articulate the roots of the tradition for the community. In the tradition of Israel, the false prophet spoke 'smooth things': that is, he was domesticated by king, priesthood and the powerful. The true prophet recalled Israel to her vocation. Hence, the role of the prophet is first to his own faith community. In any case, a prophetic call is inherent in all worship that incorporates the ministry of the Word. The faith community renews its own vocation and seeks both to relay the call to 'basic values' and to interpret their application to society and policy makers alike. There is thus a desire for dialogue, but change may be effected (if at all) through a period of disequilibrium and cognitive dissonance, for such a

---

[13] L. Festinger, *A Theory of Cognitive Dissonance* (1957).
[14] Contra R. Gill, *Prophecy and Praxis* (1981), pp. 13–30.

call may well be for changes in policy which are costly for the party in power or inconsistent with its self-interested ideology. It is not surprising if invidium, counter-propaganda and other means are used to silence an unwelcome voice; and the prophetic voice of the churches must be sure of its grasp of empirical reality as well as its moral vision, otherwise they will be severely taken to task for talking about things they do not understand! This approach is very much the model of the church 'outside the camp'.

(iii) *Perceived symbolic meaning* (Habermas)[15]

When people respond to a situation, they do so by referring to a shared system of social symbols. These symbols are patterns of shared meanings which have emerged from historical experiences, and they serve to mark out the contours and parameters of the moral world. This process is participative: everyone is involved in finding meaning. It may be controversial: there may be considerable debate over values that can be shared. Yet, as A. MacIntyre has emphasised, society has 'fiduciary foundations' which can be explored, and J. Habermas has also recognised the place of tradition. This approach of 'perceived symbolic meaning' has importance for Christian ethics. It sends us back to the Christian roots of society, among others, with a view to the rediscovery of value or, perhaps better, the recreation of contemporary value, for tradition is not something static but a living organism that grows through interaction with new situations. It is a perspective which looks to the reshaping of society, rather than simply the affirmation of the *status quo*. There is no way, however, by which churches can dictate to society what its 'fiduciary foundations' are. Tradition is, in fact, many stranded. But it does suggest the need for dialogue and debate, that value may be established.

Such a stance activates the implicit approach discussed above, although it sends the Christian ethicist (among others) back to prophetic roots. It also insists that the advocacy of moral values presupposes openness, a willingness to listen and

---

[15] J. Habermas, *The Theory of Communicative Action* I (1984).

learn, humility and compassion. The values advocated must be fully expressed in the means by which they are advocated. A particular difficulty arises with the language of transcendence, for which there is no obvious secular counterpart. But dialogue presupposes a willingness to listen on the part of *all* parties involved. There are moments within the most worldly life where the haunting challenge of human finitude or human failure cannot be silenced. There are moments in moral discussion where the perception of value pushes one into an area which transcends human manipulation. Dialogue is precisely the opening up of new horizons, the search for convergence, the preparation for disclosure. That is why Christian parties to the debate have a duty to extend the points of reference to include ultimate perspectives, while ensuring that the dialogue does not lapse into monologue at this point. Nor must it be a pre-empting of the outcome of the dialogue. Christians do *not* have the final answer to any moral dilemma, including abortion, euthanasia, homosexuality and other issues that are sometimes pre-empted by dictat. But they will always be concerned to understand, to seek a meeting of minds and sharing of perspectives as far as possible, and to witness to the truth as transcendent and therefore much greater than any attempted statement of it in human terms, yet calling all to wholeness of being.

The above perspectives suggest an exciting role for Christian ethics. All three perspectives have a certain validity, even if the first is under constant pressure from the other two. Christian ethics is inescapably involved in questions of power and social values, in relation to which it must exercise its own integrity. Political power is entirely conditioned: it appeals to the electorate, to self-interest and party interest. The religious appeal, within the socio-historical context, is to the unconditioned and the ultimate. There is also a certain comprehensiveness in Christian contributions to the discussion. At the time of the Falklands thanksgiving service, the Archbishop of Canterbury used the liturgy to express Christian perspectives of concern for those counted enemies, for healing and reconciliation. Other perspectives include environmental and global concerns, and the question of world debt, with its impoverishing and dehumanising consequences. Christian ethics may find itself simultaneously discerning truth in worldly propositions and deconstructing the self-interested claims which they may articulate. It is precisely when the debate is moved beyond the framework of immediate self-interest that Christian ethics can reinforce moral considerations.

Because of the need to address moral problems as they arise and are felt in society, this chapter cannot proceed at a merely theoretical level. The studies which follow are empirically based but bring to bear perspectives which reflect the concerns expressed throughout this book and in this chapter in particular. Different writers bring into play their own insights and emphases, but all express the interplay of theory and praxis, and strive for a disciplined method in ethics, which has been before us throughout our discussions.

The first study highlights the importance of interview and dialogue, of listening to those with firsthand experience of the empirical situation, and attempts to find amid all the conflict and complexity a way to rebuild community and foster trust, hope and renewal. It should be stated that the dialogue on which it is based took place before the 1994 cease-fire in Northern Ireland, but so far from invalidating it such a development – the beginning of 'a long hard road', as all parties agree – places a premium on the need for dialogue and understanding, and the growth of trust, which are the prime concerns of the study.

I *Justice and Reconciliation – Six Views on Northern Ireland (John N. Young)*

> Those who struggle through turbulent Jordan waters have gone beyond the glib definitions of politics or religion. The rest remain standing on either bank firing guns at one another.[1]

The year 1994 was a momentous one in the recent turbulent history of Northern Ireland. Contacts and discussions, official and unofficial, between various parties and movements – including those between John Hume (SDLP) and Gerry Adams (Sinn Fein), and those which involved the British and the Irish Governments – led to a cessation of the violent conflict and opened the way to meaningful negotiations on the future of the Province.[2] In view of the deep and historic divisions in its society, no one was foolish enough to believe that progress towards a final settlement would be easy. Such difficulties give special point to the study offered here. It seeks to explore the conflict through the views of six people who have lived and worked there; and in a land where Christian beliefs appear to be a cause of division, to see whether they also provide the seeds of reconciliation.

1 *Theories of reconciliation*

Is there a Christian ethic of reconciliation? While all Christians might agree that Jesus came to reconcile God with humanity, a superficial glance through the Gospels would provide support both for those who see Christianity as bringing conflict (e.g., Matt. 10:34) and those who see it as promoting peace (e.g., Matt. 5:9). Moltmann and Tillich are two theologians who have gone beyond the superficial by exploring the relation of

---

[1] Brian Keenan, *An Evil Cradling* (1992), p. 16

[2] The IRA cease-fire became effective at the end of August 1994; the 'Combined Loyalist Military Command' ceased operational hostilities at 12 midnight on October 13, 1994. For an account of the various parties as seen through the eyes of the interviewees, see Appendix II, pp. 168–9.

reconciliation to the very nature of God. Their studies provide us with a useful position from which to examine conflict.

Moltmann develops the implications of a trinitarian God, where each person is defined in relationship with the others. He sees the person being in the image of God only when in community with others, for this '...points to the triunity of the Father, the Son, and the Spirit'.[3] Disunity is a distortion of true personhood.

Tillich speaks of 'creative justice'. He reconciles the apparent contradictions between the concepts of love, power, and justice, by approaching them ontologically. Love is the force which reunites that which is estranged.[4] Justice defines the form of that reunion.[5] Power describes what this achieves – the power over non-being.[6] Creative justice is 'expressed in the divine grace which forgives in order to reunite'.[7] It is the justice which rises above questions of merit and tribute,[8] and speaks paradoxically of 'justification by grace through faith'. It is the form of reuniting love.[9] It is the nature of God displayed in Christ.

In our study of Northern Ireland we are looking for signs of a united community, as a visible image of a triune God. We are also looking for the reuniting love displayed in forgiveness, as a sign of God's creative justice, bringing about wholeness through reconciliation.

2. *The method*

The main data for this study are the firsthand accounts of those who have experienced the conflict. Six people with different backgrounds and experiences were interviewed in

---

[3] J. Moltmann, *The Trinity and the Kingdom of God* (1981), p. 156
[4] P. Tillich, *Love, Power and Justice* (1954), p. 25 This is love's proper work. Love also has a tragic aspect, however, which is to destroy that which prevents its proper work - this is its strange work (pp. 49–51)
[5] Ibid., p. 61
[6] Ibid., pp. 37, 49, 56
[7] Ibid., p. 66
[8] Ibid.
[9] Ibid.

some depth. It is time for the reader to meet them (names have been changed to preserve anonymity):

John – Born and has lived his whole life in Northern Ireland. He began his life in a quiet town, before working in the manufacturing industry for several years. Finally he moved into teaching and has spent most of his life working in education. He joined the Presbyterian Church of Northern Ireland in later life, eventually being ordained an elder. He has recently moved to Scotland.

Susan – Her father was a Presbyterian minister. She grew up in a small, predominantly Protestant village community, and was relatively sheltered from the conflict. Her first real contact with Catholics was when she went to university. She spent some time in teaching before leaving to study in Scotland.

Martin – A Scottish ex-soldier, who spent a total of six years on tours of varying lengths in Northern Ireland. Brought up in a Protestant home in Scotland, he became involved in the Presbyterian Church through the army, and was ordained as an elder. His life was changed, however, through a Vineyard Fellowship conference he attended when in Germany. His subsequent tours in Ireland saw his increased involvement in non-sectarian house fellowships.

Margaret – Born and brought up in a small town in Eire, she had little contact with Protestants, who were seen as belonging to another religion, and some fear, though little real understanding, of the northern situation. Attending college in Cork she met a number of evangelical Christians, including both Catholics and Protestants from the North, and her spiritual life underwent a profound change. She became a teacher, but a working visit to South Africa convinced her of the similarities with Northern Ireland, and eventually she was involved full-time in reconciliation work for a number of years, in a Christian community in Rostrevor. She has lived in Scotland for two years.

Bob – Born in Belfast, his mother was a Derry Protestant and his father Church of Ireland from Belfast. He grew up attending a Presbyterian church on the edge of a Protestant housing estate. Church was the centre of the youth culture of his day. His mother's father was a policeman, killed while on patrol with the Black and Tans in 1922. His grandmother's simple faith and forgiving spirit had a profound influence on him. He became involved in the Corrymeela Community through his local youth club leader in the days before the troubles flared up again. He left Ireland when he graduated and has lived in Scotland ever since, but used to return to Corrymeela as a volunteer for summer camps, and for some time was its representative in Edinburgh.

Theresa – Born and brought up as a Catholic in a mixed housing scheme in Newry, she had many Protestant friends (except on the 12th and 13th of July – the days of the Protestant marches). Her father died when she was young and her mother, while emphasising tolerance, instilled her with nationalist pride. She was ten when the troubles started, and the rioting and violence in Newry had a deep effect on her. In her late teens she grew dissatisfied with rigid Catholicism and began to explore other traditions. At twenty she became a 'Christian' (as opposed to a 'Protestant' or a 'Catholic'), and spent the next eleven years working for reconciliation in Rostrevor before moving to Scotland.

An attempt has been made to speak to people from diverse backgrounds, covering the same areas with each. The details and the style in which information was given varied from person to person, the result being usually a mixture of the objective and the anecdotal. Often the real insights were to be found hidden in throw-away remarks about the commonplace. The same general questions were explored with each interviewee.[10] The aim was to attempt to get behind the stated positions of the conflicting groups to find common interests that might become the basis for new direction and for their reconciliation.[11] The questions were not followed rigidly, as

[10] See Appendix I, p. 167 – written sources have only been used in support, or where they add something which has not been touched upon by the interviewees.

[11] See Appendix II, pp. 168–9.

the conversation varied according to the interviewee. Every effort was made, however, to ensure that all the important areas were covered in each case. Personally, I was surprised and startled by the depth of many of the insights which were expressed. What started out for me as a brief survey became much more of a journey into Northern Ireland and into my own faith: a journey which is by no means over yet.

3 *The Troubles*

It is possible to draw a simple picture of the conflict in Northern Ireland by balancing against each other the aims and methods of the different political bodies. This was, in fact, the way all the interviewees approached the subject, and it is the approach adopted in this study itself.[12] As we go deeper into the world which is Northern Ireland, however, we find that, while the basic opposition remains, it is reinforced over and over again in many areas of life.

(i) *The protagonists*[13]

The conflict is articulated in political language, the key question being whether the six counties of Northern Ireland should be part of Eire or part of Great Britain. Both sides have well-developed ideologies. Those who wish a united Ireland portray Britain as an alien colonial power, using its military might to maintain its illegal foothold in the North. Those who favour the *status quo* see themselves as defenders of truth and freedom, and of a beleaguered homeland against the dark forces of Catholicism. On both sides we find moderates, extremists, and para-militaries, bound together in a complex web. The existence of Sinn Fein and the DUP, for example, tends to affect the policies of the more moderate OUP and SDLP, who are '...constantly looking over their shoulders at the militants' (John). The fear of losing votes to them has made the moderates less flexible than they might have been.

[12] Fisher and Ury's method is summarised on p. 11 of *Getting to Yes* (1987).
[13] Fisher and Ury, p. 5.

(ii) *The history and culture*

The problem with arguing over positions, according to Fisher and Ury, is that one's ego becomes identified with one's position. As a result the underlying concerns are obscured and agreement becomes less likely.[14] We have seen the positions adopted by the political bodies. These positions have come to symbolise the identity of the different communities, but there are other factors which have contributed to these identities. An important one of these is history.[15]

While the outsider might find it possible to be objective,[16] the history of the North is complicated because the different communities learn their own versions. While the Catholics stress the 1916 uprising, the Civil Rights Movement, and internment, the Protestants remember the Boyne, Carson's Blood Covenant, and the Workers' Strike. Paradoxes are ignored, such as the Pope's support of William II, and the Presbyterian founder of the republican movement (Theresa). History is essentially a matter of identity. Protestants celebrate their identity in the July Marches, commemorating their history, while Catholics do the same in August. Their history justifies their position.

[14] See Appendix II, pp. 168–9.

[15] A thorough study of the history behind The Troubles would go back to 'The Plantations' of Scottish settlers in the North by King James in 1609 (Margaret). The twentieth century has had its share of significant events, however. 1916 saw the Easter Uprising in Dublin, where a handful of idealists were martyred in a successful attempt to unite the nation in the cause of independence. Two years prior to this, however, 100,000 Ulstermen had signed with their own blood a covenant rejecting Home Rule. Both events evoked powerful religious symbolism (Margaret; she also spoke of how the equation of the martyrs' sacrifices with Christ's death on the cross was repeated today in the terrorists' thinking. This is supported by the views of a convicted IRA terrorist – see *Christian* 17, 1990, p. 29). The struggle for independence and the civil war which followed caused much suffering and bitterness which is ingrained in the memories of the communities. The 1920 Partition of Ireland was a messy solution to a deep rooted conflict. The task which was left to the people of the six northern counties was an impossible one (David Bleakley in *Christian* p. 15), and the Protestant majority which came to rule through the Stormont Parliament placed the position and wellbeing of fellow Protestants before the rights of the Catholic minority (Margaret).

[16] Martin is convinced that, historically, Ulster belongs to Ireland.

There are two sets of people marching. Both feel totally right. They are saying this land belongs to me. I have a right to have it. (Theresa)[17]

The Protestant and Catholic communities in the North possess distinct cultures, yet ironically these too are influenced by the historical conflict which separates them. Protestant culture is 'barren' (Bob). The seventeenth-century Scottish Presbyterian settlers brought no recognised traditions with them apart from their church and its suspicion of worldly culture. Scottish music and dance were left behind, and these things in Ireland became associated with Catholicism (Bob). No attempt was made by Protestants to learn the Gaelic language (John). Protestants today are left with the Orange Order and the Church (Bob, Margaret).[18] Yet there is also a Catholic culture which is particular to the North.

The Catholics do not see themselves as British, yet they do not see themselves as southern either. They sense the cultural differences that are there. (Margaret)

The Opsahl Commission comments that culture in the North is used by both sides as a political weapon: the Catholic use of language and history is compared with the Protestant use of Orange Marches.[19] In contrast to southerners, the tensions in their lives tend to make northerners, both Catholic and Protestant, more introverted and suspicious (Margaret).

(iii) *Religion*
It cannot be asserted, as some church leaders have tried to do in the past,[20] that the conflict in Ireland has little basis in religion.[21] Religion permeates the distinct identities of the

---

[17] One writer speaks of the way past history is allowed to be echoed in current events: cf. T. Downing (ed.), *The Troubles* (1980), pp. 196–7.
[18] Margaret spoke of the effect of the music of Van Morrison, which incorporates much traditional music, in bringing young people into a shared appreciation of common culture.
[19] A. Pollak (ed.), *A Citizens' Enquiry: The Opsahl Report on Northern Ireland* (1993), p. 97
[20] A. McCreary, *Corrymeela: The Search for Peace* (1975), pp. 98–9
[21] See also *Christian* p. 37

communities. To study the Bible, for example, is seen by Catholics as a Protestant trait (Theresa). While the Catholic community celebrates Sunday as a holiday, Protestants prefer to 'keep the Sabbath' (Margaret).[22] All the interviewees implicated the churches' institutions fully in the perpetuation of differences. Church policies are seen to contribute indirectly to the divide. The apparent lack of any Protestant minister with a knowledge of Gaelic reflects their concern solely for their own people (John). Catholic rulings about education and mixed marriages fuel Protestant fears.[23] So too does the Catholic Church's determination to influence the State in Eire.[24] This drives the Protestant church leaders to see the link with Britain as maintaining a Protestant position in the North (John).

> The culture in which we have grown up is a religious culture, for which the churches cannot deny responsibility. They have failed to exercise the right influences. They have failed to recognise what has been happening and have failed to respond to it. Nor have they been prepared to disassociate themselves from specific acts and organisations. The Catholic condemnation of terrorist outrages is never unqualified. The Orange Order parade still marches to the local church. The church will not draw the line, and the line remains blurred, implicating all church members. (John)

Finally, there is a willingness among certain leaders openly to use religion to achieve political ends (Martin).

> Clichés bound in gold-leafed awe
> fly from Pulpit steps –
> loud-mouthed pastors
> goading on their sheep.[25]

---

[22] A completely different language is also used to talk about God – a Catholic would not be able to understand the question 'Are you saved?' (Margaret).

[23] See *Christian* p. 20

[24] See *Christian* pp. 36–7 for a summary of recent developments.

[25] From a poem by Martin Eggleton: *Christian* p. 24

(iv) *Society*

It was Margaret's visit to South Africa that convinced her that a system of apartheid was also operating in Northern Ireland. The divide affects so many areas of life that the occasions where communities are brought together are undermined by the many more when they are separated. Theresa, for example, lived in a housing scheme in Newry with a deliberate policy of mixing tenants.

> My first friends were Protestants, but they went to different schools, learned a different history, played different games,[26] and didn't play with me on the 12th and 13th of July.

Other areas were not so mixed. Theresa had an aunt married to a Protestant and living on the Shankhill. Her aunt had a biblical name which hid her identity, but Theresa had to change her own name whenever she went to visit. She also changed her name whenever she accompanied her Protestant friends to their school sports days.

Susan first thought that the way to peace lay through education. Her experience of schools, however, has led her to believe that the problems begin at home – 'it is not even something done deliberately, it just comes over'. Separate education and leisure activities do, however, continue to keep young people apart. The first time Susan got to know a Catholic was when she went to university, an opportunity missed by the majority of young people. Before students at 'Queen's' can begin to form relationships they appear to undergo a process of 'stripping the labels' and finding the real people underneath (Margaret).

There are signs of less prejudice in Protestant areas where there are only a few Catholics, such as Susan's home town where her church is used during the week by the Catholic Bowling Club. In areas of high tension, however, Bob sees an increased polarisation in all areas of life.

---

[26] While Protestant schools emphasise traditional British sports such as rugby, Catholic schools play Gaelic football and camogie (Margaret, Theresa).

(v) *A yoke of slavery*

In Northern Ireland it would appear that politics, culture, religion, social factors, and violence are all forced on to the same track.[27] 'Politics does not exist in Northern Ireland – more tribalism' (Theresa). 'West Belfast is tribal – everybody knows everybody else and which community they belong to' (Martin).[28] Tribalism seems to be deeply rooted in history and society.[29] While class is a factor, the dominant factor determining political allegiance is ethnic identity.[30] Voting seems to be determined by the accident of birth. Theresa's family was an 'SDLP family'. Whether you vote OUP or DUP depends upon where you live and whether you go to the Presbyterian or the Free Presbyterian Church (Susan). Relatively few Catholics vote Unionist, and a very few Protestants vote SDLP (John). The only exception was when the Protestant minority in West Belfast voted SDLP in a successful attempt to defeat Sinn Fein (Susan, John).

> The vote never changes. It was exactly the same, for example, in the by-elections after the Anglo Irish Accord as it was before the MPs resigned.[31] There are no real leaders in politics, and there are no good alternatives to vote for. (Susan)

Religion and politics are hard to separate.

> We always had an Easter Parade to commemorate the 1916 Uprising. I remember walking to that parade on Sunday

[27] The Opsahl Commission comments that, far from being the work of a minority, violence is integral to the whole community: see Pollak (ed.) p. 60.

[28] See also Downing (ed.), p. 193

[29] David Bleakley in *Christian*, p. 16

[30] Bob saw working class Protestants supporting the UDA, while their middle class equivalents supported the DUP. Susan, however, felt DUP support was based more on religious denomination. Working class Catholics supported Sinn Fein, but people also did so because of family connections (Margaret). Both working and middle class Catholics supported the SDLP (Theresa), and the same is said for the OUP (Bob), while the Alliance Party draws its support from both middle class Protestants and Catholics (Theresa, John).

[31] Unionist MPs had resigned in protest at the Accord and had been re-elected, demonstrating Protestant support for their actions.

morning wearing my wee lily badge. Nationalism is a religion in itself. I remember the feeling of walking in that Easter Parade – it was a spiritual thing. (Theresa)

Theresa also spoke of the confusion among Protestants when she was 'converted'.

As the 'Catholic who got saved' I felt at times like the organ grinder's monkey. Protestants assumed all the time that, being saved, I must have become a Loyalist. People couldn't cope with the fact that, despite being a Christian, I didn't share their political views. (Theresa)[32]

It is very difficult for the individual to change in one area without this unbalancing all the others. The result is a situation of inertia where it is difficult to change at all.

It is very difficult to be a liberal back home, because politics, religion, and identity are all so important. It's very difficult to question and work through things. (Susan)

When you have lived in Northern Ireland all your life, it is very difficult to break out of a single, locked-in vision. And so instead people tend to be inward-looking. (Theresa)

4 *The way forward*

We began the previous section by describing the positions of the various opposing groups, and then saw how far these positions are tangled up in the complex separate identities of the communities which support them, thus making reconciliation very difficult. In such a situation the 'principled negotiation' advocated by Fisher and Ury would seek to identify the underlying concerns which these positions obscure, by focusing on interests, not positions.[33]

---

[32] An ex-IRA convicted terrorist speaks of a similar confusion among his Catholic fellow inmates when he chose to leave sectarianism and become a Christian (in *Christian*, p. 30).
[33] Fisher and Ury, pp. 11, 42, 59

(i) *Common concerns?*

What are the interests that lie behind the conflict in Northern Ireland? Are the communities in Northern Ireland blaming each other for common socio-economic problems?[34] The Opsahl Commission sees poverty as a breeding ground for bigotry,[35] and Margaret described a society, which had endured relative prosperity through ship-building and linen, now suffering recession. Yet Theresa spoke of the Catholic community, which used to be predominantly working class, now with a growing middle class, and, whereas the Catholic poor still looked to the South for a solution to their poverty, the middle class were more realistic (John).[36]

What about discrimination and civil rights? 'Though inequality remains, things are not as bad now' (Susan). The Opsahl Commission itself comments on the small number of submissions it received on this subject.[37] We may conclude that Northern Ireland in the 90s is not the same as Northern Ireland in the 50s and 60s. What then motivates the people to perpetuate the conflict? The answer appears to be fear. A pervasive insecurity appears to characterise the Protestant community, which is embodied in their aggressive intransigence. They fear the South. They fear its supposed poverty (John), and their loss of British welfare benefits (Susan). They fear the influence of the Catholic Church on the South's government, and they fear a loss of Protestant power.[38] They fear a rising Catholic population, wresting

[34] From personal experience, a tactic employed by youth workers confronting racism among young whites in Edinburgh was to focus their attention on their own problems and point out that they shared these with young blacks. By blaming blacks they were looking for scapegoats, rather than dealing effectively with the problems themselves.

[35] Pollak (ed.), p. 79

[36] The domestic policies of the different parties were seen to be the same (Susan). Sinn Fein was increasingly tackling grass roots problems (Theresa, John), while Ian Paisley was a good MP to Catholic and Protestant constituents alike (Susan, Margaret).

[37] Pollak (ed.), p. 32

[38] See John Cooney in *Christian*, p. 37

control of Ulster.[39] They mistrust the British Government and fear their betrayal by it into the hands of the South (Margaret).

> They fear the unknown. They fear the thought that the terrorists might win in the end. They fear the cultural difference. They consider themselves British. Identity is all important. Scottish roots are all important. (Susan)

> Their existence is at stake in their minds. A united Ireland is equivalent to extinction.[40]

The fears of neither side appear to be too firmly grounded in the present. While Protestant fear is based on a pessimistic projection of the future,[41] Catholic fear is heavily influenced by the recent past. Catholics fear the Protestant State. The Opsahl Commission comments on the different perceptions of the police among Protestant and Catholic youth.[42] The latter support the IRA which has defended them against an army and police force which they see as biased against them (Margaret), and defended them against the militant Protestants, who showed their brutal power during the 'Workers' Strike' (Bob).[43] 'All sides in Northern Ireland are prisoners of a victim theology which sees the other side as the aggressor'.[44]

Do the opposing communities share common interests?

> They have shared the economic ups and downs, although there are fewer deprived areas now – more Catholic than

[39] Brian Lennon SJ writes: 'What Catholics for the most part do not realise is that Protestants are afraid. And they are afraid because for the past two centuries they have seen their power on the island gradually decline and their numbers slowly dwindle towards the North-East' (*Christian*, p. 20).

[40] Pollak (ed.), p. 40, quoting Mr Frank Curran.

[41] The Opsahl Commission gives an illustration of how this fear can pay little attention to fact. In Derry the Catholic-controlled City Council shares power with the Protestants in a manner which they feel to be entirely reasonable and a paradigm for the treatment of Protestants in a united Ireland. But this has not prevented the Protestant population from moving out: Pollak (ed.), p. 40.

[42] Pollak (ed.), p. 61.

[43] Supported by the views of an ex-IRA man: *Christian*, p. 27

[44] Pollak (ed.), p. 97.

> Protestant. They are both victims of the violence of a polarised society. There are very very few families now who have not been touched by violence. (John)

It appears that any relationship which the conflict might have had with the socio-economic situation is growing more and more remote. The agenda is now set by the conflict itself. The nature of the threat the communities face is bound up in the very identity of the communities themselves.

> There might be common problems, but they are not shared problems, that is, the two communities are not aware that they share them. (Bob)

> I sometimes imagine a sketch where there are two sets of marchers separated by a wall, and they are both shouting the same slogans. (Theresa)

We have been looking for common concerns, and have found only fear.

(ii) *Perception of trends*
Are there any signs of change in the conflict in Northern Ireland?

> They will never change. (Bob)

> Things will get really bad – I mean civil war – before they get any better. People forced into a situation will fight back. (Susan, Theresa)[45]

Change, however, was seen to be slowly taking place, particularly demographic change, as more and more young people leave – Protestants to the mainland, Catholics to the South (Bob, John).[46] There is a growing sense of the inevitable among Protestants (John), and, with the growing influence of the EEC, there is the possibility of changing attitudes to nationhood (John). People are also getting fed up with violence (Susan).

[45] A retrenchment of attitudes was in process among Protestants (Robin Eames in *Christian*, p. 7).
[46] Pollak (ed.), p. 97.

Within the Catholic community the SDLP are gaining in popularity at the expense of Sinn Fein (Susan).[47]

Yet, before the 1994 cease fire, it was difficult to be optimistic in the face of political and para-military intransigence.

> Before Christmas (1993), all of a sudden there was hope. Hope of a lasting peace before Christmas. Hope that, with the influence of Europe, the border had outlived its usefulness. But, when the violence didn't stop, this was followed by total disillusionment and weariness. (Theresa)

People are weary of conflict, but their attitude seems to be more apathetic than constructive.

> The call went out at Christmas to all churches in Newry to congregate at the town centre to demonstrate their support for peace. Only a couple of hundred turned up, whereas a couple of thousand went to the nearby shopping centre instead. A lot of people are tired, but despairing that it is ever going to end. (Theresa)

(iii) *A common theme of freedom*

According to Tillich, a love that is without justice destroys the lover as well as the loved.[48] In Northern Ireland, each community's love of itself is fuelled by its hatred of and injustice towards the other. Our interviewees have given us an indication of the dehumanisation and destruction that has resulted. Yet the unjust love we have found has been conditioned by the structures and institutions of the society there.

> My views have changed since I came to Scotland. I would never have said that my Mum and Dad were prejudiced, but over here I see things in a different light. Before, I rejected the thought of a united Ireland, but now I feel that a united Ireland is probably the only solution.... I had to get away to

[47] Wood & Wood (*The Times Guide to the House of Commons*, Times Books: London 1992, p. 92) report on the change in the Sinn Fein vote: from 13.4 per cent in 1982 to 10 per cent in 1992.

[48] Tillich, pp. 68, 78.

see things in perspective. Now I feel the need to go back and do something. (Susan)

Northern Ireland society proclaims itself to be Christian, but appears to allow little freedom to the Christian to respond, as a Christian, to the conflict within it. We have seen how division, fuelled by fear, is institutionalised at many levels in the social structure. Tillich describes such institutional authority as 'unjust authority', as it '... disregards the intrinsic claim of human beings to become responsible for ultimate decisions'.[49] 'Unjust authority' needs to be replaced with the 'authority of fact'[50] – people need to be free to deal with things as they find them, and not as they are told they are, nor as they fear they might be.

Fisher and Ury stress the need for 'creative thinking',[51] where negotiators break free from the single line upon which positions are presumed to lie, and think instead of the different options in a situation where there is no single answer. There appears to be a need to break free from the structures of authority in Northern Ireland society, which are restricting the possibility of creative thinking, and thereby restricting the options of those seeking reconciliation. Moltmann writes of the freedom achieved through sharing a 'common project'.[52] Are there common projects through which the Christian communities of Northern Ireland can break free? Are there issues they can tackle together?

(iv) *Christians breaking free*

Paradoxically, it is among the institutionally powerless of Northern Ireland that we find the greater opportunity of freedom. It is at the grass roots level that the signs are most evident of people breaking free.[53] Conversely, the higher they find themselves located within the institutions of society, the

[49] Ibid., pp. 89–90.
[50] Ibid., p. 90.
[51] Fisher and Ury, p. 59.
[52] Moltmann, pp. 216–8.
[53] It is amongst the youth of Northern Ireland, for example, that we find a willingness to share sports and leisure activities, and the traditional music interpreted by the likes of Van Morrison (Margaret).

less freedom they appear to have. This point is illustrated by institutionalised religion.

> Religion is the biggest obstacle to Christianity in Ireland. Pride gets mixed up with it. Pride in tradition. People need to stop being so defensive about their traditions. God doesn't need to defend himself. (Theresa)

> When you see faith through the eyes of the Church, you end up with its political hangups too. (John)

> Christian denominations are propping up a vision which is not in the heart of God. (Margaret)

Church leadership appears to be bound by traditions which hold people back (Martin).[54] Integrated education, for example, is seen by many as a key way to bring about peaceful co-existence (Theresa), yet the Catholic Church hierarchy refuses to recognise this. Nor does it take seriously enough the impact its ruling on mixed marriages has on the fears of the Protestant community.[55] Theresa recalled the end of a large ecumenical renewal conference which took place in Dublin in the 70s. On the Saturday specific instructions were sent out to all Catholic participants forbidding them to receive the Eucharist with the others on Sunday. Two separate eucharistic celebrations had to be set up, and the climax to a great occasion was marred. Within the Protestant leadership there is also little sign of a breaking free.

> The degree of openness to the Catholic community depends upon who is the moderator of the church that year.... It is left to individual churches to take the initiative, and the result is often tokenism. (Susan)

> There is a general unwillingness to rock the wider church boat. (John)

> It is very difficult for the leaders in any of the churches to

---

[54] Both Martin and Margaret also commented on the strong links with Freemasonry within the Protestant church leadership.
[55] See e.g., Pollak (ed.), p. 121

remain within the structures and retain their integrity. We have learned from the 70s that talking is not enough. (Theresa)[56]

In contrast, at the grass roots level there are signs of real hope.

I have a simple faith – if we believe in Jesus, we are the Church.... There is another dimension in Ireland as a whole: a Christian dimension. There is a growing number of people who are willing to say that denominations are not important enough to allow this to continue, who are willing to step outside their communal boundaries and do and say things. In the past they may have only gone so far and stopped short, but not any more. (Theresa)

Martin spoke warmly of the house fellowship that he had attended when on his last tours of duty.

They were a mixture of Catholics, Protestants, soldiers, and the odd atheist – only God could bring that about. I attended them for two years. I was making myself and my family very vulnerable and had to put my trust in the people there and in God. (Martin)

The Opsahl Commission notes the existence of lay-based house fellowships, but finds them opposed by the majority of church members.[57] John saw the solution to the conflict lying in the renewal of the churches from within. He was not alone.

God's love has got to come from the bottom, and seep up the tree through the branches .... I have seen it happening. It may take twenty years but the change will come. (Martin).[58]

---

[56] Brian Lennon had this to say on this matter: 'Sometimes in Northern Ireland people talk about reconciliation when what they really mean is "Let's all come together the way we are without changing anything". That of course is not reconciliation, but merely a way of maintaining the power that groups have' (*Christian*, p. 19).

[57] Pollak (ed.), p. 60

[58] Alf McCreary comments that while peacemaking is a slow and painful process, it is not without hope (in *Christian*, p. 5).

Christians are also among those at the forefront of the work to bring about reconciliation in society in general. The Opsahl Commission finds that the churches are producing people who are prepared to work as well as pray.[59]

(v) *Breaking free in society*
The direct relationship between institutional powerlessness and freedom to act which is seen in the church is also seen in other institutions of society. The need to hold talks with those associated with violence is seen as a necessary step on the road to peace (Susan, Theresa).[60] But when John Hume of the SDLP attempted to do so in 1993, the other political leaders were quick to draw back and leave him isolated and exposed (Theresa, Bob). Yet at the grass roots level, there is a growing number of practical peace initiatives, ranging from 'doing good by stealth' (e.g., different local churches helping each other out financially), to Women Together for Peace,[61] The Movement for Integrated Education, and Families against Intimidation and Terror.[62]

Both Margaret and Theresa had been involved in the Christian Renewal Centre at Rostrevor. This is an ecumenical community which brings people from diverse backgrounds together to share in fellowship, prayer, and regular communion, wishing to be a '...living sign of organic unity' (Margaret). Bob had been involved in the Corrymeela Community, which 'provided a neutral location where people could meet and talk of common problems such as bereavement, or the difficulties of mixed marriages' (Bob).[63] Both Corrymeela and the Renewal Centre are lay organised, and both aim to change society through the people that pass through them. The sign seen

[59] Pollak (ed.), p. 104

[60] See also Pollak (ed.), p. 60

[61] The Opsahl Commission comments on the greater likelihood of peace if more women were involved in the politicial process: Pollak (ed.), p. 119.

[62] *Peace Matters*, July 1993, p. 16, gives a number of examples.

[63] See also R. Davey, *An Unfinished Journey*, Corrymeela Press, (c.1987), and A. McCreary, *Corrymeela - The Search for Peace* (1975).

when departing the Corrymeela Centre reads: 'Corrymeela begins when you leave'.[64]

The role being played by the peace groups may be small (John), and it is acknowledged that their existence does not equal a political settlement,[65] yet their symbolic importance is great. They are signs of people breaking free, widening their options, and finding common projects. Perhaps most significant of all, they reflect a basic Christian principle: that God can use those who are on the fringes of power in society to show the powerful the way of true discipleship.[66]

Conclusions

In what way does our brief examination of the situation in Northern Ireland tie in with the Christian views of reconciliation outlined at the beginning? If we accept Moltmann's view that 'a person is only God's image in relation to other people',[67] then the disunity and conflict in Ireland stands in judgement over the persons living there and all who have had a part in bringing about the present situation. Yet we have also seen evidence that Christians are at the forefront of a grass roots determination to reunite communities estranged by conflict.

The notion of wholeness through relationship provides a Christian framework for reconciliation. Relationship implies difference. As Christians we relate to a God and to our neighbour, both of whom are different from ourselves. The challenge of forming relationships lies in the reconciling of differences. Such reconciliation requires three steps: recognising differences, dealing with any difficulties these may be causing to a lasting relationship; and forgiving any hurt, pain, and bitterness that might have resulted. We find evidence of all three steps among our interviewees.

[64] See Davey, Part X.
[65] See *Christian*, p. 38
[66] The Christian's call is not to be successful, but to be faithful (Bill Arlow in *Christian*, p. 39).
[67] Moltmann, p. 155.

The first step requires the acknowledgement that unity is not necessarily uniformity (or 'identity', as Tillich put it[68]). While communal differences are a way of life in the North, they do not necessarily have to result in antagonism. 'You didn't have to be antagonistic to be different' (Theresa). 'Catholics weren't really an issue to me. I wasn't naturally suspicious of them' (Bob). 'Roman Catholics may have different doctrines, but they are still worshipping the same God' (Susan).

Some also acknowledged the need for the second step.

In the 70s we had the attitude that differences didn't matter. So we didn't actually deal with them, and they didn't go away. (Theresa)

Corrymeela has not tried to smooth out the differences. It has tried to accept differences and to talk frankly about them. Corrymeela has been described as the place where you don't have to whisper.[69]

The third step, that of forgiveness, is seen by Tillich as the principle which underlies creative justice, and the only way to 'be reaccepted into the unity to which (we) belong', thereby affirming our very being.[70]

But mutual forgiveness is justice only if it is based on reuniting love, in justification by grace. Only God can forgive, because in him alone love and justice are completely united.[71]

Is forgiveness a gift from God? It was the simple faith and extraordinary forgiveness shown by his grandmother which laid the foundations of Bob's involvement in peacemaking: behaviour which was all the more extraordinary in a society where forgiveness is seen as an act of weakness.[72]

---

[68] Tillich, p. 111.
[69] McCreary, p. 117.
[70] Tillich, p. 86.
[71] Ibid., p. 121.
[72] Maura Kiely, herself a victim of violence through the murder of her only son, sees weakness rather displayed in the desire for revenge (in *Christian*, p. 23).

My mother told me some of the background. They were living in Belfast at the time of the curfews and the Black and Tans. My grandfather had been a policeman. He was on patrol with the Black and Tans when he was shot. In the 20s there was a very anti-Catholic riot in Belfast. Granny lived in a 'mixed' street, and it was to her the Catholic neighbours brought their statues and crucifixes to hide, so that the Black and Tans wouldn't be able to identify them. She was very upset when she learned that the Black and Tans had killed some Catholics in retaliation for her husband's murder.

If forgiveness is a gift from God, then so too is the reconciliation it brings about:

> Unity is God's gift. It is not something to be constructed, it is there to be received and demonstrated. But there are very few free thinkers – those who are 'Kingdom of God conscious'. One such is a Protestant minister I know, who regularly goes for walks with the local Catholic priest. He demonstrates in his daily life in front of the local community what he teaches about faith. (Margaret)

But there is an element of risk in reaching out to grasp unity. Theresa spoke of another young Protestant minister who had crossed the street to wish his neighbouring Catholic priest a happy Christmas, and had had his life and calling destroyed by the persecution from his congregation which had resulted. Martin has already spoken of the vulnerability of his position as he attended mixed house fellowships. In his book on Corrymeela, Ray Davey comments that reconciliation does not come without much pain and anguish.[73] Yet Tillich comments that 'the power of God is that he overcomes estrangement, not that he prevents it...'.[74] It is the power of God's love, made manifest through his Holy Spirit which seems to be producing the extraordinary in Northern Ireland, the extraordinary

---

[73] See Davey, Part X.
[74] Tillich, pp. 112–3.

which shows that it is possible to be free to love, to forgive, and to be at peace with difference.

I remember once I was leading a patrol in a border area when we stopped a bus. It was full of Catholics from a part of the South which was renowned for its IRA sympathies. We stopped them as they passed our base, and there was a number of soldiers watching, as well as surveillance cameras trained on them. There was an ichthus sign on the windscreen of the bus. I asked the lads to wait and I got on. I was wearing all my gear – helmet, flak-jacket, and carrying my gun. As I got on all eyes in the bus were on me. I realised that they were singing a renewal chorus – 'Lord Jesus, we enthrone you'. I found myself joining in. I saw their jaws dropping, as they began to realise that all of us – a soldier and a bunch of pilgrims – knew Jesus and felt we were doing God's work. The confusion, the love, and the understanding were all there for fifteen seconds on that bus. As I turned to get off again they burst into applause. (Martin)

*****

Appendix I : Interview questions

1 Personal background.
2 Assessment of current situation:
    a)   Identifying the different parties involved (political or other) –
      i Who are they?
      ii What are their stated positions?
    b)   Identifying the issues –
      i Who supports them?
      ii What are their supporters' underlying interests?
    c)   The way forward –
      i What interests / values / experiences are there in common?
      ii What is the way forward?
3 To what extent has Christianity been part of the problem, and can it be part of the solution?

Appendix II : The political bodies

The Official Unionist Party (OUP), representing the majority of Protestants, aims to bring about a more just Ulster wherein Catholics have their required civil rights, but without relinquishing Protestant power (Bob). They are the more moderate (Susan) and open (Margaret) Protestant body, and are displaying an increasing recognition of the need to acknowledge the views of the 'South' (John).[75] Martin does not see them as being very influential on the political stage.

Their moderate counterparts are the Social Democratic Labour Party (SDLP), which represents the majority of Catholics. The SDLP aims to bring about a united Ireland by democratic means (Bob, Susan, Margaret, Martin), recognising the need to co-operate with the Southern Government in so doing (John).[76] The party was formed after the recent troubles began, and has competed with Sinn Fein for the Catholic vote, especially in West Belfast (Martin). The SDLP is seen by Protestants as the more reasonable face of Catholicism – Bob and Martin both see its aims as legitimate.

At the more extreme level we find Sinn Fein and the Democratic Unionist Party (DUP). DUP, led by Ian Paisley, sees the OUP as too willing to compromise (Theresa). Ulster is portrayed by Paisley as the 'Promised Land', covenanted by God to his people, and needing to be 'cleansed' of 'anti-Christ' Catholicism, which may require 'Jericho' type battles to be fought and won (Margaret).[77] The DUP are a militant outcrop from the OUP. Their aim is to return Ulster to its pre-troubles state (Bob), keeping the South's influence 'across the border' (John, Susan), and trusting the Queen but not the British Government (Martin).

Sinn Fein have an equally powerful ideological footing. The Irish nation has been subjected to foreign British rule for centuries. At last the South has been liberated, but the six

[75] The OUP 1992 election manifesto emphasised Ulster's maintainence of constitutional power (Wood & Wood, p. 367).

[76] The SDLP manifesto stresses the need for civil rights for all citizens.

[77] The DUP manifesto stresses the need to use the powers of the state to fight terrorism.

counties of the North remain in British hands (Theresa). The 1922 partitioning of Ireland was artificial and therefore is not recognised. The views of the people of Ireland as a whole must be the basis for decision making (John). Sinn Fein is the militant expression of Catholic nationalism (Margaret, John). Claiming to represent the people (Martin), they are committed to a united (Bob, Susan) socialist (Theresa) Ireland,[78] and (at least until 1994) have not excluded violence as a means to that end (Susan). They contest constituencies throughout Ireland, but their only real support has been in the North and following the demise of the Stormont Parliament (Bob).

Beyond Sinn Fein and the DUP are the outlawed 'paramilitary' organisations. On the Protestant side there is the Ulster Defence Association (UDA) and the more extreme (John, Bob) Ulster Freedom Fighters (UFF). Bob compares these organisations with South Africa's AWB. 'They frighten me more than anything. They have considerable support and are well armed.' Their 'siege mentality' (Bob) aims to maintain the *status quo* by violent means, and to retaliate against IRA attacks (Theresa) – a ceasefire was, however, declared in October 1994. Although denials are made, they have links with the political parties (John). The Irish Republican Army (IRA), which is the predominant Catholic para-military organisation, is similarly linked with Sinn Fein (John), with whom it shares its ideology (Margaret).

The Alliance Party's non-sectarian stance (Theresa, Susan) has attempted to unite the different communities, but has achieved little support (Bob, Susan, Theresa).[79] The Conservative Party's attempt to establish itself was short-lived and resulted in persecution for the families involved (Susan).

[78] The Sinn Fein manifesto is concerned with getting the Governments of Britain and Eire to accept their aim of a united Ireland.
[79] The Alliance manifesto focuses on local government issues.

II   Caring – The Ethics of Community Care and Development   *(Pauline Steenbergen)*

To the politician, 'community care' is a useful piece of rhetoric; to the sociologist, it is the stick to beat institutional care with; to the civil servant, it is a cheap alternative to institutional care which can be passed to the local authorities for action – or inaction; to the visionary, it is the dream of a new society in which people really do care; to the social service departments, it is a nightmare of public expectations and inadequate resources to meet them. We are only just beginning to find out what it means to the old, the chronic sick and the handicapped.[1]

Our second study focuses specifically on perhaps the most vulnerable and the least understood of the groups who receive community care, namely people with mental health problems.[2] 'Caring' is a fundamental concept of Christian ethics. It is appropriate, therefore, to examine the ethical aspects of community care in relation to this constituency and in so doing to focus also on social, political and theological aspects of the problem. Throughout, reference is made to Great Britain, but the issues are not confined within national boundaries.

1 *The conception and formation of community care*

At the outset it is crucial to say that people with mental health problems were living in the community prior to legislation and before it was thought preferable to care for them in institutions. But this was not the norm. Until almost fifty years ago society

[1] Jones, Brown, Bradshaw, *Issues in Social Policy* (1978), p. 114.
[2] Chief groups are: (i) elderly people and those with dementia; (ii) people with learning disabilities; (iii) people with physical disabilities; (iv) people with mental health problems; (v) people with alcohol related problems; (vi) people with drug problems; and (vii) people living with HIV or AIDS. People may be in more than one group. On people with mental health problems, cf. J. Foskett, *Meaning in Madness* (1984).

cared for sufferers in asylums. The nineteenth-century asylum was intended to provide refuge and shelter from exploitation and destitution. It was also a product of the Victorian preoccupation with moral improvement. The result was segregation of sufferers from the rest of society: custodial care or paternalism.[3]

In the 1950s the number of residents in institutions began to decline. This is attributable to the following developments:

(i) Psychiatry was a growing specialisation in the medical field. Mental disorder was recognised as a disease which could be treated physically. New drugs and therapies were being discovered and used, shortening the length of stay in hospital for many sufferers. After-care and rehabilitation became a new focus for care. Also it was recognised that institutional care was producing psychiatric symptoms in patients, compounding their illness.

(ii) In 1959 (England) and 1960 (Scotland), the Mental Health Act brought about a huge shift in health and social policy. It was the germ of the new ethic, moving care away from the institutions. This proposal gathered momentum in the 60s and 70s. The media showed up scandals within mental hospitals and there was a growth of literature on the evils of institutions. R. D. Laing championed an anti-psychiatry movement, emphasising the role of psychology. Civil liberties were the agenda of the day, presenting a stark contrast to the repressive and authoritarian institutions. These social influences affected Government policy. In the Hospital Plan (1962), support was given to community based health care. However, despite a decline in the number of institutional residents, few follow-up services had materialised in the community even by the mid-70s. Pessimism, recession and a curb on public spending, meant that the practice of community care lagged far behind the theory.

[3] The standard book is E. Murphy, *After the Asylums* (1991).

(iii) In the 1980s awareness of the reality of community care developed. This was partly due to a growing awareness of the neglect of discharged patients. However, progress was still slow. The Government hesitated because it was neither a priority nor a vote winner. Hospitals underwent closures and cutbacks with few alternatives developed in the community. The costs involved in running old and decaying hospitals remained the same. The Griffiths Report of 1988 was a breakthrough in formulating policy and practice. It recommended:

(a) The appointment of a Minister of State for community care.
(b) Transfer of all community care to local authorities.
(c) Ring-fencing of grants partly funded by central Government.
(d) Local authorities to be empowered to buy in services from other agencies.

Not all of these proposals reached the White Paper. In 1989, the Department of Health issued 'Caring for people – community care in the next decade and beyond'. Six key objectives shaped the ethic of care which we have now:

(i)   promoting the development of domiciliary, day and respite services;
(ii) practical support for carers;
(iii) assessing needs;
(iv) promotion of independent sector services;
(v)   accountability of service agencies for performance;
(vi) new funding structure for care.

In 1990 the NHS and Community Care Act was passed.[4] Despite delays, the Act took effect from April 1993. Closures will continue and long term patients will be discharged with only acute secure wards remaining in hospital care.

---

[4] The essential components of the Act were phased as follows: inspection units (1991); complaints procedures (1991); planning (1992); assessment and case management (1993); purchasing/contracting (1993).

2 *Community care as a moral principle*

The ethics of community care and development involves a combination of principles. It is based on the belief that segregation is wrong and must be replaced. While the word 'community' suggests emphasis on corporateness, care is based on the individual's needs, rights, choices and freedom. These rights are held as a member of society, irrespective of gender, ethnic origin or physical/mental ability. Care provision rests heavily on families and is supported by the primary services. Carers, therefore, will be and are diverse. This fosters a holistic approach and collaborative care. Such an ethic is very attractive ideologically. It suggests close knit communities, like extended families, providing support in a morally acceptable way. Thus for sufferers, carers and the community, there is great appeal. However, the philosophy of community care needs further examination.

Each of the four carers I interviewed for this study, and the four individuals I know who have mental health problems, support the principle of care in the community. It is accepted that sufferers prefer to live outside of hospitals. It is not so clear that families prefer to care for their relatives at home. I would like to give three examples of the strong preference sufferers have to live in the community by sharing something of their stories.

CASE STUDIES

Jane was hospitalised at the age of ten and did not live in the community until her mid-thirties. Her memories of hospital care are painful. Once, because she threatened to break a window, she was locked in a room for a week, and her parents were refused visiting rights. She was thirteen. After living in hospital hostels, she eventually lived with her mother until the latter died three years ago. Jane is very lonely and often depressed. But she prefers to live in the community on her own.

Alex has been in and out of hospital, seeing countless professionals, and has had almost every treatment and therapy. He has always been treated as ill. He is intelligent but has great difficulty with social relations. Despite this he enjoys living in the community, though it is challenging and often distressing. He feels more misunderstood in hospital.

Robb fell when he was nine and suffered brain injuries. He got into trouble later and spent 25 years in a psychiatric prison. He lives in supported accommodation and needs daily medication. He has applied for council flats and is desperate to live on his own, partly because of his experiences in prison. However his support workers believe he would not manage and would end up on the streets. Robb has often said he would prefer this.

The preference for community care rather than hospitalisation is clear, but there is just the suggestion that it is the lesser evil. Those who originally proposed community care as an alternative to hospital care intended to improve care and services. How can community care succeed if this is not done?

The language of equal rights and choice, on which community care is based, is very appealing. But the language of rights is normative and not always practicable. How do we solve a situation when rights conflict? Local authorities are faced with this as they prioritise whose needs are most urgent. Will it be the single parent who has AIDS or the Asian man with schizophrenia? And is the right to have shelter more expedient than occupation? Care based on rights alone is difficult to administer. Furthermore these rights must be recognised by the rest of society. It is not clear that this is so.

The philosophy of rights is an individualistic ethic. This is magnified in a health care system based on market forces. The market is created by a demand (local authorities) and by suppliers (private and voluntary sector services). Somewhere in between are the sufferers and their carers. In many ways their rights are meaningless because they will be led by cost. The poor in urban and inner city areas will have less choice and less freedom and less care because of overstretched budgets. In the market there are winners and losers. What of the rights of the losers?

Much of the philosophy of community care as it is at present has been shaped by Conservative politics. Since the 80s individualism has been actively promoted, yet community care has been presented as a liberal and humane development. Of course, it serves political purposes to move health care into the private realm if it results in a cut in public spending by central Government. Official spokespersons refuse to admit that the plans are underfunded or that funding increases are below the level of inflation, and attempt to shift the blame for shortcomings to local authorities. Yet local authorities have an impossible task ahead, strait-jacketed by inadequate funds and an overwhelming remit. Responsibility has been decentralised and the Government prefer a *laissez faire* approach. Moreover, opposition parties have said very little, and have not adequately criticised the Government's philosophy of community care. There seems to be a lack of knowledge about the plans and uncertainty about the way ahead.

The general consensus from all bodies, organisations, projects, departments, authorities and the media is that community care is desperately underfunded. This has been the main worry of the carers I have spoken to.[5] Figures published by MIND show that there is a shortfall of at least £139 million. Even if taxation must be raised, more money is needed from central Government to make community care work. It is not a cheap option.

Murphy believes that the organisational problems are greater than the funding arrangements. So far there has been a lack of co-operation between local authorities, health boards and social work departments. Yet they need to work closely to provide anything like a seamless service. There is also a great deal of uncertainty and anxiety about the care plans.[6] The

---

[5] For example, Callum Stocks at the Stopover Hostel in Edinburgh fears closure and no alternative but the streets for the young homeless in his care. David Kellock, Deputy Director of the Board of Social Responsibility (Church of Scotland) told me that his department is presently in battle with the Scottish Office over resource transfers because they are unrealistic and inadequate. He and his colleagues have decided not to charge families for the shortfall, which he referred to as the care gap. Undoubtedly lack of resources will determine levels of care. The only ring-fenced grant for mental health ends in 1994. Also, no research or costing was done beforehand on the effect of Government policy.

[6] Angiolina Fraser, Department of Housing for Lothian Regional Council, professed anger about the burden placed on local authorities. They are now legally bound to assess needs and to meet them.

Griffiths recommendation for a government minister for community care does not appear to have been taken seriously. Staffing is also a problem; there have been adverts for care managers in the newspapers. More nurses are moving into the private sector and we are only beginning to realise how labour-intensive community care actually is.

If community care is *terra incognita* for the decision makers, I fear that the community itself is even less prepared for the changes. There is a lack of public knowledge and a great need for education. The media are not always helpful. We are influenced by stories such as that of the 27 year old schizophrenic mauled by a lion. Neighbours in urban areas already know of house fires, night time disturbances and frightening episodes. Many believe that sufferers cannot cope in the community. It is essential to combat fear, ignorance, and anxiety about the people who perhaps look, speak and act differently. They are in fact more vulnerable than we are. Social care is the mainstay of community care. We need to learn how to be a community for sufferers. Two weeks ago, an epileptic had a fit outside the soup kitchen in the Grassmarket in Edinburgh, where I live. None of us really knew what to do; eventually we called an ambulance. The incident emphasised the need to know what to do and what services are available: most of all to be aware of needs in our neighbourhood. This is especially true of the mentally ill. Murphy and Pattison draw attention to the fact that normalisation is not straightforward. Illness may relapse or recur. Community care does not cure the illness and we must be sensitive to this. We must also have no illusions about the state of the community sufferers are coming into. Our communities are not extended families. They are crumbling and need the rebuilding of a sense of corporateness.

Community care is based mainly on social care and not medical care. Ordinary needs are shelter, food, clothing, income, occupation and social interaction. Emotional and spiritual needs must also be recognised. Even these basic needs will be difficult to meet for many. Housing stocks in Scotland are already low and in Edinburgh 26,000 are on a waiting list; 6,000 are homeless (1993). There are several voluntary sector Housing Associations providing supported or independent flats. Yet it is all too easy to create a ghetto. Worse still are the emergency accommodation options: hostels (48 to a dorm), B&Bs, or the long stay wards of the streets. To live in a flat long-term sufferers need a lot of support, such as help with domestic chores, personal hygiene and financial matters. They also desire a lot of contact. As one chaplain at a psychiatric hospital told me, the biggest fear for patients about to be discharged is loneliness and isolation. Support and contact are vital. For instance in one Penumbra flat there are eleven sufferers and six support workers. This is highly labour intensive and also costly. One man I know got a council flat but has little support. He is frantically worried that he will not be able to pay bills and comes to soup kitchens because he cannot cook. Boredom is a common complaint and there seem to be no proposals to provide occupation as part of the care plan.

The needs and demands differ geographically. Urban areas and inner cities have the highest needs and yet this is not accounted for in the budgets given to local authorities. Neither has the Government addressed the correlation between poverty, unemployment and mental illness. Furthermore, ethnic minorities have a high incidence of mental illness. MIND says that their needs are not being fully understood or consulted. Women are also more likely to be sufferers and/or carers where the responsibility falls on families. Are their needs really being addressed? Simon Miller, of Edinburgh Association for Mental Health, said more and more single mothers with mental health problems are applying for housing. These needs give rise to the ethical question of who will fight on behalf of those with unmet needs. How easy will this be, especially in the light of cuts in funding for legal aid? I am conscious of this because the competition for care is going to grow in the next decade. The numbers of elderly needing care is rising, as are those with HIV and AIDS. Who will be our priority for care? How will we decide and who will fight for the neglected?

While many of these problems are not insurmountable, it is right to be morally ambivalent about community care. Pattison vehemently says: 'Community care might simply be a

euphemism for community neglect.'[7] This fear is not
uncommon, but the attitude is too negative. Murphy comments
that there is nothing wrong with the concept of community
care. 'For a variety of reasons we are making a hash of doing it
properly.'[8] These reasons at present are all too clear.

3 *The theological basis of the ethics of community care*

Presenting a critique of our community and its care of the most
vulnerable raises theological issues. Even if there is a tension
between medicine, social work and religion, and even if
theology's response has been nervous or inaudible, it is crucial
that its contribution is heard.

Christian ethics can help to reshape and transform
community care. A positive vision can be found in the egalitarian
and inclusive community adumbrated in Gal. 3:28: 'There is
now no difference between Jews and Gentiles, between slaves
and free, between men and women; you are all one in Christ
Jesus.' Full integration of individuals is the hallmark of the
community. It is not based on individual rights, but on
interdependence and responsibilities to others. This is
symbolised in the church as Christ's body, all parts inextricably
intertwined and dependent on one another. Community may
be defined as rootedness.[9] If this were the basis of community
care it would speak volumes to those who feel strange and are
strangers. What would this community be like in practice? An
ethics of *koinonia* should:

(a) offer love, security and significance;
(b) test shallow and inauthentic forms of togetherness,
      belonging and co-operation;
(c) judge hypocritical conceptions of community: e.g.,
      racist or anti-feminist;
(d) approach realistically the structural and institutional
      barriers in society, where genuine community requires

---

[7] S. Pattison, *Alive and Kicking* (1989), p. 118.
[8] Murphy, p. 3.
[9] A. Campbell (ed.), *A Dictionary of Pastoral Care* (1990), p. 43.

> a power balance rooted in justice e.g., problems in inner city areas cannot be isolated from wider structural facts and conflicts.[10]

This is not utopian. A community like this is essential for all of us.

This kind of blueprint has been addressed and put into practice by Christians in developing countries, as liberation theology bears witness, especially in Latin America. Feminist ethicists like R. Reuther have argued the need for base communities in the West. This need is seen to arise out of social justice issues, which Christians must tackle. Pattison is vehement about this in his book *Alive and Kicking*. He asks us in Britain to look at structural issues. The mentally ill in our society are the poor and the dispossessed. This minority is powerless and oppressed. Christians must seek justice and change political structures. Moreover their role is to restore a corporate identity and belonging. For me this is our moral vision, expressed in Christ's words and ministry. Of the sixteen healing accounts in the Gospels, eight are associated with mental illness, e.g., the epileptic boy,[11] the Gerasene man,[12] Mary Magdalene,[13] to name but a few. Jesus not only restored health, he also restored the sufferer back into the community. These acts were also the first-fruits of the Kingdom. Let us feel the implications of the words, 'I was a stranger and you welcomed me' (Matt. 25:35).

The churches must become involved in community care and in helping to change it, primarily because they must continue Christ's work and mission if they are to be true to their calling. We must indeed love our neighbour as ourselves. The mentally ill are or will be our neighbours, as they are mine in the Grassmarket. Perhaps what we can do immediately is to support and care for those in congregations who are caring for a sufferer in their family. This may involve many levels of

[10] R. Preston in *A Dictionary of Pastoral Care* (1990), p. 94.
[11] Matt. 17:14–20, Mark 9:14–21, Luke 9:37–43.
[12] Mark 5:1–20, Luke 8:26–39.
[13] Mark 16:9, Luke 8:2.

support, from respite care to simply listening and sharing the load. Ministers and church leaders have an important role in creating awareness and motivating their members. Those in churches can help to change policy and effect future improvements to community care. Yet political issues are often neglected by congregations. David Kellock, for example, claims to be frustrated by the lack of support the Board of Responsibility gets from the members of the Church of Scotland. Yet its work is very much at the front line of community issues and problems. It is also the biggest voluntary organisation in the country with amazing potential and experience.

However, some churches are struggling with the problems and doing what they can. St George's West in Edinburgh was forced to meet the needs of its parish in order to exist. Some years ago it began an open door programme. Today the lower suite of halls is used by the National Schizophrenic Fellowship, one of the main city centre projects for advice and day care. Upstairs, the restaurant opens six days a week. It is staffed by church members and people with mental health problems. Alex, who is epileptic and has never had a job, told me that, but for the provision made by the church, he'd be back in hospital: 'if this isn't Christian love, I don't know what is'. Love is perhaps as valuable as cure. Grainger says the church has a restorative function whch is a 'corporate affirmation of an underlying solidarity'.[14] This solidarity is the heart of our eucharistic celebration and should be open to all, as the offer of our hospitality.

4. *The ethics of development*

As a conclusion to her book Murphy writes:

> We must make community care work if we are to avoid slipping yet further into a pre-Dickensian era of neglect. The vision of real community care needs a united effort to push it back on to the political agenda.[15]

[14] R. Grainger, *Watching for Wings* (1979).
[15] Murphy, p. 236.

Development is crucial to make good community care happen. Murphy comments on how valuable churches are because of their rich resources. This is not just in terms of finance, but also buildings and volunteers. There is going to be an increasing need for voluntary sector services. I'd like to mention STEPS as an example of a service which may be developed in other situations.

STEPS meets in Greyfriars Kirk House in the heart of the Grassmarket. It services people with mental health problems, addiction problems and the homeless; or all three. When it started some years ago in another location, the initial aim was to teach people new skills and provide occupation: e.g., bag-making and candle-making. Over the years it has evolved as a place to find company, a meal, and refuge. Socialisation seems to be the greatest need. The ethic underlying this project is hospitality. Volunteers cook the meal and befriend the customers. Jane says her closest friends are at STEPS and they are the main source of companionship for three hours every week. Mike Sturrock, who runs the service, hopes it will continue as long as the church lends its premises and as long as it is needed.

In developing services it is essential that they are person centred. Murphy emphasises the need for consultation and participation of users in all plans. Even the best services may not cure mental illness, but can at least take away some of the pressure and loneliness from those now living outside of the hospital. One exciting development was suggested to me by a hospital chaplain who is about to begin a part-time experiment in community psychiatric chaplaincy. She will offer pastoral support to carers, statutory and voluntary. Mostly she will be available at a local health centre, offering support to sufferers in the community. She also hopes to liaise with ministers and congregations to develop their caring roles and to offer advice and support. This is an excellent development, which offers care to people where they are.

Conclusion

Reading and researching some of the aspects of the ethics of community care and development has had a massive impact on me. While I believe in the principle of community care, I am outraged by the way the present British Government has shaped, delivered and financed it. The uncertainty, combined with lack of resources and guidelines, is having a very unsettling effect on local authorities, health boards and social services, not to mention carers. However, I am impressed by the commitment of the above to do the best they can. The contribution of the churches is still patchy: they must address the needs within their communities and accept the moral responsibility to be involved. The churches have so much to offer. We must all try to make community care work well for the benefit of sufferers and carers. Undoubtedly there is a moral vision for community care and development. I think there are ways forward and hope.

Finally, I recall a man I saw in Bristo Square. He was shouting and gesticulating wildly, telling invisible voices to go away. People walked by pretending he wasn't there: pretending he was invisible. He is not an illusion. He represents the one in ten in Britain who struggle daily with mental health problems. Ethically we are asked to understand and face up to this issue. Moreover, we are responsible for welcoming and caring for the strangers and their families in our communities. Not to do so is ethically reprehensible.

III   *Some Dilemmas in Professional Ethics in the Media (Heather Wraight)*

On 3 December 1993 Princess Diana made a public statement in which she announced her intention to scale down her public duties. She made it clear that the cause was 'overwhelming ... attention' from the media. In this essay I shall look at the specific ethical questions her accusation raises for the media, and seek to relate those to media theory by looking at the areas in which they arise: the message, the medium and the messenger.

Many ordinary people think the Princess has been treated badly by the media and question how it was allowed to happen.[1] I will examine whether Codes of Practice should have prevented it or whether the problem goes deeper, to the professionalism and ethical standards of those working in the media.

Professional ethics are those standards of thought and behaviour which society expects professional people to demonstrate in their working life. This raises various questions: Who are professional people? What is a profession and do the media merit the designation? Who expects the standards? How can it be recognised whether they have been met? On what principles do people make ethical decisions and how do these apply to professionals in the media, especially Christians?

1 *Introduction*

Professional
In some contexts a professional is simply the person who is paid to do a job, so members of a church will often talk about the minister as the professional. However there is more to it than that:

---

[1] E.g., Lesley Kirby, one of fifteen street interviews printed by the *Yorkshire Evening Press* 3.12.93: 'She should have been left alone to get on with things and she should have been hounded far less then perhaps none of this would have happened.'

A profession is not only a way of making a living; it is the carrying out of an occupation to which standards of competence and responsibility are attached.[2]

Certain qualities are expected of a professional: a detailed knowledge, usually obtained by studying for a recognised qualification; a degree of competence in the practical skills involved; and to use this skill and knowledge to provide a service to others.[3] It is also commonly understood that a profession sets standards and that a professional will have developed the personal integrity and discipline necessary to make a reasonable effort to meet those standards.[4] Being a professional, however, is more than keeping the rules: 'ethical considerations ... also include such matters as character and virtue.'[5] Most professions have some kind of mechanism whereby the members can be held accountable for meeting standards, but they cannot legislate the motivation which drives an individual to want to act professionally. Those areas of employment most often thought of as professions include medicine, law, teaching, engineering and theology.[6]

While modern society has chosen to add the media to this long established list, it may be asked whether this is justified on the criteria given above. Many journalists receive a formalised training, but until the last few years there was almost no specific training in broadcasting available in Britain outside the BBC.[7] Even though training is now available, it is not a legal requirement and skills are still frequently learned 'on the job' rather than within the formal framework applied to the training of a lawyer or accountant. The service which the media provides is also different: the medical profession deals with those who are sick, and the law provides a service to those

[2] *A New Dictionary of Christian Ethics* (NCE), p. 502.
[3] NCE, p. 502.
[4] NCE, p. 503.
[5] NCE, p. 38.
[6] *Collins Concise English Dictionary*, p. 597.
[7] *Community Service Volunteers* produce a list of training courses of all kinds related to the media. In a decade or so the list has grown from a single A4 sheet to a sizeable booklet.

seeking justice, but the media provide a service not for a specific segment of the population, but for anyone who wishes to buy a newspaper or turn on their radio or television.

The role of the media is more like that of shopkeepers than doctors, yet shopkeeping is not considered a profession. The media, with the possible exception of newspapers, do not have the long established tradition of the other professions, nor the structures of professional accountability. Issues, particularly ethical ones, which others resolved long ago,[8] are still being wrestled with by the media.[9]

The mass media represent a recent addition to the professional world in comparison with the other professions and seem still to be struggling with basic ideas in professional ethics. However, whether or not the media is a profession in the strict sense, the general public expect the media to behave in a professional way.

Professional ethics
Professional ethics concern the standards and behaviour which are expected of a professional who is carrying out his or her job in a responsible manner:

> Professional ethics do not concern the general obligations of human beings to other human beings as such, but canalise certain of these obligations in relation to the functional requirements of carrying out a particular kind of service.[10]

These obligations are therefore seen to be fulfilled or not by the people who are served by the profession. In the media virtually everyone in society is a recipient of the service offered, from the Queen who is said to listen to BBC Radio 4's *Today* programme, to the tramp who sleeps under discarded newspapers. The ethical dilemmas which arise in the media

---

[8] Hippocrates of the medical profession's Hippocratic Oath lived in the fifth century BC.

[9] The British Press Complaints Commission *Code of Practice* was ratified as recently as October 1993.

[10] NCE, p. 503.

are not confined to studios and Press Rooms, they are manifestly also in the public arena.

The situation of Princess Diana illustrates this fact. Her case was not debated solely in the higher echelons of the media, as might be the case if, for example, a doctor had been accused of unethical conduct. For some time after her announcement, it was a topic of general conversation and was discussed and analysed in school classrooms and by almost every newspaper, radio station and TV channel in Britain.[11] The Princess placed the responsibility for her proposed withdrawal from public life squarely on the media. We shall look at reaction in the first 24 hours after her announcement as seen in four radio programmes and four newspapers.[12] The debate soon moved to other issues such as the future of the monarchy or the possibility of Prince Charles and Princess Diana being divorced. However this is not an excuse for those in the media to avoid the issues raised by her accusation.[13]

Her case highlights ethical dilemmas at three levels which merit further examination:

the external i.e., the message: what the public read in their newspapers or see and hear broadcast.

the internal i.e., the medium. These are the pressures which are part of the job. Journalists and broadcasters have to contend with them although the general public is not usually aware of them.

---

[11] I listened to several phone-in programmes on various radio stations, watched documentary programmes on television and read articles in feature magazines. Few of them made even a brief mention of the issues raised for the media.

[12] BBC Radio 4: News bulletin, 18.00, 3.12.93
Any Questions, 20.05, 3.12.93
The World Tonight, 22.00, 3.12.93
Today, 07.00, 4.12.93
Newspapers: *Yorkshire Evening Press* 3.12.93
The Guardian 4.12.93
The Daily Telegraph, 4.12.93
Daily Mail, 4.12.93

[13] See n. 11.

The personal i.e., the messenger: the individuals who have to wrestle with, and balance, these issues, and how they do so. This is where motivation is crucial: why does a person make ethical decisions in a particular way, and on what basis does each analyse the factors involved and reach a conclusion?

Media

For the purposes of this essay, the media are those which are the main sources of news: newspapers, television and radio.

2. *External ethical questions – the message*

The Princess's situation raises many ethical issues about the gathering and dissemination of news and information, such as privacy, the public interest, obtaining material in a dishonest way, sensationalism and the 'snowball effect', buying material, truth and accuracy, comment and conjecture, discrimination and bias.

These issues raise many practical questions; specifying these shows how complex are the dilemmas which journalists face every day. What they decide shapes how they obtain their information and what they write or broadcast. It is therefore the outcome of such decisions which the public reads or sees and on the basis of which it judges whether the media are acting professionally.

Most of these issues are at least alluded to in the Press Complaints Commission Code of Practice (PCC Code), the introduction to which states that:

> All members of the press have a duty to maintain the highest professional and ethical standards … this involves a substantial element of self-restraint by editors and journalists…. The Code applies in the spirit as well as in the letter.

In her statement Princess Diana blamed the media for subjecting her to overwhelming pressure. Her proposed solution was simple: that she be allowed more privacy. To the Prime Minister, Harriet Harman MP and others this seemed a reasonable request. But Diana is a 'public figure': as such does she forfeit her right to privacy (PCC Code 4)? Where do 'public' and 'private' begin? When Diana asks for more space to have a private life, what is she expecting, and will that bear any relationship to what the media expect?

She is an immensely popular public figure, but 'something in which the public is interested' is not the same as something which is 'in the public interest' (PCC Code 18).[14] The distinction seems to get blurred when the person involved is a 'public figure'. Does the public have a 'right to know' as much as possible about Princess Diana simply because she is Princess Diana?

Some sections of the media, particularly the tabloid press, have acted as though the answer to that question is positive; that they do have the right to say anything they like about a person, particularly one of such great public interest. However, was the amount of speculation about the state of the royal marriage legitimate (PCC Code 4)? Laying aside for the moment the manner in which they were obtained, should the tapes of private telephone conversations between Camilla Parker-Bowles and the Prince, or the Princess and her 'close friend' (the so-called 'squidgy-gate' tapes) have been published (PCC Code 5)? Were these disclosures a responsible exposure by the press of events the public needed to be aware of, or was it sensationalism? Was the public informed about these matters because it was important that they know or was it primarily to sell more newspapers?

What about the money involved? A French paparazzi claimed he would expect £100,000 if he were to take an exclusive picture of Diana. Who would decide to pay him that money, and why (PCC Code Introduction)? The fitness club manager who took the photos of Princess Diana using a concealed camera (PCC Code 8ii) admitted that his motive was purely financial,[15] yet a newspaper was prepared to buy and publish

[14] Hiebert, Ungurait, Bohn, *Mass Media VI* (1974), p. 528.
[15] *Daily Mirror*, 8.11.93: 'I am not ashamed of the fact that I am going to make a lot of money out of [the photos]. In the hard cold world of commerce, the barometer of success is money.'

them. The Camilla Parker-Bowles tapes and the 'squidgy-gate' tapes were obtained dishonourably, but before the Commission's Code of Practice was ratified: does that make them acceptable? Is it ever right to use material which has been obtained in a dishonourable way, whatever the motive (PCC Code 7i)?

When the gymnasium pictures were published almost all the other newspapers reproduced them – as part of their denigration of the Mirror Group for using them.[16] Was that necessary for the public to be adequately informed, or was it giving in to what is known as 'the snowball effect'? Should discriminating editors yield to the pressure to print or broadcast a story because their competitors have done so?[17]

Ingrid Seward, interviewed on *The World Tonight* on Radio 4, proposed that when the Princess blamed the media for putting her under such pressure she was not telling the whole truth. However, in pursuit of that truth various possibilities were raised, some of which were presented as fact even though they were in direct contradiction to one another (PCC Code 3): e.g., whether there was pressure or support from Buckingham Palace. Can the public believe all that they hear or read in the media? How do journalists discover the truth?[18] If there is more behind the statement than Diana admitted, do journalists have a responsibility to find out at any cost, or should they respect the Princess's request for privacy?

Discrimination in the media is ruled out on the grounds of race, colour, religion, sex or sexual orientation (PCC Code 15). Those who are anti-royal or anti-establishment frequently use prejudicial or pejorative language about people like Princess Diana because she is royal and therefore perceived to be different. Should they be allowed to discriminate on the grounds of social class when they could not make similar statements about, say, blacks or homosexuals? This illustrates that journalists or broadcasters have their own biases

---

[16] E.g., *The Guardian*, 8.11.93. Princess Diana sued the owner of the gym and in March 1995 she obtained an out-of-court settlement which included an injunction against the photographs ever being published again.

[17] A. Boyd, *Broadcast Journalism* (1988), p. 165.

[18] G. Priestland, *The Dilemmas of Journalism* (1979), p. 30.

(background, education, politics etc.) which they bring to work with them. When the matter was discussed in *Any Questions* on Radio 4, it was easy to recognise who was royalist and who was not, but bias is not always as easy to discern.

These are important issues which conscientious journalists struggle with. The late Gerald Priestland, journalist and broadcaster, was for a time a Religous Affairs Correspondent for the BBC. In his book *The Dilemmas of Journalism* he wrote about a similar situation and the questions that he, as a Christian, wrestled with then:

> In the Unites States, President Lyndon Johnson firmly believed that it was the mass media that led to the failure of his war effort in Vietnam and ultimately obliged him to renounce a further term in the White House .... Richard Nixon had much the same convictions about the press .... A Christian correspondent of any human sensitivity was bound at some time or other to ponder whether it was right for the media to destroy the careers of these two leaders.... The beginning of a Christian understandinng of journalism is that the truth is very much more than the obvious facts ...[The journalist] will hardly – if he is a Christian – communicate messages that are malicious, obscene, cruel or patently false.[19]

It is important that all journalists wrestle with the issues of what messages they communicate and how they communicate them. Priestland's Christian faith caused him to question the actions of the media in this and other instances. His particular perspective led him to certain conclusions, which might well be shared by other journalists with no Christian commitment. However there are more fundamental issues inherent in the media themselves.

3 *Internal ethical questions – the medium*

Ethical questions arise at another level of which the general

---

[19] *The Dilemmas of Journalism*, pp. 26, 30, 46.

public is mostly unaware. These are the issues created by the nature of the media and the practice and structures of the industry.

Modern technology has made the broadcast media possible and has dramatically changed the print media, but the technology itself creates ethical problems. That it is technically possible to do something, such as use remote control cameras, does not make it right (PCC Code 7i). However there are even greater issues than this. The number of outlets is multiplying, particularly with the growth of cable and satellite radio and television. Material must be found to fill the newspapers' pages and the broadcasting hours. As journalists have more reports to file, they have less time in which to research the stories.[20] All material must also be produced by a deadline and probably with a finite limit on the budget, as Boyd illustrates in *Broadcast Journalism*: 'In a radio newsroom that is squeezed for staff, the only stories that will be chased are those that will yield an acceptable result within the available time.'[21]

These sorts of pressures are a daily fact of life in media offices, but they tend to squeeze out ethical thinking: there is just no time for it, as Rutherford-Smith argues in *Questioning Media Ethics*[22] and as Gerald Priestland points out: 'Perhaps the worst treason is that too many able journalists who enter television allow themselves to be seduced by its technology.'[23]

That finite limit on the budget is another pressure. Survival of a programme or newspaper may depend on ratings or circulation figures, particularly in the current economic climate in which some newspapers have already been forced to close. Mary Kenny in *The Daily Telegraph* said, 'Diana's picture sells anything'. However, Rutherford-Smith believes it is important to guard against economic necessity becoming the main driving force when making ethical decisions about choice of material,[24] while Boyd shows the potential outcome of such thinking:

---

[20] Michael Burke, *From Our Own Correspondent*, BBC Radio 4, 4.11.93
[21] *Broadcast Journalism*, p. 169.
[22] B. Rubin (ed.), *Questioning Media Ethics* (1978), p. 295.
[23] *The Dilemmas of Journalism*, p. 32.
[24] *Questioning Media Ethics*, p. 296.

When profit motive replaces news value there is pressure to
pander to the lowest public taste for fear that audience and
advertisers alike will desert ... that pressure spills over into
the newsroom.[25]

Issues such as accuracy and privacy which relate to the message,
can all too easily be overwhelmed by the insistent demands of
the medium. With such pressures to contend with, someone
has to take ultimate responsibility for what is presented to the
public. The editor or producer cannot blame a journalist, or
hide behind the decisions of others (PCC Code, Introduction).
It is the editor's responsibility to ensure staff adhere to the
approved standards: the editor of the *Daily Mirror* did later take
responsibility for publishing the photos of Princess Diana in
the gym.[26] The struggle in the press is to remain free, yet to act
in a responsible way. It was a contentious issue in the USA when
Mass Media VI was written: 'What underlies such debate is
nothing less than the question of how best to balance freedom
and responsibility.'[27]

   True freedom of the press includes not only the rights of the
journalists and owners to publicise their own views but also the
interests of the audience and readers. One of the advantages
of private ownership as against a government controlled
monopoly is the breadth of opinion it affords: people have
access to opposing viewpoints, even if they need to buy another
newspaper to find it.[28] In Britain the press are often partisan,
which the Press Complaints Commission recognises while
putting constraints on its expression (PCC Code 3). The
broadcasting media in the UK, in contrast to, say, the USA, are
not partisan in the same way. Nevertheless, total objectivity,
although a wonderful ideal, can never be achieved, not only
because of the personal bias of the journalist but also because
of the editorial policy of the organisation. That is no excuse for
abandoning the attempt, as Andrew Boyd points out: 'The

---

[25] *Broadcast Journalism*, p. 169.
[26] *Daily Mail*, 8.11.93
[27] *Mass Media VI*, p. 524.
[28] *Mass Media VI*, p. 523.

journalist's duty is to recognise the inevitability of bias without ever surrendering to it.'[29]

4. *Codes of Practice – a solution?*

The social and cultural context in which the media work is another powerful influence. There are four major theories of the way political systems and media systems interrelate:[30] the authoritarian system, the communist system (and similar), the libertarian system, and the social responsibility system. It is the last named which obtains in Britain.

The social responsibility media system is organised and to some extent regulated by Codes of Practice, some of which have already been quoted. If they could be adhered to strictly, even enforced, would that solve the problems of both the message and the medium? Unfortunately not, for several reasons.

In the UK Codes of Practice are not legally binding, although the Press Complaints Commission is seeking to introduce an element of compulsion by getting their Code of Practice written into contracts of employment of newspaper editors.[31] In this way an editor who broke, or allowed his paper to break, the Code could theoretically be dismissed for breach of contract.

Codes by their very nature are either so ambiguous that it is easy to find loopholes in them, or so detailed that they do not fit specific situations and therefore can be avoided as Rutherford-Smith describes:

> Codes, if they are to endure, must be cast in general terms applicable to a variety of unforeseen future events. This essential ambiguity in legalistic ethical formulations not only gives them endurance; it also provides loopholes for those interested in conforming only to the letter of the law.[32]

---

[29] *Broadcast Journalism*, p. 161.
[30] Cf. F. Siebert, T. Peterson, W. Schramm, 'Four theories of the Press', *Mass Media VI*, p. 607.
[31] *The Daily Telegraph*, 13.11.93
[32] *Questioning Media Ethics*, p. 287.

He highlights another difficulty: Codes can actually make people less responsible rather than more. It is possible to abdicate personal responsibility by acting 'strictly by the book'. As the writers of *Media Ethics* point out,[33] this is one way to avoid thinking about ethical dilemmas or facing the effect of decisions. This is one of the struggles for the Press Complaints Commission as they try to make voluntary regulation work, rather than have a Privacy Law imposed upon them by Parliament.[34]

The problem lies not so much with the Codes *per se* as with the people whom they are supposed to regulate, as G.F. Woods points out:

> A person does not become a genuine professional when he accepts the standards for some reason other than his own belief in their excellence as professional standards.[35]

The writers of *Mass Media VI* agree that ethics cannot be reduced to Codes of Practice' lists of what should or should not be done:

> Media ethics may be more usefully thought of as a process rather than a result. The crucial question for the communicator is: 'How should I go about deciding what I ought to do in any given situation?'[36]

5 *Personal ethical questions – the messenger*

One way of looking at ethics is to look at what a person is: the motive for behaving in a particular way. Woods argues from a Christian perspective that maintaining professional standards is a necessary component of the personal standards required by the Christian faith. The various contributors to *Mass Media VI* write as professional communicators, yet they also make it

---

[33] Christians, Rotzoll, Fackler, *Media Ethics: Cases and Moral Reasoning* (1991), p. 414.
[34] *The Daily Telegraph*, 13.11.93
[35] G. F. Woods, *A Defence of Theological Ethics* (1966), p. 60.
[36] *Mass Media VI*, p. 527.

clear that ethics have to do with voluntary conduct, with what the person chooses to do and why he or she makes that choice.[37]

There is a fine but distinguishing line between applying professional standards and behaving in a professional way as Woods shows:

> A person does not become a genuine professional when he accepts the standards for some reason other than his own belief in their excellence as professional standards ... He must freely identify himself with *the kind of person* [emphasis added] who admits and employs the proper standards of his profession.[38]

When the Mirror Group published the now infamous pictures, not only were they breaking the Code of Practice of the industry, but the conduct of the people responsible for the decision to publish was described by Lord McGregor, Chairman of the Press Complaints Commission, as dishonourable.[39] They appear to have considered the sensationalism of a scoop and the likelihood of selling more papers as more important than observing a Code of Practice.

People who are recognised as professional rarely make ethical decisions in a haphazard way: consciously or unconsciously they base their decisions on specific ethical principles. Some of the major ones are outlined in *Media Ethics*.[40] These are:

Aristotle's Golden Mean 'Moral virtue is appropriate location between two extremes.'[41] This approach specifically emphasises that what a person is is more important than what he or she

---

[37] *Mass Media VI*, p. 521.

[38] *A Defence of Theological Ethics*, p. 60.

[39] Lord McGregor, Chairman, Press Complaints Commission, quoted in *The Guardian*, 9.11.93; cf. Pat Healy, NUJ Ethics Council, in a letter to *The Daily Telegraph*, 10.11.93.

[40] *Media Ethics: Cases and Moral Reasoning*, pp. 11–21. On this, cf. chapters 1 and 2 above.

[41] *Media Ethics*, p. 11.

does. 'The mean is not only the right quantity, but at the right time, toward the right people, for the right reason, and in the right manner.'[42] The extreme treatment of Princess Diana would be to print everything that can be found out, whatever the means used to unearth it, or to ignore her totally. Perhaps the Golden Mean would be to continue to report about her when she does appear in public, but otherwise leave her alone, as she has requested.

Kant's Categorical Imperative   'Act on that maxim which you will to become a universal law.'[43] So, what is right for one is right for all. The obligation of the good conscience is to do its duty for the sake of duty ... even to the sacrifice of all natural inclinations and social standards.[44] Ideally, this approach encourages obedience to guidelines such as Codes of Practice. It is said to have greater motivating power because, if it is used objectively, the decisions made will not alter according to moods or other such transitory variations. After the photos in the gym incident a broadcasting company set up 'Peeping Tom' cameras to spy on two of the people responsible for their publication.[45] They were not pleased: thereby demonstrating that their decision to publish was not based on universality!

Mill's Principle of Utility   'Seek the greatest happiness for the greatest number.'[46] People using this principle determine what is right or wrong by considering what will yield the best balance of good over evil. It has a lot to do with giving people happiness or pleasure: there is no doubt that many people derive pleasure from seeing or reading about Princess Diana. In that sense publishing any information about her is 'in the public good'. The problem with this approach is that it depends on those involved making accurate assessments of the possible consequences. If the Press had realised that the

[42] *Media Ethics*, p. 13.
[43] *Media Ethics*, p. 14.
[44] *Media Ethics*, p. 15.
[45] *The Guardian*, 9.11.93.
[46] *Media Ethics*, p. 15.

amount of pressure they put on the Princess would lead to her desire to withdraw from public life, perhaps at least some editors would have made different decisions. As a close friend of the Princess put it, 'They have killed the goose that laid the golden egg.'[47]

Rawls' Veil of Ignorance   'Justice emerges when negotiating without social differentiations.'[48] One definition of the 'Veil of Ignorance' is 'asking that all parties step back from real circumstances into an "original position" behind a barrier where roles and social differentiations are gone'.[49] The aim is to be totally fair to everyone; to negotiate and discuss decisions in a state of imagined equality. Taking this principle, if editors could have genuinely put themselves in the shoes of the lonely, disillusioned woman struggling with separation from her partner, would they have treated her more sympathetically? It is interesting to note that nearly all of the editorials in the immediate aftermath of the Princess's announcement were sympathetic towards her.[50]

Religious Tradition   'The Judeo-Christian tradition, so formative for Britain as for many other cultures, sees each individual as important: "you shall love your neighbour as yourself" (Luke 10:27).' Ultimately humans stand under only one moral obligation: to love God and humankind. All other principles, such as obedience, justice or peace, though connected to this central one, are considered to derive from it. The question must be asked, 'Who is my neighbour?' (Luke 10:29). To answer this requires looking at a broad canvas, beyond party or even professional loyalties. On the one hand, Princess Diana as 'my neighbour' deserves fair and balanced treatment from the media and a positive response to her request for privacy. On the other hand, the readers and

[47] Christopher Soames quoted in *The Guardian*, 4.12.93.
[48] *Media Ethics*, p. 17.
[49] *Media Ethics*, p. 17.
[50] E.g., Editorial, *Yorkshire Evening Press*, 3.12.93.

audience are also 'my neighbours',[51] many of whom are fascinated by what Mary Kenny called an 'aura of stardust' which surrounds the Princess and do not want her to disappear from the public eye altogether. The media owe them whatever news or pictures of the Princess become available without using unethical means to obtain them.

Conclusion

Christian ethics is concerned with professional ethics as a whole, as well as with the distinctive perspectives which Christians can bring to the media. It is impossible to separate acting professionally from acting ethically: the person who is truly professional in attitudes and actions is motivated by personal standards. The professional has a commitment to excellence. All who work in the media face the same dilemmas in gathering and disseminating the message, and the same pressures created by the medium. Those who seek to act professionally often come to the same conclusions in seeking to resolve those issues. The differences lie in the grounding of the principles used in making a decision, and in the area of motivation.

The actions of Christians will not be influenced primarily by whether a Code of Conduct is written into the contract of employment, or by the ethos that 'we don't do that here'. Rather they will be guided by a Christian self-understanding and a Christian view of the world they serve: a view which promotes distinctive character, qualities and motivation, and therefore informs professional commitment. The people who are the subjects of articles or programmes (e.g., Princess Diana) are 'neighbours' and as such should be treated with respect. The readers or audience are also 'neighbours': not an anonymous mass to be manipulated for profit or ratings.

---

[51] E.g., Robert McLeish, a former Head of Local Radio Training, BBC, said that for the Christian broadcaster we should first love the Lord our God with all our heart etc. and secondly love our audience as ourself. (In a lecture given on several occasions to an annual radio training course sponsored by the Evangelical Missionary Alliance.)

Codes of Practice or an understanding of the media cannot create moral behaviour. They are only truly effective when the people using them are already motivated 'to maintain the highest professional and ethical standards' (PCC Code, Introduction).

IV Integrity – Disclosure of Life Assurance Commission: a case study in Christian values (David Molyneaux)*

The problem with charging structures, from the consumer perspective, is that the vast majority of life and pension products charges, in the shape of life office expenses and commissions paid to advisers and sales staff, are loaded into the first two or three years of a policy's term. For example, with a typical 25 year, £100 a month endowment policy, the adviser would receive £1,245 in 'initial commission' loaded into the first three years of a policy's life, plus a further £655 in 'renewal commission' spread over the entire policy term.... The potential effect of such front end loading is to emphasise the sale, possibly at the expense of the client getting a product appropriate to the circumstances.[1]

[Good] past performance provides companies with a powerful selling point [but] excellent fund management is only part of the story as Government figures show [1990 Department of Trade and Industry Returns].... These reveal that many companies doing well in the performance tables have much higher than average numbers of customers cashing in policies early. That is, they are able to provide excellent past performance figures primarily because of the number of policies surrendered.[2]

---

*I should like to acknowledge information supplied in early 1994 by Equitable Life, Legal and General plc, The Prudential Corporation plc, Scottish Widows and Standard Life in preparing this article. I have also found material of particular help in *City Ethics*, the newsletter of the St James Ethics Centre in Sydney. The views expressed are my own.

[1] *The Accountants Magazine*, the journal of the Institute of Chartered Accountants of Scotland, September 1993

[2] *Sunday Telegraph*, 10.11.1991. Figures for 1990 show that in the case of some large and well respected life offices, for every person whose policy continued to maturity nearly *seven* surrendered their policies early.

1. *Overview of the issue*

These quotations show the emergence in the early 1990s of a little known and unsatisfactorily resolved ethical dilemma of unusually wide significance. Life assurance and pensions affect directly or indirectly almost every person within the UK, whatever their ethical or religious values. It is perhaps of particular relevance to Christians because caring for widows, orphans and for the elderly – 'fathers and mothers' – is a deeply embedded theme within the Bible. Moreover, many of the major entities within the industry which organises the 'arrangements' to provide this service, were established with Christian principles in mind.[3]

Before the present disquiet, the industry appeared an unqualified success and a source of rightful pride. Despite what seems to be a particularly British aversion to saving,[4] the life assurance industry has been remarkably successful at collecting savings and organising the provision of some security for many who might otherwise be disadvantaged. At the end of 1993, life companies held assets of more than £400 billion, up fourfold compared with ten years earlier. They are selling eight million new policies a year in the UK and collecting £35 billion in premiums from individuals. Meanwhile they are paying out £30 billion annually in benefits.[5]

Yet complacency as to integrity and therefore competence is no longer possible. Life assurance companies large and small, irrespective of whether mutually owned by their policy holders or by separate shareholders, have been forced by the independent regulator to pay substantial fines or even suspend all sales staff for weeks at a time for 'retraining'. Ironically, mutuals owned by the policy holders but geographically spread

[3] The Prudential Corporation's centenary publication (1948) – *A Century of Service. The Story of the Prudential 1848–1948*-refers to the Rev. D. Worthington and Rev. James Gillman, two founding chairmen.

[4] Statistics show that Britons save only around 3.5 per cent of income compared with an average of around 9 per cent for similarly developed countries. Source: *Financial Times*.

[5] Cf. *Financial Times*, 2.4.1994, article by Barry Riley and a useful source for the historical review.

throughout the UK, are now particularly distanced from proprietorial scrutiny and pressure, except by regulators whose concern can only be with existing rules. If regulators do have cause to levy fines on mutuals, it is the policy holders who, ultimately, pay.

A situation which saps the public confidence in entities founded on trust should challenge the spiritual, as well as the potential material, wellbeing of all those who manage and derive employment or income from them. It should prompt the question 'How have *we* let this happen?' – particularly among those claiming generations of probity and moral rectitude.[6]

This article is a brief review of what is a complex subject with a long history and a wide diversity of practitioners and practices. Inevitably it is with some sweeping generalisation that it attempts first to summarise how the position has developed. It then examines the arguments against and for the disclosure of commission payable on life assurance to see whether or not this is a root ethical issue. Enhanced disclosure is now seen as the solution being stipulated by the Regulators in spite of opposition by many in the industry.[7] It then aims to consider professional and business ethics within the wider context of theological and biblical teaching.

It does *not* address whether saving matches a basic human concern. The teaching of the Sermon on the Mount may be interpreted as warning against excess concerns. In an imperfect world, accumulated savings can be liberating from anxieties. This article therefore assumes that saving and insurance are acceptable Christian objectives without further debate on a potentially far wider issue.[8]

---

[6] This article was written in Edinburgh, a city described by *Investors Chronicle*, 8–14 April 1994, as the UK's 'second financial centre where canny Scots steeped in generations of probity and financial nous take very good care of your money'.

[7] The Independent Financial Advisors Association was quoted in the *Financial Times* of 24.7.1993: 'We are somewhat disappointed that the Chancellor sees commission disclosure as vital to the consumer.'

[8] Reconciling the purpose of the Life Assurance and Pensions industry with Matt. 6:19–21 and particularly 6:25–34 could be an article in itself. However,

2. *A brief history*

'Good advice' and 'trustworthiness' are two of the most sought after and precious elements in any service. The life assurance industry has sought to make these valuable commodities appear to have no cost and no price. Yet, because of their intangible nature and only long-term ability to prove their worth (or otherwise), most individuals are unwilling to pay a price which reflects the real value of trustworthy advice.

Willingness to save against an eventual foreseeable problem must come even before investment is possible. Because of their paternalistic origins, many of those societies set up to arrange life assurance and pensions seem to have adopted the view that the first priority was to encourage people to save for their own good. It was far less appealing to dwell on the complex and potentially subjective areas of what could constitute good investment advice and how it should be paid for. The essential was to set in place a means by which the habit could be initiated.

For many decades, society and UK government policy have supported the overall objective and provided two main political favours to the life industry in return for encouraging thrifty practices. Until 1984, there was a long-standing tax incentive, of about half the standard rate of income tax. Pensions continue to enjoy substantial tax reliefs and these are a significant inducement to the habit of regular saving for the future.

The other favour was exemption from the investor protection laws introduced in the 1930s. Life company representatives

as W. D. Davies and D. C. Allison write in their commentary on Matthew (*ICC*) 1988 (T&T Clark, Edinburgh): 'If Jesus – who may have lived out of a common fund (cf. Jn. 12:6; 13:29) – appeared to belittle the consuming tasks of obtaining food and clothing, it was only because he had something even more arduous in mind, namely, seeking the Kingdom of Heaven. And certainly he did not have many illusions about an easy world. The bird will fall to the ground (Matt. 10:29) and the righteous will inevitably suffer (cf. 5:10–12; 10:16–23)'. Given the imperfections of an earthly kingdom, the pension and other arrangements which should efficiently *minimise* the need for caring about the future would seem consistent with the content if not the detail of the passage.

were permitted to continue selling door-to-door and collecting premiums without disclosing policy costs and charges. The arguments for this were probably teleological: the 'overall good', that many people should have such policies, outweighed concerns that this could give rise to potential abuse from those motivated by 'avarice, greed, robbing and injustice'. A deontological approach would have given higher priority to avoid these.

Eventually, keeping undisclosed the commissions and other selling costs became more significant than the tax advantages. The industry lobbied hard and successfully to minimise disclosure in the changes, introduced by the Financial Services Act 1986, to many aspects of the savings and investment management industries. The end result was a complicated, bureaucratic regime which has tidied up some areas but left a major loophole for misunderstanding at the interface with the general public. Various forms of 'soft' disclosure were conceded but it was only in 1995 that a formula for disclosure *in cash terms at the point of sale* was introduced, following Treasury insistence in July 1993.

Life companies aim to persuade customers to sign up for long periods, usually of between 10 and 25 years, for apparently commendable reasons. This provided greater security for the customers, not just because of the discipline of a monthly instalment enforcing greater prudence, but also because regular periodic saving has smoothed out the investment risks inherent in the variable markets for stocks and shares. This also benefited the companies because it gave them greater commercial stability and enabled them to implement long-term capital investment and employment strategies.

However, as a by-product, it also enabled inefficiencies and over-manning of inadequate sales teams (whether independent or tied to a particular company) to be sustained and perpetuated.

For managements, such sales teams are justified *economically* by the initial problem that few people will readily sign up for 25 year contracts, and *morally* by the perceived wisdom that it is in the reluctant customer's interest to be persuaded to purchase what is ultimately in his/her interest. To be effective, this has usually required a salesman to operate on a one-to-one basis during a specific visit to the home or office of an individual. Inevitably this is an expensive business (as in the cost of an emergency plumber's visit) but without immediately obvious benefit or guarantees. If the visitor is indeed an expert in financial planning, he/she is likely to have had a period of unremunerated training and will want commensurate pay. Moreover, a typical salesperson may only sell one or two contracts a week and therefore look for commission (or the employer for income) of hundreds of pounds on each to justify an otherwise fruitless activity.

For a time, commissions were restricted but this control was abolished, in recognition of the drawbacks as well as the benefits of a cartel. As a result, it became even more important to disguise selling costs. The fear was that whatever the marketing skills and techniques of the salesman, the awareness of the raw data of the size of the salesman's interest in the contract (and the substantial costs of terminating early) would be a large deterrent to the would-be purchaser.

The position of advisers/sales staff and Life Office managers seems, in general, to be as follows:

> For each person sold a policy which they took to maturity, many more did not. Meanwhile most of these could have invested better elsewhere. This suggests that some of them had not been properly advised of the risks and/or were sold inappropriate products. Others may have been wrongly advised to surrender a policy, perhaps when moving house, rather than continuing the existing policy.
>
> Advisers/salespersons have incentives which encourage these practices because they receive the great bulk of their commission within the first two years (average policy life, seven). There is no commission if no sale but also few drawbacks in that there is often no contact after the sale, or at time of surrender, with the original policy holder. A new salesperson has an inducement to advise surrender to encourage a new policy.
>
> Management of Life Offices have no incentives to

discourage this. All policies contribute to minimise shared administration costs, and so large numbers of early surrenders, at low or nil recovery, benefit those who continue. This flatters the most widely used industry statistics (maturity values on past investments) which in turn helps generate future sales. As a generality it will be those who are less likely to be able to afford to continue who benefit those who can, which seems unjust (in spite of Luke 19:26). The argument against higher surrender values is that these might be an encouragement to the abortion of the policies, and so directly against the original purpose. Moreover, although most managements may try to persuade for continuity, they cannot dictate or override individual circumstances. Indeed, arguing *for* continuity by management can appear, superficially, to be self-interestedly biased.

This situation may be limited to certain types of policies but it raises starkly the question whether casualties need to be so high. Commission arrangements do seem to play a part. Some offices do achieve ratios of one for one or better. These seem to be those which have in the past made more use of dedicated sales forces, remunerated only in part with commission, rather than sales persons or independent financial advisers, who are remunerated almost exclusively by commission or settled expenses.

This brief history suggests that the issue of disclosure of commission is significant, for it is the *objectivity* and *quality* of the advice at the time of originating the policy which will give the best prospect of most nearly matching the policyholder's needs.

3. *The debate over disclosure*

The 1986 Financial Services Act made changes within the industry but, following intense lobbying, a compromise required little change in respect of disclosure of commission to the general public. Subsequently, such disclosure has been only at a late stage and in an obscure part of the documentation.

However, in the view of the Office of Fair Trading and of the Treasury, announced in July 1993, greater openness of disclosure to *potential* customers was seen as the principal solution to the problems of conflict of interest arising in the life assurance and pensions business. This relies on the idea of *caveat emptor* as being the best regulatory means. From January 1995:

> Disclosure requires the nature and value of commission to be prominently and promptly stated to the potential policyholder.
>
> There is statutory obligation that the calculations relating to the disclosure be verifiable, whereas in the past oral statements voluntarily made by salespersons could be misleading or simply untrue.

The change by way of disclosure is not a radical development. It has always been open to a potential purchaser to question how the 'adviser' is reimbursed for his or her time and work. Few seem to have done so. Many who might rigorously dispute, say, a car service bill, when itemised, will calmly pay a single figure for a less defined financial service, perhaps because few like to admit a failure to understand matters of their personal finances. Others, once emotionally committed to a transaction, do not want to question further those they are trusting.

The industry has argued specifically that fuller disclosure will be unhelpful. It used the following grounds:

> Disclosure could be counterproductive by distracting consumers from addressing more important information such as their ability to pay the premium or the office's record of performance.
>
> Given the volume of information already available, particularly involving several possible products and different companies, there might be a surfeit of confusing figures which would not only prevent focus but be completely daunting.
>
> A comparability of commissions will be very difficult to achieve. A direct salesforce might receive a combination of salary and commission, whereas some independent advisers

may receive remuneration either wholly by way of a direct payment of commission or else by many alternatives such as gifts of equipment, settlement of expenses and supplementary bonuses for certain levels of sales. All such arrangements will make it very difficult to determine the exact amount fairly attributable in respect of a specific life assurance transaction for comparison with alternatives.

Elaborate computer systems will need to be adapted, at a high cost to the consumer, in order to disclose this information.

Life offices and pensions may become competitively disadvantaged whereas alternative savings media, such as unit trusts or PEPs, might gain inappropriate purchasers.

Sales agents' 'right' to privacy in respect of their personal affairs might be infringed.

Because of the extensive and historical use of commission as an incentive within the industry, the problems which these arguments represent generated further considerable debate on *what* should be disclosed, *how* it should be disclosed and the *timing* of the disclosure. In addition, information such as the life office's ability to sell *appropriate* products (as represented by persistency rates) is also being prepared for publication, but clearly this will be of limited value unless the implications are recognised by readers.

Another, superficially persuasive, argument is that if a car salesperson does not have to disclose commission, why should an insurance agent? However, the car salesperson is presenting a tangible product for inspection and test drive both before and immediately after the sale, unlike a long-term life product. The public expectation is that he/she will champion the merits of the car, within the broad criteria outlined by the visiting customer, by reference to the car's demonstrable attributes: not by reference to projections based on subjective assumptions. Crucially, the car salesperson, while expected to be honest, is not expected to analyse closely the individual customer's ability to pay, or to consider objectively a range of options, or ask whether a car is needed at all.

It is possible that the car salesperson may need to provide

some form of warnings, such as the prohibitive expense of insurance on a powerful car to a person under age 25, or he/she may be interested in the credit worthiness of an individual purchasing on hire purchase. However, if the salesperson were to ask detailed, normally confidential questions about finance or salaries, or suggest alternative purchases such as holidays, ask about long-term plans and aspirations, even the contents of wills and inheritance plans within the family, most customers would see this as no part of the automobile transaction. By contrast, for the life assurance or pension salesperson, such matters are an integral part of determining not just an appropriate but the *best* arrangement for their client. There is a *relationship* of trust in which a client has the right to believe that the agent is advising in his/her best interests *and these interests have complete priority*.

The core of the debate is the *nature of the relationship* between the adviser and the individual. The life assurance person is not operating like a supermarket till checkout operator simply to process quickly and efficiently, in a sales driven industry, the results of a decision made first and foremost by the customer. Hence the pricing policy of the product and the remuneration paid to the individual adviser (not to a distribution operative) may be potentially relevant. If the adviser wishes to be seen as a 'professional' then, in the current meaning of the term, he or she needs demonstrably to be acting in the interests of the client, irrespective of his or her own interest.

No such trusted adviser to a client relying on the objectivity of the advice should, in such a relationship, sell a product which is inappropriate or inferior but pays higher commission. In such circumstances, despite the difficulties listed above, disclosure seems a prerequisite if the relationship is to be credible. The policyholder can then judge its relevance for him/herself.

Alternatively there might be an arrangement whereby commission is simply removed from the industry. All persons involved with the advising or sale of insurance products would have an hourly charge rate for their costs. They would need to agree with the potential client the amount of time which they might expect to spend involved in research, discussion and administration and give estimates of what this might cost.

Hence the customer would be charged a fee proportionate to the skills and time involved rather than an arbitrary amount, involving as it does an incentive for the premium to be made as large as possible. However, this too has drawbacks in that it might deter individuals with relatively small premiums from receiving *any* advice, for the following reasons:

> The cost might appear prohibitive. Moreover, to be fair to the sales person this fee would need to be paid whether or not any assurance contract was entered into. This might be very difficult to collect if there were no ongoing relationship.
>
> Since the bill for professional time would be payable in full in the first year, it might cause the individual to defer taking out a life assurance/pensions contract until the fee could be afforded. At least under a commission arrangement the terms are agreed and entered into and the arrangement for spreading the cost of the advice is handled by the company over two or more years. This may be more convenient to the individual.

A separate, hybrid solution has existed for some time in that a number of advisers inform clients at the outset of the commission arrangement but agree to a fee on a time/skills basis. The agent then uses the commission to offset, either using surplus commission as a means of purchasing greater benefits for the client or looking to the individual to make up any shortfall. The spread nature of commission may make this still a confusing arrangement and clearly the agent must make explicit his/her intentions at the start of the process.

Another initiative, whose growth may be stimulated by the requirement to make explicit the impact of commission and charges, is Guaranteed Equity Products, based on the use of options and derivatives of the stock market. These may come to replace, in future, traditional life assurance and pension policies for they can offer many of the benefits but fewer uncertainties. In short, disclosure has applied pressure to develop solutions which better suit needs.

What is most clear from this brief review of life assurance commission is that failure to disclose is not a simple evil nor is disclosure a panacea despite the banner headlines. There is no single solution to the circumstances. It gives rise to three areas for further consideration:

(i)   the general ethical considerations raised by the historical circumstances which the life assurance industry has experienced;

(ii)   a comparison of professional ethics with those of business; and

(iii)   the social and political means of control.

The proposed solutions involve an extensive structure of regulation and prescriptive guidelines attempting to create orderliness and fairness within a competitive environment. The semblance of honesty and trustworthiness can command a high premium but the substance has on occasion shown itself to be less than justifiable. It raises the question: *must trustworthiness now be imposed by legal sanction?*

4. *Ethical analysis*

The foreseeable and hoped-for consequences of addressing one aspect of the issue, by way of more disclosure, may be that savers will be less vulnerable to crippling costs for terminating contracts which they should never have signed. A salesperson will be under greater pressure to be more thorough, more clear and more open.

However, other foreseeable consequences may be that far fewer people will be persuaded of the benefits of any form of longer term saving or provision and there could be a further sharp decline in the proportion of savings to income. Moreover, a structural shift in the UK's investment market towards one-off and more volatile investment media could reduce the stabilising influence of long-term funds on the stock and gilt markets. These are already prone to short-termism and fluctuations which do not benefit the mass of ordinary non-specialist investors without the use of complex options and derivatives. Such products may now become even more necessary and common. *Accidentally,* or *incidentally,* greater accountability may have several unintended influences. This is symptomatic of teleological ethical solutions and not a new problem.

A reading of Luther's *Trade and Usury*[9] suggests that there is little different in the ethics which relate to this situation than to those of his contemporary merchants. It was difficult and complicated then and is no easier now. The worth of the advice on a 25 year policy will only become known at some distant date in the future and indicators (such as the current performance of a company's policies) may depend more on the ability of managers 25 years earlier than those at present. There are many variables. Teleological ethical decisions continue to require an awareness and balance between actual, foreseeable, intended and accidental consequences. It is difficult to imagine that the results of the system, as now widely revealed in the 1990s, were intended or even foreseeable to those who laid its foundations based on teleological decisions.

The deficiency lies in a failure by successive generations of actuaries, managers, brokers, and to an extent the general public, to recognise that the costs of providing the advisory service were becoming disproportionately high in relation to the benefits. The ability of the public at large to generate the demand for change was cloaked by a legally permitted absence of disclosure, hence successive governments also bear some responsibility. *The practices, once accepted, were not subject to repeated challenge.*

An act-utilitarian argument for the *status quo* is not difficult to discern.[10] The policyholder and his/her family stand to benefit and various forms of employment are maintained. But with general and rule utilitarianism it is difficult to see how those individuals, *who were in full possession of the facts,* could have seen the situation as fair, or even efficient. The *actuality*

[9] As set out in R. Gill, *A Textbook of Christian Ethics* (1985), pp. 205–23
[10] On 'act utilitarianism', see chapter 1 above, p. xx, n.7; and cf. Fairweather and McDonald, *The Quest,* pp. 44–6.

was that many of their fellow citizens were entering arrangements that were to prove unsustainable.

Nevertheless, it seems that the sense of 'everyone benefits so why change the system' long prevailed among many leaders of the industry. Probably for themselves, most of those who were in a position to understand the arrangements would have had the commission converted to their own future benefits. It was the ignorant or strangers (i.e., those clients who were not privileged and so were not informed) who did not benefit. Senior industry representatives can seem reluctant to admit convincingly to any past shortcomings in ethical matters, arguing that commission, undisclosed, was the norm, and so acceptable. We might represent this kind of defence as: '*You were a stranger* (to this subject) *so I took you in* (to my advantage) *but to do so was such a matter of course that I did not think about it*'; and compare it with Matt. 25:31–46, where the same words have a completely different meaning!

It may seem harsh to make such generalisations. The motives of many involved in the industry in accepting commission may have stemmed from a genuine belief that they were providing a valuable service to the best of their ability. It is, however, difficult to see why, if this was the case, disclosure could have been so long resisted. It is difficult to avoid the suspicion that there was (and is) embarrassment about letting the facts be known. Perhaps having once accepted commission, an implicated individual was (is) committed to supporting the system.

It is for this reason that this article is primarily directed at the *longstanding failure to disclose* rather than whether the amounts paid as the commission were excessive or not. For, as Luther was well aware, providing a fair prescription for price is difficult and specialist, if possible at all.

By contrast, emphasising the deep deontological need to avoid dishonesty, or the appearance of it, can be done by anyone who recognises it. Many individual, ordinary salespersons or agents could have independently and quietly changed the system by volunteering their own commission data, on their own initiative to their own clients. It would have needed, perhaps, older (and wealthier) salespersons to show a lead. Undoubtably it would have involved risks of loss of family income and status and the probability of some personal sacrifice. Some people will have done this but their numbers were too few to make a wide impact.

Surrender/persistency rates may have been more complicated for individual initiative and a certain loyalty to the institution may have prevailed, although clearly it is a relevant concern for the would-be policyholder to consider fully the implications of such ratios. The conclusion must be that the majority, together with their senior managements, seem to have chosen to say and do little to challenge or amend arrangements, or to encourage imaginative, improved alternatives.

There was no vision to see ways of bringing change – or even the consequences of not so doing. That is the subject which, with the privilege of hindsight, needs to be examined for the lessons it can teach. Why did collective inertia and past precedents stunt private initiative? The ethical role of the individual within business/professions now needs to be considered.

5. *Professional and business ethics*

This distinction is secular rather than Christian. Increasingly in practice it is blurred but not necessarily towards higher standards. To the extent that a profession constitutes the carrying out of an activity to which standards of competence and responsibility are attached, all Christians, as a *profession* of their faith, should have an integrity with regard to their conduct.

Moreover, the 'affective neutrality'[11] of professional ethics requires the professional to behave in a manner which provides the best possible for his/her client irrespective of his/her own interests or emotional involvement.

---

[11] Talcott Parsons, *Essays on Sociological Theory* (1949), cited under 'Professional Ethics' in *A New Dictionary of Christian Ethics* (1987).

In short, the professional may, on occasion, be required not just to 'love his/her neighbour' but to go beyond this. As in John 15:12–13, it should if necessary involve willing self-sacrifice of his/her own interests for the benefit of others, just as Jesus, as the Christ, in an infinitely more important way, did for all mankind.

Even for wholly secular occupations, professional ethics are part of an aura of quasi-religion. There may be a canon of knowledge, credal statements, tests, promises, special clothes, titles and meetings exclusive to the initiated – just as in an ecclesial institution. As with Christian ethics, any professional ethics are, at their core, about relationships.

By contrast, traditional business ethics are not only more loosely defined but have often been coupled with expressions of unease over the nature of trading. Plato did not consider it a suitable activity for Guardians.[12] Traditional church teachings of the Middle Ages on such subjects as 'just price', 'usury', 'property' and 'work' were part of a larger framework which involved an awareness of ambiguity. Thomas Aquinas did put forward various arguments on prices and cheating which seem to presuppose the concept of a 'fair price'. Selling goods at a profit was in accordance with moral law for without this there could be no tradesmen, and crucially, no food or commodities for any but the self-sufficient. Nevertheless a monastic detachment reflects his sense of superiority and good fortune in not needing to be directly involved, for he says:

> Trading, considered in itself, has a certain debasement attaching thereto, insofar as, by its very nature, it does not imply a virtuous or necessary end.[13]

Without digressing into Max Weber's classic account of Protestant and Reformed developments, the Protestant response seems to stress the individual Christian's calling and

---

[12] Plato, *The Republic*. The general citizen body, who carry on their trade, profession or craft, do not participate in the Government; cf. T. A. Sinclair, *A History of Greek Political Thought* (1967), ch. VIII.

[13] Thomas Aquinas, *Summa Theologica*, cited on p. 93 of J. P. Wogaman, *Christian Ethics - A Historical Introduction* (1994).

integrity together with the capacity and responsibility for charitable uses for business-derived earnings. Although there have been papal encyclicals and also World Council of Churches' pronouncements suggesting broader themes, McDonald,[14] having cited Brunner,[15] noted that there is also an argument that gives:

> Frank recognition that the business world has its own symbolic system which the businessman must follow or perish. Eschatological visions do not make company policy! The Christian, like any other, is at the mercy of this ruthless impersonal system, but any opportunity of expressing human value should be gratefully accepted![16]

Perhaps it is the 'commodity' rather than the service nature of the normal business product which enables a greater divorce by the business practitioner from personal *relationships*. In business or trading, loving of people and abstinence from self-love are harder to achieve because the relationships are briefer and less intimate. The more tangible nature of goods or products, which can be assessed for quality or value by the customer him/herself, creates less of an atmosphere of trust and reliance. The customer becomes a potential challenger or competitor rather than client expecting 'good faith'. The onus is clear in '*caveat emptor*' and the seller is absolved, if necessary, thereby.

Perhaps because of this, less 'high standards' are expected than in the professions, for they are 'people businesses'. Perhaps the corporate, institutionalised conscience should be expected to be more remote and disconnected from face to face and normal conceptions of moral agency. As a result, in business there is a climate which expects individuals, however reluctantly, to compete with apparently fewer scruples.

This may seem realistic but it is not thereby sanctified. Niebuhr spoke of the 'impossible possibility'. Jesus' teaching was rigorous, unconditioned and yet universal with high vertical

---

[14] J. I. H. McDonald, *Biblical Interpretation & Christian Ethics* (1993), p. 151.
[15] E. Brunner, *The Divine Imperative* (Eng. tr. 1937), p. 434.
[16] J. I. H. McDonald (1993), pp. 151–58.

reference points, not those that are horizontal. It may be unobtainable and 'interim' compromises a necessity. Nevertheless, it provides a transcendent possibility even while humans have to recognise that no humans can, of themselves, transcend their own limitations. It is by aspiring at this level that Christians in business, as well as in the professions, can most readily choose how best to respond, within the range of options between confrontation and collusion but motivated by Christian beliefs and ideals.

The car salesperson referred to above may have a relationship with a customer which is less intimate and so less responsible but this still gives no licence for lies, cheating or deception. Instead, he/she can help the prospective customer come to a sensible choice. It would be a fatal presumption, irrevocably to separate ethics from business and treat each as operating in a different sphere from other human activities, for business is a part thereof, no more and no less. Likewise, '*ethics affects all spheres. It is about people having the integrity to challenge themselves and society around them when on slippery slopes.*'[17]

The prophetic role may be far from easy but there are encouraging signs that, with ever improving communications and the dissemination of information, it may be becoming easier. Long term, reliable relationships are recognised as prerequisites of 'quality' programmes. No longer is business ethics an unchanging arena, worthy of disdain and pious expressions of concern coupled with vague advice.

Churches and Christians who walk by on the other side, or heap opprobrium from a distance, do a positive disservice to fellow Christians and to the world as their neighbour. If they themselves are not directly engaged with these thorny issues they need to understand, to support and to encourage with particular love and humility. Sanctimonious shuddering and self-satisfaction are clearly far from the Christian ideal[18] – as

---

[17] Hugo de Waal, Bishop of Thetford, quoted in the *New Civil Engineer*, 5/ 12 May 1994, referring to ethics, in this instance as an ethics adviser to the Institute of Civil Engineers.
[18] Luke 18:9–14 could not be more explicit that the tax collector, conscious of his failings but involved with worldly affairs, went home justified before

also is cynicism, seeking the appearance of worldliness, but unaware of the pain which many in both business and the professions feel, for '*it is a far more difficult task to be a Christian accountant than to be a Christian bishop [or minister]*'.[19]

Nevertheless, there appear to be several areas where the Christian can have an input. This may mean focusing on management as the moral agents and drawing the prophetic–critical aspect of biblical moral inquiry towards whatever seems to offend against agapism – love 'uncaused' by any existing attribute in its object – or Natural Law. These include:

the development of critical awareness among individuals so that they think through the ethical aspects of their actions;

the development of critical ethical analysis of the institution in its specific role and practices;

the encouragement of analysis of the institution's co-operative function within society (i.e., for 'mutuals', for its policyholders and potential policyholders);

the integration of disparate and cross-discipline thinking so that the broader consequences of any chosen course of action receive due consideration.

Moreover, ethical statements are becoming ever more common, setting out principles which managements can expect to be evaluated, even though a few do so with little intention of immediate, full compliance. Commission within the life assurance industry itself gives hope. The protests and legislation over the perceived failings of the industry could become a classic example of how laxness and failure to realise, then act, upon ethical matters can be disadvantageous and unsustainable. Despite the impressions given (so far also in this article), there

God rather than the Pharisee who was proud to have remained ritually pure and remote.

[19] James Thompson, Bishop of Bath and Wells, quoted in *Accountancy Age*, 26.5.1994, when addressing Chartered Accountants, on his receipt of the Founding Societies' Centenary Award of the Institute of Chartered Accountants of England and Wales.

is a number of life assurance companies which have never paid commission to intermediaries. Through avoiding the high costs of commission, these have managed to provide apparent out-performance in comparative statistical tables of costs, by a factor of up to ten.

In Autumn 1993, one of these was named by one of the UK's most respected retailers as its chosen partner in an 'over the counter pensions service', where the emphasis will be on openness and disclosure. This combination created a potentially significant development within the retail sector of the pensions industry, for it may successfully challenge the larger, more traditional companies which had for so long preferred not to adapt. It may be that future generations on ethics courses within business schools will be shown this as an example of where an 'unnecessary' entrepreneurial opportunity was presented to a formidable non-traditional entrant into a market. The now recognised failure by the major existing assurance companies to realise that an ethical concern, unaddressed, could develop into a serious weakness, may encourage those faced with giving timely warnings in other industries.

6. *Ethics and regulation*

The solution of the government has been to *impose* regulations relating to disclosure. There have been difficulties, and many months taken to formulate exactly what was required. In the end, this may still produce a figure of limited use. Ethics has become caught up in a rush to regulate by reference to detailed, comprehensive rules and avoidance of loopholes.

The scope for individual judgement is then specifically limited. This may create comparability and the semblance of fairness but broad rules, expressed in terms of principle, and recognising the prospect of ethical development, might be more robust and flexible. These would seem better suited to the varied demands of the very large number of people, specialists and non-specialists, who have an interest in life assurance and pension matters.

If it were to be possible to compel compliance for the spirit as well as the letter of the law, rules would be a wholly satisfactory solution. However, such codes of practice are not a substitute for individuals examining their consciences in proper ethical ways and acting accordingly. Some, fundamentally honest, people will fail inadvertently to comply with the detail of the law but nevertheless suffer penalties for so doing. Others, less honest, may instinctively manage to find new loopholes, or in certain instances, for a while, blatantly ignore the rules altogether.

The interplay of rules, personal judgement and intention is a theme at the heart of current discussion on many diverse activities.[20] It mirrors a debate which occupies much of the Old Testament, the Gospels and Epistles, and literature concerned with Natural Law. True Christian *koinonia* provides the faith and the motivation to hold rules and judgement in tension.

It is necessary to recognise that honesty does not always pay. Ethics too may not always pay in the short-term, opportunistic sense. But, on a longer term view, the need is for an ethical climate to be established in which dishonesty and misconduct are not equated with success. Motivation, training and remuneration arrangements need to be such that they have, and encourage, clear integrity. This seems to be the long-term priority for the industry beyond disputes over the formulae for reluctant disclosure. It is to the practical adoption of such values that Christians need to give every possible support.

Conclusion

Ultimately business and professional (separate or combined) ethical statements, programmes and courses are only allies

---

[20] For example, in auditing, as a senior accountant wrote in the *Financial Times* of 14.4.1994: 'We can either move towards a system where fair presentation simply means that accounts comply with the rules, or we can try to revitalise the process of financial reporting so that judgement has a greater role to play and the myriad facets of a business are synthesised into something more than the *sum of a cook book's parts*. We, as auditors, have to convince the financial community that we have the qualities to exercise the judgements required, in a proper, timely and consistent way.'

and helpful pointers. The Christian in business and/or a profession must be clear for him/herself as to the ethics appropriate within the faith community and be willing to engage in dialogue with others – listening, questioning and discussing. By this means the shared social symbol system of Christianity can be used as a common reference point for support or challenge of the ethics of any practice within any corporation or entity, large or small. Ethical issues, if not always ethical solutions, are accepted by many as a widespread and common concern and this interest must not be ignored.

It is sad that major financial institutions, proud like others of their reputation for innovation as well as reliability, seem not to have provided any clear and unequivocal initiative in the unsatisfactory area of their professional business by promoting openness of relationships with those they were founded to serve. However, it is all too easy merely to criticise with hindsight. The Christian perspective must be to see that the lessons are understood and applied elsewhere in the future. Christian values do have a *vital* role in business and professional life, not least in the willingness to examine and admit to tension, to recognise and regret past and present inadequacy of ethical practice, and to persevere in the expectation of better to come. In short, Christian ethical values combine faith, hope and love, and Christians continue to need for *themselves* to reappraise *all*, even time honoured, practices by reference to these three.

FOR FURTHER READING

INTRODUCTION AND CHAPTER 1

Philosophical, theological and historical perspectives

Attwell, R. A., *The Ethics of Environmental Concern*, Athens Ga., 1991.

Clark, S. R. L., *How to Think About the Earth. Philosophical and Theological Models for Ecology*, London 1993; *The Moral Status of Animals*, Oxford 1984.

'Ethics and Ecology', *Studies in Christian Ethics* vol. 7, no. 1, Edinburgh 1994.

Fairweather, I. C. M., and McDonald, J. I. H., *The Quest for Christian Ethics*, Edinburgh, 1984 (esp. chs 1 and 2).

Ferguson, J., *Moral Values in the Ancient World*, London 1958.

Fletcher, J., *Situation Ethics*, London 1966; *Moral Reponsibility*, London 1967.

Frankena, W. K., *Ethics*, Englewood Cliffs, N. J., 1973.

Gill, R., *A Textbook of Christian Ethics*, Edinburgh 1985.

Keeling, M., *Foundations of Christian Ethics*, Edinburgh 1991.

Lehmann, P. L., *Ethics in a Christian Context*, London 1963.

Long, E. L., *A Survey of Recent Christian Ethics*, Oxford 1982 (esp. Parts I and II).

McDonagh, S., *To Care for the Earth*, London 1990.

MacIntyre, A., *After Virtue: A Study in Moral Theory*, London 1981.

Mahoney, J., *The Making of Moral Theology*, Oxford 1987.

Midgley, M., *Beast and Man*, Ithaca 1978; *The Ethical Primate. Humans, Freedom and Morality*, London 1994.

Nash, J. A., *Loving Nature. Ecological Integrity and Christian Responsibility*, Nashville 1991.

Nygren, A., *Agape and Eros*, London 1954.

O'Connor, D. J., *Aquinas and Natural Law*, London 1967.

Outka, G. H. and Ramsey, P., *Norm and Context in Christian Ethics*, London 1969.

Pope John Paul II, *Veritatis Splendor. Encyclical Letter*, London 1993.

Ramsey, Paul, *Deeds and Rules in Christian Ethics*, Edinburgh 1967.

Robinson, N. H. G., *The Groundwork of Christian Ethics*, London 1971.

Ross, W. D., *The Foundations of Ethics*, Oxford 1960.

Ruether, R. R., *God and Gaia*, London 1993; *New Woman, New Earth*, New York 1975.

Selling, J. and Jans J. (eds), *The Splendor of Accuracy*, Kampen 1994.

Smart, J. J. C. and Williams, B., *Utilitarianism For and Against*, Cambridge 1973.

Stivers, R. L., Gudorf, C. E., Evans, A. F. and Evans R. A., *Christian Ethics: A Case Method Approach*, Maryknoll, N. Y., 1990.

Tillich, P., *Love, Power and Justice*, Oxford 1954.

Wilkins, J. (ed.), *Understanding Veritatis Splendor*, London 1994.

Wogamon, J. P., *Christian Ethics — A Historical Introduction*, London 1994.

Woods, G. F., *A Defence of Theological Ethics*, Cambridge 1966.

Biblical interpretation and ethics

Bauckham, R., *The Bible in Politics*, London 1989.

Birch C. B., and Rasmussen, L. L., *Bible and Ethics in the Christian Life*, Minneapolis 1989.

Chilton, B., and McDonald, J. I. H., *Jesus and the Ethics of the Kingdom*, London 1987.

Dunn, J. D. G., and Suggate, A. M., *The Justice of God*, Carlisle 1993.

Fiorenza, E. S. (ed.), *Searching the Scriptures: A Feminist Introduction*, London 1994.

Fowl, S. E., and Jones, L. G., *Reading in Communion*, London 1991.

Houlden, J. L., *Ethics and the New Testament*, Harmondsworth 1973.

Kelsey, D., *The Uses of Scripture in Recent Theology*, London 1975.

McDonald, J. I. H., *Biblical Interpretation and Christian Ethics*, Cambridge 1993.

Marxsen, W., *New Testament Foundations for Christian Ethics*, Edinburgh 1983.

Ogletree, T.W., *The Use of the Bible in Christian Ethics*, Oxford 1983.

Rowland, C. and Corner, M., *Liberating Exegesis*, London 1990.

Schrage, W., *The Ethics of the New Testament*, Edinburgh 1988.

CHAPTER 2

Bonhoeffer, D., *Ethics*, London 1958.

ten Boom, C., with J. and E. Sherrill, *The Hiding Place*, London 1976.

Cupitt, D., *The New Christian Ethics*, London 1988.

Dussel, E., *Ethics and Community*, Maryknoll, N.Y., 1978.

Fairweather I. C. M., and McDonald, J. I. H., *The Quest*, ch. 3.

'Feminism and Christian ethics', *Studies in Christian Ethics*, vol. 5, no. 1, Edinburgh 1992.

Gilligan, C., *In a Different Voice: Psychological Theory and Women's Development*, London 1982.

Hampshire, S., *Two Theories of Morality*, Oxford 1977.

Häring, B., *The Law of Christ* (3 vols), Ramsey, N. J., 1961; *Morality is for Persons*, London 1972; *Faith and Morality in a Secular Age*, Slough 1973; *Free and Faithful in Christ* (3 vols), Slough 1978–81.

Harrison, B., *Making the Connections. Essays in Feminist Social Ethics*, New York 1985.

Hauerwas, S., *A Community of Character*, Notre Dame 1981; *Suffering Presence*, Notre Dame/Edinburgh, 1988; *Character and the Christian Life*, Trinity 1975.

Johann, R. O., *The Meaning of Love*, Glen Rock, N. J., 1966.

Keeling, M., *The Foundations of Christian Ethics* (see above).

Long, E. L., *A Survey* (see above), part III.

McIntyre, A., *After Virtue* (see above).

O'Donovan, O., *Resurrection and Moral Order*, Leicester 1986.

Porter, Jean, *The Recovery of Virtue*, London 1994.

Tillich, P., *Love, Power and Justice* (see above).

Welch, S., *A Feminist Ethic of Risk*, London 1989.

CHAPTER 3

Achtemeier, E., *The Committed Marriage*, Westminster 1976.

Bernard, J., *The Future of Marriage*, Harmondsworth 1976.

Church of Scotland Board of Social Responsibility, *The Future of the Family*, Edinburgh 1992.

Craven, E., Rimmer, L., and Wicks, M., *Family Issues and Public Policy*, London: Study Commission on the Family, 1982.

Curran, D., *Traits of a Healthy Family*, Ballantine 1983.

Davis, C., *Religion and the Making of Society*, Cambridge 1994.

Davies, J. (ed.), *The Family: Is It Just Another Lifestyle Choice?*, London 1993.

Dominion J., 'Sexuality and the family', *Studies in Christian Ethics* 4.2.1991, pp. 42–52 (with a response by R. Franklin).

Egan, G., *The Skilled Helper*, Monterey, Calif., 1975.

Foucault, M., *The History of Sexuality* I, Harmondsworth 1978.

Fletcher, R., *The Family and Marriage in Britain*, Harmondsworth 1966.

Gillis, J. R., *For Better, For Worse: British Marriages, 1600 to the Present*, Oxford 1985.

Hauerwas, S., *A Community of Character* (see above), esp. Part Three.

Hewitt, P., and Leech, P., *Social Justice, Children and Families*, London 1994.

Jenkins, G., *Cohabitation: A Biblical Perspective*, Nottingham 1992.

Leslie, G., *The Family in Social Context*, Oxford 1976.

Oppenheimer, H., *Marriage*, London 1990.

Richmond, G., *Successful Single Parenting*, Eugene, Oreg. 1990.

Spinnanger, R., *Better Than Divorce*, Logos, 1978.

Turner, P., 'Undertakings and promises or promises and undertakings?' *Studies in Christian Ethics* 4.2.1991, pp. 1–15 (with a response by D. Wiltsher).

Thatcher, A., *Liberating Sex: A Christian Sexual Theology*, London 1994.

CHAPTER 4

Babuscio, J., *We Speak for Ourselves: the experiences of gay men and lesbians*, London 1988.

Countryman, L. W., *Dirt, Greed and Sex*, London 1988.

Coleman, P., *Gay Christians: A Moral Dilemma*, London 1989.

Cotter, J., 'Same sex relationships', *Studies in Christian Ethics* 4.2.1991, pp. 29–41 (with a response by D. Atkinson).

Dominian, J., *Sexual Integrity*, London 1988.

Duberman, M., Vicinus, M., and Chauncey, G. (eds), *Hidden From History: Reclaiming the Gay and Lesbian Past*, Harmondsworth 1991.

Fletcher, B., *Clergy Under Stress: a study of homosexual and heterosexual clergy*, London 1990.

Forrester, D. B., McDonald, J. I. H. and Tellini, G., *Encounter with God*, Edinburgh 1983.

Hanigan, J. P., *Homosexuality: the Test Case for Christian Ethics*, New York 1988.

Moberly, E., *Homosexuality: A New Christian Ethic*, Cambridge 1983; *Psychogenesis: the early development of gender identity*, London 1983.

Moor, G., *The Body in Context*, London 1992.

Nelson, J., *Embodiment*, London 1989.

Ranke-Heinemann, U., *Eunuchs for the Kingdom of Heaven: the Catholic Church and Sexuality*, Harmondsworth 1991.

Reidy, M., *Freedom to be Friends: Morals and Sexual Affection*, London 1990.

Spong, J. S., *Living in Sin?*, San Francisco 1988.

Stuart, E., *Daring to Speak Love's Name: A Gay and Lesbian Prayerbook*, London 1992.

Turner, B., *The Body and Society*, Oxford 1984.

Wright, D., *The Christian Faith and Homosexuality*, Edinburgh 1994.

CHAPTER 5

General

Bellah, R. and others, *Habits of the Heart: Middle America Observed*, London 1985.

Bonhoeffer, D., *Letters and Papers from Prison*, London 1953; *The Cost of Discipleship*, London 1959.

Brunner, E., *The Divine Imperative*, London 1937.

Festinger, L., *A Theory of Cognitive Dissonance*, Evanston 1957.

Forrester, D. B., *Beliefs, Values and Policies*, Oxford 1989.

Gill, R., *Christian Ethics and Secular Worlds*, Edinburgh 1991; *Prophecy and Praxis*, London 1981.

Habermas, J., *The Theory of Communicative Action* I, London 1984.

Lebacqz, K., *Six Theories of Justice*, Minneapolis 1986.

Moltmann J., *The Trinity and the Kingdom of God*, London 1981.

Niebuhr, R., *The Nature and Destiny of Man* (2 vols), London 1944.

Noyce, G., *Pastoral Ethics*, Nashville 1990.

Parsons, T., *The Social System*, Tavistock 1952; *Essays on Sociological Theory*, Free Press of Glencoe 1954 (first pub. 1944).

Preston, R. H., *Church and Society in the Late Twentieth Century: The Economic and Political Task*, London 1983.

Ramsey, P., *Who Speaks for the Church?*, Nashville and New York, 1967.

Rawls, J. B., *A Theory of Justice*, Oxford 1973.

Tillich, P., *Love, Power and Justice* (see above).

Wogaman, J. P., *A Christian Method of Moral Judgment*, London 1976.

Northern Ireland

Akenson, D. H., *Education and Enmity: The Control of Schooling in Northern Ireland 1920–1950*, Newton Abbot 1973.

Downing, T. (ed.), *The Troubles*, London 1980.

Eames, R., *Chains to be Broken: a personal reflection on Northern Ireland and its people*, London 1992.

Fisher R. and Ury W., *Getting to Yes*, London 1987.

Greer, J. E., 'Education reform in Northern Ireland', *British Journal of Religious Education*, 13.3.1991.

Hadden, T., *The Anglo–Irish Agreement: commentary, text and official review*, London 1989.

Interchurch Group on Faith and Politics, *Living the Kingdom – faith and politics in the Northern Ireland conflict*, Belfast c.1989.

Keenan, B., *An Evil Cradling*, London 1992.

McCreary, A., *Corrymeela: The Search for Peace*, Belfast 1975.

McGarry, J. and O'Leary, B. (eds), *The Future of Northern Ireland*, Oxford 1990.

O'Leary, B. and McGarry, J., *The Politics of Antagonism: understanding Northern Ireland*, London 1993.

Pollak A. (ed.), *A Citizens' Enquiry: The Opsahl Report on Northern Ireland*, Dublin 1993.

Whyte, J. H., *Interpreting Northern Ireland*, Oxford 1991.

CTPI,* 'Northern Ireland – A challenge to theology', Fitzgerald, G., McDonagh, E., McCaughey, T., Morrow, J., Hurley, M., Wright, F., O'Brien, K., Occasional Paper no. 12, Edinburgh 1987. (* For CTPI, see end of Further Reading.)

Community care and development

Forrester, D. B., *Christianity and the Future of Welfare*, London 1985.

Foskett, J., *Meaning in Madness*, London 1984.

Grainger, R., *Watching for Wings*, London 1979.

Jones, K., Brown, J., Bradshaw, J., *Issues in Social Policy*, London 1978.

Mulholland, M., 'Sexuality and the mentally handicapped: The law's response', *Studies in Christian Ethics* 4.2.1991, pp. 53–63.

Murphy, E., *After the Asylums*, London 1991.

Pattison, S., *Alive and Kicking*, London 1989; *A Critique of Pastoral Care*, London 1988.

Schroten, E., 'Sexuality and the mentally handicapped: The perspective of moral theology', *Studies in Christian Ethics* 4.2.1991, pp. 64–67.

CTPI,* 'Care, community and state', Holloway, R., Marshall, M., Forrester, D. B., Occasional Paper no. 30, Edinburgh 1994. (* See end of Further Reading.)

CTPI,* 'The Market and Health Care', Jenkins, D. E., Bates, A., Riddell, A., Kelly, B., Occasional Paper no. 19, Edinburgh 1990. (* See end of Further Reading.)

Media

Arthur, C. (ed.), *Communicating Faith in a Technological Age*, Cardiff 1993.

Boyd, A., *Broadcast Journalism*, Oxford 1988.

Belsey, R., and Chadwick, R. (eds), *Ethical Issues in Journalism and the Media*, London 1992.

Christians, C. G., Rotzoll, K. B., Fackler, M., *Media Ethics: Cases and Moral Reasoning*, New York 1991.

Curran, J. and Seaton, J., *Power Without Responsibility: The Press and Broadcasting in Britain*, London (4th ed.) 1991.

Elvy, P., *Opportunities and Limitations in Religious Broadcasting*, Edinburgh 1991.

Fore W., *Television and Religion*, Minneapolis 1987.

Hiebert, R. E., Ungurait, D. F., Bohn, T. W., *Mass Media VI*, New York 1974.

The Press Complaints Commission, *Code of Practice*, London (issued on 27th October, 1993).

Priestland, G., *The Dilemmas of Journalism*, Guildford 1979.

Rubin, B. (ed.), *Questioning Media Ethics*, New York 1978.

Weber, D., *Discerning Images: The Media and Theological Education*, Edinburgh 1991.

CTPI,* 'The future of broadcasting in Britain', Eldridge J., Elvy, P., Marjoribanks, B., Webb, P., Weber, D., Occasional Paper no. 24, Edinburgh 1991. (* See end of Further Reading.)

Business ethics

Atherton, J., *Christianity and the Market*, London 1992.

CTPI,* *Capital: A Moral Instrument?*, Edinburgh 1992. (*See end of Further Reading.)

Gray, J., *The Moral Foundations of Market Institutions*, London 1992.

Griffiths, B., *The Creation of Wealth*, London 1984.

Harries, R., *Is there a Gospel for the Rich?* London 1992.

Niebuhr, R., *Moral Man and Immoral Society*, New York 1932.

Owensby, W. L., *Economics for Prophets*, Grand Rapids 1988.

Preston, R. H., *Religion and the Ambiguities of Capitalism*, London 1991; *The Future of Christian Ethics*, London 1987, esp. pp. 115–156; *Religion and the Persistence of Capitalism*, London 1979.

Sedgwick, P., *The Enterprise Culture*, London 1992.

Williams, O. F., and Houck, J. W. (eds), *The Judaeo–Christian Vision and the Modern Corporation*, Notre Dame and London 1982.

Weber, M., *The Protestant Ethic and the Spirit of Capitalism*, New York 1958.

Wilkie, G., *Christian Thinking about Industrial Life*, Edinburgh 1980.

CTPI,* 'Justice and the market', Hughes, G., Campbell, T., Atherton, J., Sinclair, D., Occasional Paper no. 21, Edinburgh 1990.

* CTPI: Centre for Theology and Public Issues, New College, University of Edinburgh, Mound Place, Edinburgh EH1 2LU.

INDEX